STILL POINT *of the* TURNING WORLD

CAROL ANN WILSON

STILL POINT *of the* TURNING WORLD
The Life of Gia-fu Feng

Amber Lotus Publishing
Portland, Oregon

Published by Amber Lotus Publishing
P.O. Box 11329, Portland, Oregon 97211
800.326.2375 • www.amberlotus.com

Amber Lotus Publishing first printing: 2009
10   9   8   7   6   5   4   3   2   1
Printed in Korea

Library of Congress Control Number: 2008943488

Cover and book design: Barbara Tada
Front cover composite photographs: Courtesy of Carmen Baehr and Carol Wilson
Back cover photograph: Jane English
Author photograph: David Chrislip
Editorial services: Meadowlark Publishing Services, www.larkonline.net

Amber Lotus first edition ISBN: 978-1-60237-296-2

To

the memory
of my sister
Margaret Susan Wilson
who remains in my heart

and

my mother
Earline Wilson
whose courage inspires me daily

*Right now, here, this is the best version of the story
I can assemble. Who's to say it's the right one?
The facts—haven't you heard it said?—are as clay in the hands
of the potter! I can only give you this sum of what I have heard
mixed with my own opinions of the matter.*

—*NICOLE MONES*
A Cup of Light

CONTENTS

FOREWORD

In the summer of 1967, we lived in a flat on Cabrillo Street, two blocks from Golden Gate Park in San Francisco. I had just returned home for lunch after playing baseball at Rossi Playground, when Gia-fu unexpectedly appeared at our front door. Never a fan of small talk, Gia-fu—or Uncle Jeff, as we called him—excitedly asked me if I wanted to go for a ride. Parked out on the street was a Triumph sports car. At fifteen and never having ridden in a sports car, I was as thrilled as anyone could possibly be. Tires screeching, no seat belts, we set off to turn Golden Gate Park into an imaginary racecourse.

Little did I know that Uncle Jeff had no idea which trails were legal for cars and which trails were strictly for pedestrians and horses. All were poorly marked at that time. So, blindly weaving in and out on those trails, missing trees and large rocks by inches, we drove around the park for what seemed an eternity. Miraculously, we did not run over any walkers or horses that day, including the mounted police who used to patrol the trails. Even more miraculously, the car did not hit any trees or boulders along those rough, narrow trails. It was not until I read Carol's manuscript some forty years later that I realized Gia-fu's driving skills were universally belittled. For all these years, since the day he treated me to that special ride, I thought Uncle Jeff was, among his many other skills, an anonymous stunt driver. There was no doubt Uncle Jeff was not just a typical relative.

Nor did he lead a typical life. Carol Wilson's biography of Gia-fu is an extraordinary effort that traces the improbable life of Uncle Jeff. Fate brought him to this country at precisely the right time. The cultural and social changes Gia-fu experienced in his first days living in this country laid the course for his destiny.

I think no one in our family can really put a finger on exactly what Gia-fu's vocation was. We know that he translated Lao Tsu and taught tai chi. According to my mother—Gia-fu's sister, Lu-tsi—he was an accomplished calligrapher, tutored by the masters during his youth in China. We now know that he was adept at identifying the people whom he ultimately partnered with to complete the most important projects during and after his life—people like Jane English, Margaret Susan Wilson and the unsuspecting Carol Wilson who never met him.

I also know he did not like being a "master" to those he lived and interacted with. I believe Jane English was most perceptive in calling him a teacher of his art. I'd like to add entertainer to the list of descriptions. If translating Lao Tsu was his calling, performing was his hobby. By this I mean not the ballroom dancing described in Carol's early chapter, but his charismatic ability to lead us in romping Golden Gate Park's unmarked racecourse and in salsa dancing up Pikes Peak. And I think he approached his translations the same way, riveting the reader with calligraphy and graphics, followed by an intimate recital of insight on ancient Chinese philosophy.

In all this, Carol Wilson is the heroine in my eyes. Compiling someone's life as it touched different continents during tormented political eras from scattered bits and pieces and retelling it is quite a feat. Perhaps it is destiny that this book was completed. It is evidence that a strong will is present for this story and its message to be told. It's a small, peaceful statement that the Taoist principle is not lost despite all the political upheavals and social prejudices that marked the past century.

For me, Uncle Jeff is still the mischievous, somewhat eccentric guy who entertained us during those long, boring summer days. He's also the teacher who gave me access to the *Tao Te Ching* that someday my sons will be able to read, and which I will never pretend to fully understand.

— DEXTER WOO
Uncle Gia-fu's nephew

ACKNOWLEDGMENTS

This journey of thirteen years began with a single, albeit solid, nudge. That nudge came from my mother, Earline Wilson, whose confidence in me exceeded my own, and for this I continue to be grateful. Each step of the way brought longtime and new friends and colleagues to my aid, and I thank you all.

Even before I undertook this challenge, Clara Reida worked with my late sister, Margaret Susan Wilson, to edit Gia-fu's original manuscript. Their work made it possible for me to take it up. When it became clear that I would take on the task, José Mariman and Elizabeth Parmelee transferred the entire manuscript to the computer so that I could begin to work with it. Putting the three hundred pages of stream-of-consciousness writings into some semblance of chronological order required the brave of heart, and thankfully, Andrea Hart is brave.

Encouragement has come from many. From the beginning Gary Holthaus, Carmen Baehr, Lloyd Alexander, Steve Harper, Pierre DeLattre, Steve Arney, John Daniel, Celia Barnes, Ellen Price, Richard Clark, John Goodlad, and Elizabeth Martin offered support as I struggled to make some sense of how to tackle the job. Bonnie Walters even went so far as to give me Chinese language tapes so I could communicate directly on trips to China. It was a great idea, but the dog was too old to learn this new trick. Thankfully, Deann and Jim Pierson, who so graciously hosted David and me while we were in Shanghai, also introduced us to Feng Li, a delightful young doctor of traditional Chinese medicine who not only served as our guide and translator on that first trip but remains a dear friend.

Even to scratch the surface of understanding another's life, one must learn about it from multiple perspectives. Finding those perspectives required help. Jane English has been stellar in this area, introducing me to some of Gia-fu's family and many others from his life. Jane has been helpful in every possible way, even encouraging me to talk with Amber Lotus Publishing about this book. Leslie and Lawson Day and Tim Campbell of Amber Lotus, three individuals who reflect both compassion and aesthetic sensibility, are a joy to work with. Aleta Florentin has my admiration and gratitude for managing the project so aptly, Sheridan McCarthy and Ali McCart for their eagle-eyed editing, and Barbara Tada for bringing her sensitivity and artistry to the book's design.

Tom Bellamy introduced me to leaders in Denver's Chinese-American community, and Ann Foster traveled with me to talk with family and friends, lending another ear to understanding some of the complexities encountered along the way.

To all who agreed to be interviewed—and some to have your memories prodded and examined multiple times—you have my undying respect and gratitude. Many of you appear in the book, so I'll let the reader delight in discovering who you are.

Guidance in the historical context has come from Loren Crabtree, who launched me on a course of reading about China; William Wei, who helped me better understand the Chinese experience in the United States; and William Doub, who provided multiple resources, background, and insights and has tried very hard to keep me from making big mistakes. If I've done so despite his efforts, I claim them as my own. I thank Lloyd Alexander for the realization that historical context was needed.

Members of Gia-fu's family have talked with me about Gia-fu and the family, and for this I am most grateful. They helped me understand the person behind the stories. Feng Yun ke and Dexter Woo have lent encouragement and support, and Dexter and Kathleen Woo have supplied some wonderful photographs. For those who wish to remain unnamed, thank you. For those who are no longer with us, my gratitude remains in my heart.

Mertis Shekeloff, Sunita—known in the book as Sue Bailey—Richard Hoffman, and Jane English have also lent photographs, and these photos speak to aspects of Gia-fu that words cannot.

To so many, I owe my thanks, and probably much more. Dean, whom we miss very much, and Mildred Chrislip, Sherry Sirotnik, Barb and Hue Martinez, Cori Mantle, Lauren Pelon, Bill Donley, Michael Holland, Bruce Allen, Carolyn Servid, Dorik Mechau, Jayne Satter, Diane Thornton, Linda Hansink, and Pam Durr, you are indeed good friends and wonderful family. And I must not forget to thank Ken Cohen for those enlightening conversations during the Island Institute symposium in Sitka, Alaska.

Just like the hiker who thinks she's reached the summit only to discover it's only the next ridge, so have I thought on various occasions that I had almost arrived at my destination. Through the candor of friends such as Jaye and John Zola, I learned that I had not. Jaye and John read many drafts before they convinced me to find a guide who knows the territory. They went further and introduced me to someone whose wisdom, intuition, and experience made it possible for me to finally complete this book. Laura Goodman has been the guide, therapist, and mentor who led me out of the wilderness into really writing the book and stayed beside me the whole time. She deserves a medal.

Throughout the journey, David Chrislip, my life partner, has also been a partner in researching and bringing this book to light. He has read more drafts than one can imagine. Together we've traveled across the United States, and to China three times, visiting people and places that would provide more clues to the enigma called Gia-fu Feng. In all of this, he has brought his wisdom and humanity to the search, ensuring that my journey of thirteen years was not alone.

Finally, to you, Gia-fu Feng, you who left us, as your friend Tran Van Dinh so eloquently described, "for a long session of tea and poetry with Lao Tsu." Many times you've heard me as I stood by your grave asking about you and also asking, "Gia-fu, do you have any idea what you've done to my life?" And recently as I stood there, through the crack of a thunderbolt I thought I heard, "Well, Carol, just look what you've done to mine."

— CAROL WILSON
January 24, 2008
Boulder, Colorado

PROLOGUE

Nestled in scrub oak and native grasses, Gia-fu Feng's grave lies down an unkempt trail west from Custer County Road 387 in south-central Colorado. Left of the grave head, a carved round laughing Taoist figure supports a Chinese gong. Just above the grave lies a marble head-stone, engraved with these words from Chuang Tsu's *Inner Chapters*:

> *When the master came, it was at the right time.*
> *When he went away, it was the simple sequence of his coming.*

White rock crystals, primarily quartz, cover the grave below the marker, which rests unencumbered by fence or posts. Fastened to a nearby tree, a few bells chime softly in the breeze.

On the hilltop above the grave sits his hut, built somewhat in the style of Chinese hermitages. Gia-fu (pronounced Jah Foo) lived here for seven years, until a few weeks before he died. An eccentric building, it is fashioned of weathered wood and ample glass for light and warmth. Steep steps and a small enclosed east-facing porch lead into the second of three levels. Essentially a simple and straightforward sitting area, it also served as Gia-fu's sleeping space. A ramp, so narrow and close to the ceiling that only a very small figure can use it with ease, slants upward to an also very small loft. Back down from the sitting/sleeping room, another ramp leads to the ground level, which consists almost entirely of a bathing area. Altogether, the house measures about two hundred square feet.

From the sitting room, as from the porch and grave, the view to the north encompasses hazy mountains rising from the plains. Smaller mountains cluster around the highest, Pikes Peak, then slope outward and downward from it.

To the east, the land rises gently, climbing upward into a large meadow. Late spring and early summer fill the meadow with wildflowers, serene companions to a natural rock memorial commemorating the life of Margaret Susan Wilson, late heir to Gia-fu's estate. Lovingly placed there by our mother in 1992, the memorial lies halfway up the meadow in full view from the hut.

To the south, the land becomes more contoured as the Wet Mountains begin their evergreen-cloaked ascent to approximately ten thousand feet. Westward is the same, punctuated only by a small stream, aptly named Middle Hardscrabble Creek.

From Gia-fu's grave, the trail continues westward, splitting just past the creek. Its south turn eventually finds San Isabel National Forest. To the north the trail circles back to the county road. Both segments pass somewhat close by many of the more than twenty huts sprinkled across Stillpoint's 166 acres. Some huts remain in usable condition; others sag from years of neglect. Each hut holds memories: of its builder, of the people who lived there for long periods, and of those who were just passing through.

About a quarter of a mile up the trail to the west sits a larger cabin called the teahouse. Situated on a slope amid tall ponderosa pines and the ubiquitous scrub oak, the teahouse is a rustic construction of logs and secondhand windows. From outside it resembles a pioneer cabin with its logs of various lengths and a rusty stovepipe, more than a little askew, anchored to the roof by an equally rusty piece of baling wire. The stovepipe connects inside to a wood-burning stove, which stands off center in the larger of two rooms. A makeshift ladder leads to a loft, leading, in turn, to a small deck. One enters the front of the teahouse through a small enclosed porch. In addition to housing a small family—a couple and a baby—the teahouse also served as a central community meeting place, housing predawn meditations and early morning community meetings.

Middle Hardscrabble Creek runs below the teahouse, its soft burbling reminiscent of distant conversation. Upstream about three miles, long after the land becomes San Isabel National Forest, water leaps over a cliff in a respectable waterfall.

This idyllic land was the third in a series of places that bore the name and held the community of "Stillpointers." The land holds a special story, that of a man who had a dream and brought that dream to reality in his search for community, for honesty, and for simplicity.

In September 1994, nine years after Gia-fu's death, Jane English and I stood beside his grave. Jane, Gia-fu's common-law wife of twenty-plus years ago and partner in the Manitou Springs Stillpoint, as well as in the *Tao Te Ching* and *Inner Chapters* translations, had come for a short visit. The sky was piercingly blue, a stunning backdrop for the thickets of copper-colored scrub oak burnished by the late September afternoon light. The blanket of white quartz on the grave glistened in the sun's slant-ing rays. Jane had never seen Gia-fu's grave and had come, perhaps, to tie up some long-unraveled loose ends; I was there because Stillpoint was now my responsibility.

Jane looked at the grave and the headstone the Stillpoint community had placed there, studying them both for a long time. Then, with a slow shake of her head, she said, "No. That's not right."

She paused as I stared at her, surprised and startled by her words. "What?" I wanted to know. "What's not right?"

"This verse. 'When the master came ...' It's not right. This thing about the master, I think it's a little off the mark, because I don't think he really was a master." Her voice was low, a study in contrasts with its lilting musi-cal quality, deliberative and thoughtful. "I think he was a teacher, but he was an ordinary human being who had his faults and his difficulties and his problems. And some of them he dealt with well, and some of them he didn't deal with very well. He wasn't an enlightened master or anything, but he was a very good teacher."

Astonished, I turned her words over in my mind. Finally, I asked, "So, what's the difference between a master and a teacher?"

For me, this question turned out to be a giant step toward learning who Gia-fu was; it helped me begin to understand who he was not. Until this moment, it never crossed my mind that he was not a guru, some sort of spiritual leader. I realized that my sister, Margaret Susan Wilson, whose ashes rest in the meadow above Gia-fu's grave and who was my link to this place and to Gia-fu, had never talked about him very much. Or if she had, not much stayed with me. My sister and I were attached at the heart, and we shared a great deal of what was important in our lives. But between occasionally assuming the other would surely know certain things and sometimes being protective of each other, we left gaps in what we actually knew. What I knew about Gia-fu was that, according to her, he was the leader of an intentional community and translator of Chinese classics. Undoubtedly, through the years she had mentioned other odds and ends of things, but nothing that altered my abstract assumptions. Events of the sixties, seventies, and early eighties focusing on myriad spiritual leaders had filled in blanks I had not even recognized as such. Now, standing at this meadow's edge, my erroneous assumptions were being exposed, quite literally, to the light of day. The effect of Jane's words was doubly profound because she had been very close to Gia-fu for a time, and although that time had been two decades ago, I thought she had special insight into his character.

"Hmmm. The difference between a master and a teacher," Jane said. "That's an interesting question." Again she paused, then continued. "I'm not sure what the formal distinction is, but I think it has to do with this: A teacher knows and can teach, but a master not only knows and can teach but lives what he or she teaches. A master walks the talk. Gia-fu didn't necessarily do that."

Walking the talk, I thought. What talk did Gia-fu not walk? What talk did he walk? Who was this man?

"But what I said about Gia-fu being a teacher, I'm just thinking that probably because he was from a totally different culture, he could really see what was going on with people in this country. He wasn't entangled in it. I don't know, it's just my conjecture that he could probably point out things that people were doing because he didn't have those same patterns in himself."

Jane gazed across the meadow toward Pikes Peak. Medium-length brown hair, shining in the bright sunlight, framed her pensive face. Turning back to look at the grave, she continued. "But there was nobody who could really point to him and say, 'Well, what about you?' People just didn't do that ... I guess the point is, I think a lot of people idealized Gia-fu. And, you know, he had his warts and his bumps and blind places."

Jane's reaction to the headstone provoked me to push beyond my assumptions, to seek answers that invariably resulted in more questions. At that point, I began to realize that in researching Gia-fu's life I would have to explore many different aspects of his relationships and much more deeply than I'd thought. My work on this book began with a personal interest, an obligation I felt came to me along with the responsibility for Stillpoint and urging from my mother to complete Gia-fu's autobiography. In 1986, Susan first brought me to Stillpoint, and it was with her that I stood by his grave, feeling an initial sense of awe about who Gia-fu must have been.

My sister's and Gia-fu's initial meeting occurred in 1978. From dramatically different backgrounds, both approached life in original and unorthodox ways. Susan—law student, fierce and tenacious fighter for social justice, with bachelor's and master's degrees in Asian studies—and Gia-fu, self-described rogue, teacher, philosopher, Gestalt therapist, and Taoist sage. Both were possessed of fiery tempers and extraordinary gentleness, and the eight years of their friendship brought out the full range of these qualities in both. In a world that counts success by financial accomplishment, each sought to live authentically by digging deeply into themselves, living simply, and helping others. In keeping to this path, both touched and enhanced many lives because they could see beyond themselves and reach out to others. When Gia-fu died in 1985, he left Stillpoint and his other worldly matters in Susan's hands.

Then in 1991 Susan died, and her sudden, devastating loss brought responsibility for Stillpoint to me. It was years before the remaining legal and financial matters were resolved, and once they were, other questions began to arise. One such question was what to do with the partial autobiography Gia-fu had left, and which Susan, with the help of friend Clara Reida, had been editing. Once Gia-fu's and Susan's complicated estates were settled, the idea of undertaking a biography began to take hold in my mind. Background and skill became secondary to taking on a fresh challenge, and that challenge unexpectedly proved to be healing. I see now, as I could not then, that I was driven by a need to know this man and

5

the impact of his friendship and legacy on my sister and the importance, on many fronts, of having this knowledge and understanding.

I began work on Gia-fu's biography with his approximately three hundred pages of partially edited stream-of-consciousness writing, primarily about his early years in China, and an already noted very narrow, awed view of the man. As the years unfolded, they brought contact with Gia-fu's students, acquaintances, friends, and family, in the U.S. and China. The succeeding decade brought both deep friendships and passing interviews.

In San Francisco, David, my life partner, and I first met Gia-fu's eldest sister, with whom we had a lovely visit, and his next-youngest brother, who became like family to us. There were nine siblings altogether. In China, David and I traveled to Shanghai and stood in the old Feng family home and in their summer villa. Through our interpreter, we talked with people who had known the family during the difficult years of the Cultural Revolution. We visited Gia-fu's youngest brother and his wife, with whom we formed a deep and abiding bond. Led by Gia-fu's nephew, we climbed Taishan, one of China's Five Sacred Mountains noted in the *Tao Te Ching*, walked through the Gates of Heaven, and smelled the burning incense in the Temple of Azure Clouds. We strolled along country roads with the family, who introduced us to ancient Taoist temples and other intriguing places such as Three Laughing Place and Fairy Cave. They took us to Qu Fu, Confucius's birthplace and home of the Kung (Confucius's) family, and we walked through seventy-seven generations of Kung family tombs set amid myriad fabulous and ancient trees. Also in the mix were books about Chinese history and philosophy, the Japanese invasion and occupation of China, religion, spirituality, the many specializations and schools of Taoism, Quakers, the Beat poets, Gestalt psychotherapy, encounter groups, recent American history, the history of America's treatment of the Chinese in this country, and biographies of all sorts, all of which connected to Gia-fu in some way. Surprisingly, many also connected to my sister, causing me to wish I had known these things when she was still here.

From these many sources, Gia-fu's life in China and the United States began to take meaningful shape in my mind—and in my heart. In the process, left behind was the initial simplistic impression of Gia-fu as a revered master-of-something-I-didn't-know-about. In its place came an appreciation of the exceedingly complex nature of a man who was many different things to many different people—bumps, warts, and all.

And so I try to tell about this man of contradictions, this fiery, gentle, wise, and sometimes crazy, multifaceted man who provoked many and helped many. A man who, in seeking peace and resolution in his own life full of upheaval and displacement, found a place of stillness within himself and sought to share it with others.

Yet because of the interwoven lives, I cannot tell his story without, in the end, telling of my sister, whose life and legacy have so shaped my own life, through Stillpoint and, more importantly, through who she was. T. S. Eliot, in his poem "Burnt Norton," captures the essence of both their lives, and of the place.

At the still point of the turning world ... there the dance is.

The dance was there, and it emanated out from that center. Now I am here as steward of this place and its memories, and I walk the land always mindful of its interconnected, inseparable stories. It is a bittersweet role I was given and finally came to embrace, for this is a place of quiet beauty, and that beauty evokes a deep longing for what cannot return. The stillness holds those memories, and in the quiet of my deepest self, the dance continues.

CHAPTER ONE

SEEKING
GIA-FU

The Tao that can be told is not the eternal Tao.
The name that can be named is not the eternal name.
The nameless is the beginning of heaven and earth.
The named is the mother of ten thousand things.

—from Chapter 1, *Tao Te Ching*

I look at a photograph of Gia-fu Feng taken in 1965 at Esalen Institute in Big Sur, California. He is standing on the beach, waves breaking behind him, his right hand raised about chest high, directed forward, his eyes focused on his hand.[1] A slight smile touches his lips. The hand position and focus on his hand suggest he is demonstrating a tai chi movement. He is dressed in a white turtleneck and a dark-colored V-neck sweater. His dark, short hair, tousled by the sea breeze, frames a face that is clean shaven. He looks very young for his forty-six years. Innocent, almost.

Another photograph sits on my desk, in sight of my every move. It shows Gia-fu with slightly longer hair around his receding hairline, a longish beard, and eyes that hold incredible longing, longing that breaks my heart. I don't know what this longing means or even exactly when this photograph was taken. In the background are hills that look like those across from Stillpoint, but he is too young to have been there then. He must be nearing his mid-fifties.

A third photograph lies in view, taken circa 1978. In this one, Gia-fu is sitting on a cushion in a classic meditation position, left hand raised about chest high, eyes looking slightly downward. Somewhat longish, unruly hair frames a balding crown. A long, full beard adorns his face. His look could be described as wisely contemplative. Closing in on sixty, one can begin to be wise.

Something Gia-fu said in a book about Gestalt therapy founder Fritz Perls seems to fit these photographs. In describing Perls, a man older than Gia-fu who influenced him greatly, Gia-fu paraphrased Confucius: "When you are fifteen you start to learn; when you are thirty then you stand up, at forty you are out of confusion; and at fifty you know the destiny; at sixty you are so desireless you can really listen, you are untemptable; and by the time you are seventy then you do whatever you want without worry about right or wrong."[2] Perhaps these words also describe how Gia-fu saw himself. Perhaps he even saw his destiny.

These photographs recorded moments in Gia-fu's life, just three moments. They reflect life events, illuminating Gia-fu, and as they illuminate him, ten thousand things begin to appear—and as other facets of this man reveal themselves, ten thousand more. I keep thinking about how his brother Chao-hua told me early in my search to understand Gia-fu that people are multifaceted, and Gia-fu even more so. After that 1995 talk with Chao-hua, as I continued to explore, each facet seemed to reflect its own innumerable dimensions.

Other photographs have also helped guide me in learning about Gia-fu and writing this book. Photographs of him with Jane English in the early seventies. Also pictures of him with members of his family on his 1975 trip to China at the end of the Cultural Revolution, his only return to his homeland, the first time he or anyone else was allowed to go back. The Cultural Revolution, that exceedingly turbulent time from 1965 to 1975, brought incredible destruction, especially to large, well-educated, wealthy families such as Gia-fu's. Families with these characteristics were considered "capitalist-roaders," a deadly label during that decade. That trip back evoked grief and depression for Gia-fu; he learned less than he wanted to learn but more than he could bear. Reconciling his early years in China with those new realities proved a momentous challenge for this man who had gained so much hard-earned wisdom to guide his life and help others. But not enough to ease this newfound pain.

There are dozens of photographs of Gia-fu during his adult life, and some taken on his 1975 return to his homeland brought a new level of meaning and fresh insight to my long quest for a suitable way to write about Gia-fu's life.

In many pictures taken during the 1975 trip, Gia-fu and his fellow travelers pose beside various statues of Mao Tse-tung. This could have been due to the omnipresence of Mao statues, but possibly it reflected a conflict simmering inside Gia-fu, a conflict I could not grasp prior to a heart-wrenching talk with some of his family members thirty years later. We talked about Gia-fu, by then a foreigner, a man who could not under-stand what his family had endured during the Cultural Revolution, who could not accept their inability to change it, and who feared he might un-wittingly contribute to their suffering. This was a piece of Gia-fu's internal life that had puzzled me from the beginning of my research eleven years earlier. Only after that conversation did I finally begin to understand just how torn Gia-fu was about his family and his homeland. I knew then to look deeper into the research material I had collected through the years.

Transcripts of interviews I've had with people who knew Gia-fu during his sixty-six years fill two file drawers. Some knew him very well and over a long period, others not as well or for shorter times, but each had a compelling perspective on who he was and what he was trying to do. Some were more flattering than others. Someone suggested it was a waste of time to write about Gia-fu because he wasn't famous enough to have a book published about him. Others said they couldn't wait to read the book. Each interview revealed more details, ten thousand multiplied, it seemed, by Gia-fu's sixty-six years. I spent hours in the interviews and countless hours more poring over them, looking for clues, themes, patterns, pattern breakers, insights.

Then there were the three-hundred-plus jumbled pages, tattered, dog-eared glimpses of a life so different from my own, the pages my sister and Clara Reida had begun editing in 1989. Written in a stream of consciousness, Gia-fu's story sidles from one decade to another within a paragraph, then back again, and to yet another decade in the next. There is also, I discovered after working with friend Andrea Hart to organize this version, a condensed, more coherent account, entitled *One Hundred Pages of Feng, 1919–1949*, his years in China. This one showed up on my doorstep soon after David and I returned from our first China visit in 1997, probably left by former Stillpointer Jerry Coulter.

Early on I asked publisher friend Lloyd Alexander, a person who had known Gia-fu well and the one who introduced my sister to him, if he thought the manuscript could be published. After reading the three-hundred-page jumble, he told me that it needed context. "Unless the reader were very familiar with Chinese history, and even recent U.S. history, she would be lost," he said. I was fairly familiar with recent American history, but I didn't know much at all about Chinese history. Baffled about how I was going to turn Gia-fu's manuscript into a book, I nonetheless continued searching for a way to do it.

More information and many more sources awaited exploration, including interviews, letters, references to books in which Gia-fu is mentioned, or descriptions of incidents in which he was involved, or observations that he made, such as the quote from the Fritz Perls book. Contact with his friends, acquaintances, family—Colorado, New York, California, China,

England, Germany. Chinese history, recent U.S. history. Where was I to begin in all this, and how was I to make sense of it for myself and for others? There's an Inuit food, *muktuk*. It's whale blubber and skin, and the longer you chew on it, the bigger it seems to get. Trying to write Gia-fu's story, I realized, was my muktuk. When and how would I break it down and start to swallow? And when, I asked myself, would I do this, given my consuming professional life in public education? At that time, I was executive director of the Colorado Partnership for Educational Renewal, a member of the National Network for Educational Renewal.

Then one fortuitous blue-skied autumn afternoon in October 1994, a few weeks after Jane English and I had been to Stillpoint, my work took me up the interstate to Colorado State University. There I found myself in the well-ordered, pleasantly modest office of Liberal Arts Dean Loren Crabtree. The dean, a scholarly, kind man, greeted Nancy Hartley, dean of the CSU college that included teacher preparation, and me. He took his seat behind his tidy desk, and Dean Hartley and I sat facing him, his well-stocked bookshelves a fitting backdrop.

Leaning forward, Dean Hartley initiated the discussion by saying that liberal arts and education at CSU enjoy good relationships between the colleges and with the public schools. "But there's more we can do," she added.

With that the three of us were off on a lively exploration of ways to strengthen those relationships. Dean Crabtree considered and named professors and their various content areas amenable to working with teachers in the public schools. "And, of course, my area of study is recent Chinese history," he said.

I stared at him. I tried not to stare at him. I took a breath. I couldn't breathe. I couldn't believe what I thought I'd heard. And somehow I knew the heavens had opened and dropped opportunity right into my lap. Trying to pay attention to what Dean Hartley was saying, I found my eyes searching the book titles on the shelves behind Loren Crabtree. *My Country and My People* by Lin Yutang; *The Gate of Heavenly Peace* by Jonathan Spence; *Chinabound* by John King Fairbank. Lots of books with China or China references in the titles. I had to stop myself from reading the titles and pay attention to that important discussion.

Talk ceased for a moment. Willing the discussion finished, I breathed out what seemed an interminably held question. "Dean Crabtree, have you ever heard of Gia-fu Feng?"

Without hesitation he said, "Well, yes. I have his translation of the *Tao Te Ching* on the coffee table at home. It's the best of the more than three hundred translations out there. I use it in my classes, and my students love it!" Then he paused. "Why do you ask?"

Quivering, unable to believe my luck but knowing somewhere deep down that it was real, I told him. I told about the manuscript, about Stillpoint, about my sister's connection to Gia-fu, about how I wanted to write the book but needed help—expert, scholarly help. And I asked if he might be willing to help me.

Pleased to assist, in the year that followed that meeting and revelation, he launched me on a course of reading that began to fill gaps in my knowledge and create context for Gia-fu's early life in China. The sources were endless, and the reading continued well beyond that year, turning into a decade of research. And somewhere along the way I began to feel it just might be possible to swallow a bit of that muktuk.

The reading was only a beginning, really. So much more remained. Looking at the photo of Gia-fu at Esalen, snippets of a conversation with Ananda Claude Dalenberg tugged at my mind, so I pulled out the file containing the 1997 interview with him. Rereading the transcript of that meeting in San Francisco brought back more clearly the question he raised.

That rainy afternoon we spent together, Ananda Claude, a Zen priest and a large man with a full graying beard, who appeared as Alvah Goldbook in Jack Kerouac's *Dharma Bums*, spoke in a gentle tone belying his full, resonant voice. In the mid-1950s, he told me, he along with Gia-fu and others had created and lived in the East-West House, a cooperative established to extend the East-meets-West approach of the Academy of Asian Studies. He talked about how quiet and easy to be with Gia-fu was, and about his involvement with the Quakers during their years together in San Francisco. Also how Gia-fu had begun to get interested in the old Chinese religion.

Then in the early 1960s, Gia-fu went to Esalen. "I visited a couple of times there, and it was a different personality. I hardly knew him. Well, I knew it was Gia-fu, but from his background I didn't expect it, from the days I knew him."

This indicated a dramatic shift I hadn't known about. Before that 1997 interview with Ananda Claude, I had thought that the flow from San Francisco to Esalen was a smooth, even one. I realized then, for the first time, that there were things about the Gia-fu before Esalen and the Gia-fu after that didn't add up. If I was going to write this biography, I needed to know what had happened.

I searched, analyzed, asked others to analyze. Prodding events and accounts before Esalen and after, I began to discern seeming shifts in personality. I detected the beginnings of an evolution toward something well beyond Gia-fu's quiet, well-bred East-West House persona. There were also presages early on of the teacher he would become. Looking far back into his boyhood, there were clearly even seeds of the self-described rogue he was to become. I saw, too, in the eventual leader of the Stillpoint community reflections of the patriarchal figure of his father. Back to his beginnings and to his end. But none of the story was neat or tidy, nothing complete. In the myriad details and large chunks of information, gaps yawed and contradictions loomed. Ten thousand facets, multiplying themselves.

Sixty-six years, captured by moments in photographs, in Gia-fu's written memories and in the memories of others. And although one could never have predicted where and how Gia-fu would live his life or where it would end, in looking closely at the whole of it I now see that the seeds of who Gia-fu became were in him all along. As Mary Catherine Bateson suggests in *Composing a Life*, looking back one can see patterns that cannot be seen as one's life is unfolding, for we improvise as we live our lives, bringing what we have within us to bear on whatever comes our way.[3] And what Gia-fu had within him was, as it is in all of us, shaped in part by his family, his early environment, and events throughout his life. But these were not the only forces. A desire for freedom, an ideal, a longing for something more—an inner longing, one that drove him outward to different places and then inward to the deepest parts of himself—seem to underlie both the sudden changes and the gradual transitions in his life.

In telling what I hoped would be the coherent, compelling story of this man I didn't know and who has touched my life so profoundly, I knew I must reflect those facets that most enchanted, puzzled, and provoked me along the way. I hoped to do this by exploring the multiple formative influences, punctuated by transformational events and circumstances in his extraordinary life. I've ordered this story chronologically, used as much as possible from Gia-fu's own manuscript, and incorporated numerous other sources. I have been selective in what I have included, choosing what has seemed to me most directly related to the people, places, and experiences that ultimately led Gia-fu to the freedom he sought: his dance, his center, his point of balance, his stillpoint.

CHAPTER TWO

TRADITION
& PROSPERITY

Stand before it and there is no beginning.
Follow it and there is no end.
Stay with the ancient Tao,
Move with the present.

—from Chapter 14, *Tao Te Ching*

Images linger, suspended in time, as I contemplate Gia-fu's written memories of his early life in China. Some of these images are etched in fine detail; others have been sharpened through conversations with his siblings. In reconstructing a life, such images matter. Picture an early-morning ritual in the three-story Feng home on Avenue Foch in Shanghai's French Concession. The year is 1929. Father Feng Chong-ching lies in his bed. A wooden bed frame of elegantly simple design supports the full-sized bed, which, along with several other beautifully carved traditional pieces, furnishes the room. Propped up by several plump pillows, Feng Chong-ching drinks black tea from his tall glass and contemplates his children.

Having had their morning "wash-ups," Gia-fu and his brothers and sisters arrange themselves around their father's bed, offering morning greetings and awaiting attention, perhaps some instruction about how they should study or behave for the day. Feng Chong-ching speaks at length to his children. The children speak only when asked, and when they do speak to him, they call him Dea Dea, the Chinese equivalent of Dad or Daddy.

A dizzying range of ages and array of faces and names cluster around Feng Chong-ching. Of his nine children, seven are here. Gia-fu, third brother, middle child and ten years old, stands by next-to-youngest, fourth brother Chao-hua, eight; Lu-tsi, third daughter, six; fifth and youngest brother, Zhao-shu, five. Four-year-old Wan-tsi is fourth daughter and youngest child. Of the four older siblings, only the two girls, Mei-chi, thirteen, and Pei-chi, eleven, stand here awaiting their father's instructions. The two older boys, twins Chen-fu and Chen-shu, now fifteen years old, are away at boarding school.

Father Feng, a highly successful banker and financier, provides well for the family and, as evidenced by this scene, commands great respect. In the family he is primarily responsible for decisions about moral growth and education: hence his morning instructions and admonitions to the children. A strict man and in the Confucian fashion, he takes his family responsibilities seriously. Also a nervous, high-strung man: in Gia-fu's eyes, he has "a colossal temper, typical of a stern patriarch."

Other dimensions of Feng Chong-ching directly affect his children. He writes accomplished calligraphy, much of which he taught himself, reflecting his love of learning. That he respects and values education ensures his children will be thoroughly and well taught. He sends them to the best schools, boarding school awaits most of them, and he hires scholarly tutors to teach them English and the Chinese classics during summer months. This is an uncommon effort, beyond the bounds of duty, or perhaps reason, in the eyes of Feng Chong-ching's friends. But the children benefit from this extra effort, and even enjoy some aspects of it. Gia-fu is keen on Chinese classics.

While the children are with their father, mother Wei Han-chuen, whom Gia-fu loves dearly, spends the morning organizing the maids and servants, an important part of the Chinese extended family, for the day—for their shopping, cooking, laundry, dusting, and cleaning, as well as helping to look after the children. She is responsible for the home and therefore for those who work in it. The servants' and family roles are clearly prescribed. Even now, in the first third of the twentieth century, the Fengs reflect China's traditional view of the family as the stronghold, the central social unit. It is to the family that duty is directed.

Seniority throughout the family counts. The Confucian ideal of filial piety as the root of virtue and origin of culture is at work here. The children look up to their father and mother. Younger siblings look up and defer to older brothers and sisters, which can be reassuring in its definitiveness and maddening in its expectations for those less inclined toward order. For Gia-fu, just turned ten, this isn't a problem—yet.

After talking with his children, Feng Chong-ching has breakfast—a bowl of congee, a rice porridge, in keeping with the mild diet he needs for his chronic stomach problems—and leaves for his work in Shanghai's booming financial district. Because of the chaotic times, with warlords vying for power and crime difficult to control because of the many foreign jurisdictions in Shanghai, Feng Chong-ching takes precautions to avoid the all-too-common occurrence of well-known figures being kidnapped and held for ransom. He wears dark glasses and his hat pulled down close over his forehead as he enters his big American-made limousine and is chauffeured to the Da Ching Bank.

Feng Chong-ching's success in the banking and financial world draws respect from many, including his children. He had moved to Shanghai at the age of thirteen with his father, Feng Ying-shan, a consultant-manager with a big firm in northeast China near Harbin. The move from their ancestral land, Yu Yao, Chekiang, a hundred miles southwest of Shanghai, deep in the Yangtze Valley of thick rice paddies, brought the thirteen-year-old Feng Chong-ching into an apprenticeship at the Da Ching Bank, an institution of the Ching Dynasty (1644–1911).[1] While it was hardly unusual for a thirteen-year-old to work or enter an apprenticeship, it was indeed something out of the ordinary for him to become a banking apprentice in this prestigious institution.

Because of his intense loyalty and diligence, he was rapidly promoted to top positions. His rise was accelerated when, during the change of currency from silver to bank notes, he contributed numerous innovative ideas, which impressed the bank's upper managers, including Mr. Song Han Chuang and Mr. Bai Sang Sung. He found strong support as he went to all of China's major cities to exchange the silver for bank notes, and by the age of forty had risen to a top position in the bank. Feng Chong-ching is fond of telling his children about "getting up at dawn, pulling up my socks while my eyes were still closed, to race to the railroad station to supervise the transportation of bank notes."

After the Revolution of 1911, which freed China from Manchu rule and ended more than two millennia of its imperial history, the Da Ching Bank became the powerful Bank of China. Feng Chong-ching, now president, is considered one of the founders of this bank in Shanghai.

Astute about human relationships and possessing, according to his third son, "tremendous guts, plus a little luck," Feng Chong-ching has a large network, including contacts influential with the president of the republic and other key leaders. His position affords him influence on the bond market, which is active and highly speculative in Shanghai during the late 1920s and 1930s.

In contrast to Feng Chong-ching's worldly-wise day, Wei Han-chuen's routine reflects her old-fashioned upbringing. She prefers staying at home, available to the servants and the children when they're not at school. Her responsibilities for this huge, beautiful home, large family, and many servants require constant vigilance. To Gia-fu, she seems to be the first one up in the morning and the last one to bed at night. Late at night Gia-fu can hear his mother's bound feet drag as she approaches his bed to check on his bedding and bedroom windows. She does this with each of her nine children, even the older ones when they are home from school.

Gia-fu not only loves his mother, he admires her ability to keep track of all the complicated social customs, for to Wei Han-chuen fall the social responsibilities inherent and essential in traditional Chinese society. The numerous prescribed protocols include, for example, the sending of presents and the giving of tips to servants bringing presents, a seemingly constant activity. She has at her fingertips the names of, and special foods for, the twenty-four different annual festivals based on the change of seasons, among them New Year, Spring or Ching Ming, August Moon, and the Midsummer Festivals. She must also keep in mind the many rites and rituals for weddings and funerals, and the complicated science of nomenclature for all the various kinds of kinship among the paternal and maternal uncles and aunts, their respective wives and husbands, their sisters and sisters-in-law, their children, every possible variation of cousins and nephews and nieces and nieces' husbands, and so on. Gia-fu is in awe of her ability "to tell at a glance at a funeral how many sons, daughters, daughters-in-law, sons-in-law, and grandchildren the deceased man has following his coffin by noting merely their different signs of mourning."

Gia-fu and his siblings love and admire their mother for many reasons, her kindness not the least of these. An old-style Buddhist, Wei Han-chuen embraces compassion and kindness as a way of being. Through another lens, she personifies what is called *jen*—Confucian virtues of kindness, benevolence, and human-heartedness.

This morning, now that she's given initial instructions to the servants, Wei Han-chuen sits at her dressing table. Her hair-combing maid stands behind her combing her long, beautiful hair. Their visit with their father over, the children traipse noisily in and out of her room to say good-bye and ask for pocket money before leaving for school. This lively scene produces a crescendo in the early morning activity; then everyone settles down to the day's work before them. For Wei Han-chuen, it's the smooth functioning of the home; for Feng Chong-ching, it's staying on top of the fast-paced, high-stakes world of finance; and for all but the very youngest of the children, it's their studies.

Within the family, a sense of order based on tradition prevails. Beyond the family, however, the Fengs' environment is in flux in a city and a country undergoing explosive change. It helps to understand that the forces now changing and shaping China are linked to events of the past, to external influences that, especially during the mid-nineteenth century, devastated the Middle Kingdom, the name the Chinese gave their vast and varied country. (Indeed, they believed it to be the center of the universe.)

As did so many other countries during that period, China suffered humiliating defeat and ruinous setbacks at the hands of Western nations wanting to take advantage of its markets and resources, including its people. The early Opium Wars from 1839 to 1842 were part of the disasters. The British introduced opium to China, creating a drug market among the Chinese. China's attempt to resist was unsuccessful, an unfortunate outcome that affected the country far into the twentieth century.

This particular instance of aggression, the Opium Wars, resulted in Shanghai's becoming a "treaty port" as a legacy of the 1842 Treaty of Nanjing, with two foreign concessions or settlement areas being established. Other foreign zones, such as Portuguese, American, and German, came later. In these foreign zones, the foreigners' respective legal systems replaced Chinese law, resulting in a "jurisdictional tangle" that drew merchants, missionaries, settlers, traders, and many others wanting to avoid the law. The International Settlement, dominated by the British and the French Concessions where the Fengs now live, almost completely surrounds the original Chinese city of Shanghai.

Given the various jurisdictions, the resulting legal confusion, and the near-constant conflict between warlords, it is difficult to know who is in charge of which areas. Further confounding matters, territories and boundaries are set by the underworld but not always respected. In one incident at their home, the Feng children find themselves ducking under the table to avoid stray bullets fired by a roving band of marauding soldiers.

Shanghai, because of its location on China's eastern coast at the mouth of the Yangtze River on the East China Sea, has long invited trade, growing up like many modern cities where interior river commerce meets sea trade. It sits in a temperate latitude, with a climate similar to Washington, DC. It is so ideally set for all kinds of enterprise that it has become the scene for an increasingly multifaceted commercial, cultural, social, intellectual, political, and underworld life. Journalist Stella Dong asserts that in the 1920s and 1930s, which was "Shanghai's prime, no city in the Orient, or the world for that matter could compare with it."[2] In the center of this vivid, electrifying environment Gia-fu and his family live.

Shanghai's exponential growth from 1910 to 1930 sees its population triple. By now in 1929, the Chinese and foreign population combined is almost three million, with 1.5 million Chinese and almost ten thousand foreigners living under Chinese jurisdiction. The French Concession is home to almost a half million Chinese, including the Feng family, and twelve thousand foreigners. The International Settlement as a whole holds just short of one million Chinese and thirty-six thousand foreigners. In Shanghai's odd way, this leads to approximately 1.5 million Chinese living under foreign law.

Industry is also booming now. World War I has caused Western merchants to focus their attention and money on Europe, thereby encouraging the Chinese to invest their own funds and even to buy Western firms. Chinese and Japanese money successfully back scores of new industries capitalizing on resources as varied as soybeans, flour, oil, cotton, silk, rubber, coal, and opium. Numerous Chinese banks have come into being to handle the massive money flow of those who, like Feng Chong-ching, have worked hard and long, as well as that of the many overnight entrepreneurial millionaires.

Gia-fu loves both the traditional and international aspects of Shanghai, and especially loves exploring it with his uncle, one of his father's younger brothers, an attractive young man who is a friend to the boy. This uncle finds roller skating great fun and enjoys taking his nephew out for this and to explore the wonders of Shanghai. Sometimes he takes Gia-fu out to rent Chinese storybooks from the sidewalk peddler. These books, unlike Western comic books, include lots of Chinese history and social events.

23

Vividly illustrated with pictures and humorous comments, among these are some of Gia-fu's favorite classics—*Three Kingdoms, Monkey, Dream of the Red Chamber*—many of which have been translated into Western languages. Gia-fu and his uncle often spend hours reading nonstop, forgetting to eat or move around, sometimes ending up with stomachaches from hunger and prolonged inactivity.

They also go to the Chinese opera, where Gia-fu envies his uncle's skill in listening, crucial for really appreciating this event. He observes the experienced audience sitting sideways, facing the upper right-hand corner of the stage in order to concentrate and discern the quality of the voices. Although Gia-fu doesn't feel he is a competent listener yet, he enjoys it for the beauty, emotion, and historical content. Later in life he will sing Chinese opera for friends on the other side of the world.

In addition to Chinese culture, Gia-fu and his uncle enjoy the vast cultural variety Shanghai offers. They eat ice cream and French pastries and also take in the music and dancing of the many Russians in Shanghai, a group exerting a significant cultural influence on the arts. They are here in great numbers. The White Russians, who are ex-nobility and traders, fled Russia during the Revolution. The Red Russians, also numerous in Shanghai, are primarily former diplomats.

History, literature, arts, culture—Chinese and others—draw Gia-fu's attention. They fascinate him, and this fascination will last a lifetime. However, his love of the humanities will cause conflict within the family in a few years when his interests and his father's wishes collide. But for now, spongelike, he soaks it all up.

Feng Chong-ching's ideas about a complete education include balancing Western influences in the formal schools with the classics, taught by special tutors. He engages these tutors for the two-month summer vacation, which the Fengs spend at their alternate residence in Shanghai's suburbs. This is a spacious, multistory flat that is part of the bank's luxurious housing compound for its employees. Gia-fu idealizes this place as "immersed in the beautiful surrounding of tranquility... an ideal setting for studying Chinese literature" and reminiscent of a "Chinese painting, [with] a lonely old sage in a cottage above a murmuring stream." Indeed, quite possibly this idealization is at the root of where and how he will choose to live in his later years.

The two summer months spent at the villa are hot. The children, a troop of servants, chauffeurs, gardeners, bodyguards, and others go off to live with the old tutor, Master Chuan, who is a scholar of the old school and a member of the Han-lin Academy, an honor somewhat comparable to that of Rhodes Scholar in the West.[3] The Academy admits only a small, select group who have the highest scores in the imperial civil service exams. Academy members frequently write commentaries on the classics and compose official documents. They are often appointed to high, desirable official positions. Feng Chong-ching truly wants the best for his children.

An old-fashioned man, Master Chuan doesn't keep up with Shanghai's rapidly Westernizing customs. Gia-fu notes his manners at meals, particularly how he grabs a pair of chopsticks and, without waiting for the others, digs into the meat dishes. Good manners dictate that one must not take from one dish only so that others can enjoy it, but Master Chuan seems oblivious to this. Additionally, his nearsightedness causes him to bend so low over his food that his head almost touches the table. Sometimes his nearsightedness tempts the children into hiding his glasses when he occasionally naps in the classroom during the hot afternoon hours.

But before the children have breakfast, before even brushing their teeth, they must do two sheets of calligraphy. Sleepy-eyed, they grind their ink blocks against their ink stones and start copying their respective pieces of stone engraving, the originals of which were set down by the great calligraphers of dynasties past—Tang, Song, and Ming.

Later in the day Master Chuan examines their work, rewarding the good inscriptions with a red ink circle in the upper right hand corner. The bad ones receive a diagonal stroke from upper left to lower right corners. The children always compare numbers of circles and strokes respectively to figure their scores.

Yet another early-morning task for Gia-fu and his siblings is the chanting of particular sections of the Chinese classics as they ready themselves for their recitation for Master Chuan. Early mornings, therefore, are filled with preparation, not only for their studies but also dressing properly for their other tutor, Miss Gawler, whose brother is the British commissioner of the Shanghai Customs. Miss Gawler arrives at nine a.m. each day to teach the children two hours of English conversation. Often the children are unprepared for her because they are completing Master Chuan's assignments. They are not as alert as they might be because they have stayed up late into the night. Youngest brother Zhao-shu saves the day, however, as he is always the first ready and awaits Miss Gawler's arrival with a cup of tea while his siblings rush to be in their seats before class begins.

Late afternoon music lessons provide a welcome break from English conversation and from memorizing and chanting Chinese classics. Gia-fu specializes in the er-hu. A two-stringed fiddle with a horsetail hair bow, the er-hu is played held upright leaning against the thighs or held between the knees. Five Chinese music notes are five tones, each represented by a calligraphic character. Master Chuan chants out the sounds and taps out the beats by slapping his knees, waving his hand, or jerking his head. Little does Gia-fu know that following Master Chuan's instructions will make it possible for him to play the er-hu in undreamed-of situations throughout his life, such as in writer and artist Pierre DeLattre's downtown San Francisco Beat coffee shop in the late 1950s, or at Esalen Institute in the 1960s. For now, he enjoys playing and gives it his complete attention.

This special tutoring contrasts sharply with the children's formal schooling and especially Gia-fu's boarding school experience. He attends boarding school for much of primary middle school and senior middle school, each of which is three years. After middle school, he will take exams to enter university. In the boarding school there is less flexibility or opportunity for diversion. Gia-fu's father is on the school's board of directors, but avoids exercising undue influence for his sons. The school emphasizes academic achievement and accompanying heavy homework, and allows the boys to go home only one weekend a month. Their families, however, can visit the other three weekends. As mother Wei Han-chuen seldom goes out, Gia-fu's nursemaid often visits him on these weekends, bringing treats mostly of freshly cooked food such as *chiao-tzu*—meat dumplings, similar to wontons but oilier and usually pan-fried—sweetmeats, chickens, and peanuts, always Gia-fu's favorite. He shares with his friends, who vary from time to time as relationships change.

Gia-fu's next-youngest brother, Chao-hua, is also at the boarding school, and when they go home for extended holidays or vacations, they share a room on the top floor of the Feng home. Youngest brother, Zhao-shu, also shares the room with them and enjoys hearing the older boys talk about their experiences. Later, when they are in their teens, he will learn from their conversation about the girls they like.

In the boarding school Gia-fu notices that social groupings stay within class lines. With about forty boys in one class, sixteen in one bedroom, and a gatehouse with two or three gatekeepers, the social environment seems to him "not unlike a prison setup." Going beyond the gatehouse requires special permission, meaning a direct request to the dean, a formidable undertaking. The strictness may be in part due to kidnappings and other dangers to be found on Shanghai's streets, but only in part.

Knowing the stern and authoritative nature of their dean, who often patrols the dormitories after the nine fifteen lights out, the boys cease their chattering the instant they hear his footsteps. The dean has the authority to expel anyone from the school, and the boys wisely fear and respect that power.

The students here are diligent and disciplined, holding the nation's highest record of passing entrance exams to leading universities. Gia-fu, for his part, does well in school. He is a good writer, in the Ku-wen-yen style, which means literary language and includes many allusions and allegories of the classics. Perhaps Master Chuan's influence can be seen here. Drawn to literary and artistic studies, Gia-fu finds these studies also complement his continued interest in history.

His athletic ability, however, remains undeveloped for the moment. He still remembers when he first arrived at the school the year before and ran away from the ball so he wouldn't get hit, causing his fellow students to laugh at him. Another student, Da-Ling, with whom Gia-fu developed an immediate friendship when they enrolled in the school at the same time, protects Gia-fu from the torments of other classmates. While the shortest student in the class, Da-Ling is extremely athletic and watches out for his friend Gia-fu, the second shortest and quite the opposite of Da-Ling in athletic ability. Gia-fu rewards him by sharing his treats from home, which are especially appreciated by Da-Ling, whose family lives far from Shanghai in Szechuan Province in the Upper Yangtze Valley.

During holidays Gia-fu and his family celebrate the various festivals—twenty-four each year. Except for the annual out-of-town trip for Spring Festival, mother Wei Han-chuen goes out only at New Year's when the whole family has dinner out and attends a theater performance. At these dinners, nursemaids sit behind each of the younger children, helping them when needed. Gia-fu remembers when he was younger and his nursemaid sat behind him, eating only when the family had finished their meal. In his later years, he will feel guilty about this, but for now he accepts it as a normal part of family life.

The lunar calendar determines the New Year, and for the first fifteen days of it the Feng home is completely refurbished. Everything is cleaned. Rare and expensive wall hangings replace the old, to be removed after the fifteen days and stored until the next New Year. The children have learned how to behave appropriately at these special times and in special places, so very few scoldings or confrontations occur.

Throughout the year, during the ancestor-worship rituals and feasts, all the relatives come to visit. Gia-fu thinks the adults maintain "an atmosphere of solemn reverence" during these times, leaving the younger family members with a certain sense of freedom and peace.

Next to the New Year or Spring Festival, which celebrates the new lunar year and anticipates the coming of spring, Ching Ming Festival is the biggest annual event. Ching Ming occurs in April, the fifteenth day from the Spring Equinox. Ching Ming, "Honoring the Dead" Festival, celebrates spring's arrival, thereby simultaneously paying tribute to the dead and welcoming new life. To celebrate and honor their ancestors, the Feng family journeys to their ancestral home in Yuyao south of Shanghai in Chekiang province. On January 10, 1919, Gia-fu was born near here because his mother is from a neighboring village and had returned to her family home for the birth.

To get to their ancestral home, the Feng family as a whole takes a steamer and travels south overnight from Shanghai to the coastal city of Ningpo. While on the steamer, except for the very young children, each person has a little cabin to himself, and the family has a reserved room in the dining hall. The food is Western, leaning toward the Mediterranean style, with sandwiches neatly cut in small squares, butter balls, hors d'oeuvres, oxtail cabbage soup, and breaded tongue—Gia-fu's favorite. After leaving the steamer, they take a train, then a sampan, a small boat sculled by oars, to reach their destination.

The family arrives at the family home, which in classic Chinese style includes numerous buildings and a pavilion near a pond a little away from the main compound. With a long row of six houses joining together, the compound itself is quite large. Father Feng Chong-ching, Grandmother, and Fourth Uncle each have a separate house. A courtyard lies in front of the long, wide patios that are covered with long beams and curly eaves. Farther down, a narrow path leads to the garden, which is enclosed by a high stone wall.

The whole family visits the ancestral tombs, dating from the eleventh century. They engage in the proper ceremonies, called "sweeping the tombs," and then for several days take hikes and have picnics. Each night brings a feast, and the courtyard fills with relatives and neighbors. These feasts include a dish that Gia-fu finds the most interesting and delicious: half-hatched eggs. He eats so many of the little chickens that he gets a stomachache.

Games and playacting are part of the festivities. Typically Chinese, the games are based on the individual rather than teams, another reflection of the Confucian emphasis on individual and family, not society as a whole. A game Gia-fu particularly likes includes guessing the number of fingers the opponent will hold up out of his or her fist, which are then added to numbers from his own fist. When it's his turn, he calls out the number in a dramatic voice, since the goal is to "scare the other person out of his or her wits, so that he or she loses control of the number of fingers being stretched out, and one gets his number, so to speak." These games require bravado, with significant shouting and gesturing, and leave the players little room for embarrassment. Gia-fu's extroverted side resonates to these games.

Life for the Fengs stays full, celebrating the myriad festivals and special events, observing rituals, and attending to the responsibilities and vicissitudes of their respective daily lives. It is the latter that now concerns

Gia-fu, who at fifteen finds himself in a spot of trouble. Having become friends with the family's young chauffeur, Gia-fu accepts the young man's half-joking offer to show him how to drive. What teenage boy can resist such an offer? Certainly not Gia-fu. He accepts, climbs into the Buick convertible, and with instructions from his friend, starts the engine. But releasing the clutch and pressing a little too hard on the accelerator bring an unexpected reaction from the car. Gia-fu's astonishment at the car's sudden backward movement, the car being in reverse gear, is matched only by his horror at feeling the jolt of an equally sudden stop as the car plows into a tree, denting both the back bumper and the back fender.

Terrified of his father's reaction, Gia-fu worries for himself as well as for the young chauffeur. Naturally, his siblings take it upon themselves to reinforce this worry, causing Gia-fu to fret even more. But nothing happens and several months pass. Then one day, as Gia-fu walks by the car, he notices that the fender and bumper have been repaired. The relief he feels almost equals the trauma of the experience, which will haunt him for years and affect his driving, a fact to which many friends will attest later on.

Now as Gia-fu enters his senior year in high school, his classmates elect this popular young man to be class president and treasurer. In some ways it seems a natural choice, his father being a banker. But his popularity seems more attributable to his sociability. He enjoys people and people enjoy him. He likes to go out, and does so occasionally. One such occasion is what he calls a night's fling at a nearby dancing parlor. He is fascinated by the glamorous taxi dancers, those attractive young women who will dance with one for a fee. The taxi dancer sizes a person up by appearance and manner and then gives the degree of physical closeness she feels should be accorded. A person's money doesn't mean much, but manners and taste mean a great deal.

Money apparently does means something, since Gia-fu spends all his classmates' dues on the taxi dancers, the money for which he, as class treasurer, is responsible. Realizing the ramifications of his actions, albeit too late, he feels desperate. Scared stiff to tell even his mother because he fears his father's "considerable wrath," Gia-fu also fears losing face among his peers. To him, this is another "terribly traumatic experience."

Having nowhere else to turn, he finally decides to confide in his mother and ask for her help. Even so, Gia-fu waits for just the right time to tell her. To Gia-fu's great relief, his mother comes through for him, giving him the money "without a word." She could tell that he was in trouble. She also knew he was suffering and "was truly repentant."

The year is 1935. Gia-fu, now in his senior year at boarding school, is studying for the daunting university entrance exams. Tension pervades the campus as students cram for the exams. All other classes have left for the term so the teachers can focus on helping the seniors prepare.

Late one night as he sleeps, Gia-fu hears a knock on his door, an unusual occurrence at midnight. Shaking off his slumber, he jumps up and moves quickly to see who's there. It is someone who tells him his chauffeur is waiting at the gate for him. Gia-fu must dress and go immediately to the hospital. His mother is dying.

Overcome with anxiety and barely able to dress himself, he manages to get his clothes on and dashes to the car, throwing himself into the back seat. The chauffeur drives to the hospital as fast as he can and pulls up to the entrance, where Gia-fu jumps out of the car and runs inside the building. Knowing his mother is on the sixth floor, he runs up the many flights of stairs to where she lies.

He passes his father, who sits quietly on a chair in a room adjoining his mother's. As he enters his mother's room, he sees all his other siblings kneeling on the floor beside her bed. He's too late. She's gone. Her body lies there, a look of peace gracing her face. Gia-fu touches her leg and finds it still warm. He bows his head and kneels beside his siblings.

Wei Han-chuen, forty-seven years old, had an inflamed gallbladder, which had threatened to burst. There had been many consultations with Chinese, American, and German specialists, including Gia-fu's Fifth Uncle, his father's second-youngest brother.

Dr. Fox, the American doctor and reputedly the personal physician to T. V. Soong, brother-in-law to President Chiang Kai-shek, advocated surgery. Dr. Bacht, the German doctor and professor at Tung-Chi University where Fifth Uncle studied for his medical degree, thought the risk involved in surgery equal to the risk of the gallbladder bursting. He therefore suggested sulfa drugs to control the inflammations. Fifth Uncle sided with his former teacher, and that had settled the matter.

But the drugs did not control the inflammation, and it became too late for surgery. The gallbladder burst and now Wei Han-chuen is gone. Through Gia-fu's grief and despair, his mother's last words to him swirl in his mind: "Study hard and don't fail your father's wishes."

Devastated, the family prepares for the final rites. Notice of Wei Han-chuen's death is printed in the papers. A large traditional funeral follows. Wei Han-chuen's portrait sits on an altar surrounded by wreaths and papery gold Chinese characters pinned to silk hangings, sent by friends, relatives, and neighbors. Hired mourners sit behind a curtain wailing, vocally expressing the family's grief. Wearing white, coarse-clothed gowns and white hats made by a special tailor, the children, except for Gia-fu, sit quietly. Despite the hired wailers, Gia-fu himself wails for hours, voicing his anguish at his mother's death. Bereft at the time of her death, throughout his life Gia-fu will often find his mother appearing in his dreams. Her image lingers.

CHAPTER THREE

BIRD IN
THE CAGE

Happiness is rooted in misery.
Misery lurks beneath happiness.
Who knows what the future holds?

—from Chapter 58, *Tao Te Ching*

Gia-fu lives in misery. He has lost his beloved mother, and now he must ready himself for the Chiao-Tung University entrance examinations. Chiao-Tung University, considered the MIT of China, prepares engineers and other professionals in technological fields, exactly the careers Feng Chong-ching wishes for his five sons. Three of them will become engineers, another an architect. For now, Gia-fu tries to follow his father's wishes.

Gia-fu thinks his father "a man of strong will and very stubborn at times. Once his mind [is] made up, he [is] slow to change." A self-made man, Feng Chong-ching expects hard work and steady application toward success from his children, leaving little doubt about his expectations. But in his frequent recountings of their accomplishments and achievements, there's also little doubt that Feng Chong-ching is a proud father who relishes his children's successes and enjoys showing them off to family and friends.

Gia-fu ardently wants his father's approval and loves getting it. He also fears the consequences of not living up to his high and very specific expectations. The memory of his mother telling him not to fail his father's wishes haunts him. He's stunned by her death, by the cavernous gap now in his life, by the shock of losing her so suddenly and so early in his life. He most certainly doesn't want to fail her memory, to let her, of all people, down. He must study. But he can't focus. He grieves for his mother. His interests and his heart lie in the liberal arts, and he deeply resents studying for engineering school. But terrified, heartbroken, unfocused, denied the chance to follow his own wishes, he knows he still has to study for these exams. Though he does try very hard, mustering all the effort he can, in the end it isn't enough. He fails the entrance exams.

Feng Chong-ching refuses to give up and will not let his third son off the hook, insisting that Gia-fu attend the university anyway. Because successful completion of all freshman courses will allow a student to become a "regular" sophomore, he uses his influence to have Gia-fu enter as an auditing freshman.

Such is the power of Feng Chong-ching's determination for Gia-fu to pursue engineering studies that both the family and servants get behind the effort. They, too, want Gia-fu to show his father that he is indeed competent, and they believe he can do it. With the household's support, Gia-fu secludes himself with the single aim of focusing on his studies.

As in other winters, the servants scurry around doing the chores that keep the household running during this long season of study. Despite the lack of heat in their own quarters, they carry on with the laundry, washing vegetables under the cold-water faucet, and myriad other daily tasks. Only the combined sitting and dining room contains a large, heat-generating coal stove. Gia-fu and his siblings stay as close to fireplaces as possible, burning coke or charcoal in their respective rooms to keep warm, aware all the while of the servants traveling the cold hallways to bring tea, food, hot water, or whatever is needed. At this point in his life, Gia-fu appreciates what the servants do for him, but he also takes their efforts as his due, little knowing how very differently he will think later, how he will deplore race and class disparities and promote egalitarian relationships.

Unaware, therefore unconcerned, about such matters for now, Gia-fu sits by the fire in his room, books stacked in various piles, papers strewn around him, as he tries to comprehend the equations and theories on the pages before him. Physics, chemistry, calculus, trigonometry... He looks up as one of the servants enters the room, bringing him a tray of tea and hot, spicy soup, which will warm his insides. Muttering, "Xie xie," thank you, as the servant places the tray beside him, Gia-fu turns his bleary eyes back to the dreaded pages.

The servant travels back down the staircase, never touching the beautifully carved mahogany banister, hardly noticing the cold that pierces the large, stone walls of the house. Outside, the temperature hovers in the low thirties Fahrenheit. Inside it is warmer, but the dampness and chill seem to penetrate to the bone. A quiet ensured by the servants' hopes for Gia-fu's success has settled over the house. By the fire, Gia-fu continues with the task before him, struggling to concentrate, trying hard to study these dry, technical subjects, devoid of the color and adventure of the history, literature, and culture he loves.

Notwithstanding his genuine attempts to succeed, the late-night cramming sessions, and family and servants' efforts to support him, Gia-fu fails his courses. He is not allowed to return to Chiao-Tung University. There will be no degree from the MIT of the East for Feng Chong-ching's third son.

This turn of events, difficult and disappointing as it is, pales in comparison to what is happening in China, events that divert Feng Chongching's attention from Gia-fu and his studies. Now in 1937, just as Gia-fu is finishing the academic year and learning he is not to return to the university, Japanese hostile action in North China escalates.[1] Having seized Manchuria in 1931, the Japanese have now progressed to a full-blown invasion of China—one that will dramatically affect the Feng family during the unforeseen eight years of occupation.

On July 7, 1937, at Lou Kuo Bridge, also called Marco Polo Bridge, ten miles west of Peking, the Japanese open fire on the Chinese. The Chinese successfully resist the attack, which will be considered the first battle of World War II, although war has not yet officially been declared. This will become known as the Incident of Lou Kuo Bridge (Lugouqiao), or the Incident of Seven Seven, referring in Chinese fashion to the auspicious date.[2]

Decades later, journalist Iris Chang will observe that Americans think World War II began with the attack on Pearl Harbor on December 7, 1941, Europeans think of September 1, 1939, when Hitler's Luftwaffe and Panzer divisions launched the blitzkrieg assault on Poland, and Africans credit Mussolini's invasion of Abyssinia in 1935. Yet Asians trace the beginning to Japan's 1931 occupation of Manchuria and refer to the July 7, 1937, incident as the first battle.[3]

For now, as Gia-fu's academic future moves along its unpredictable path, the Feng family watches closely as national events unfold. By July's end, 1937, the Japanese have seized the bridge and solidified their control of the Tianjin-Peking region. Then in their continual move south, on August 13, the Incident of Eight Thirteen, they attack Shanghai. In an attempt to shift attention from North China, China's Nationalist (Kuomintang or KMT) government under President Chiang Kai-shek (known as the Generalissimo) orders an attack on Japanese forces in Shanghai, with disastrous results. The Japanese intercept the Chinese plans and are prepared. Even worse, the Chinese bombs miss their Japanese targets and fall instead on Shanghai. Hundreds of civilians die as a result. The fighting is fierce, and although the Chinese fight heroically, the Japanese prevail and the Chinese army retreats westward.[4]

Then in November, the Japanese launch an attack on China's new capital, Nanking, but they find that Chiang Kai-shek and almost all of the Nationalist government officials have moved west to Hankow, Changsha, and Chongqing. In December Nanking falls to the Japanese, and the subsequent slaughter and cruelty that follow have few precedents. Iris Chang will later record that the fatalities will surpass the numbers killed by the Romans at Carthage or the Christian armies of the Spanish Inquisition. They will even go beyond the 100,000 prisoners slain by the Timur Lenk at the 1398 Delhi massacre. "Tens of thousands of young men were rounded up and herded to the outer areas of the city, where they were mowed down by machine guns, used for bayonet practice, or soaked with gasoline and burned alive." The savagery and cruelty of the Rape of Nanking lasts for six weeks, with up to three hundred thousand civilians raped and murdered. For China as a whole, in the eight ensuing years of the Sino-Japanese war, more than ten million Chinese people will die.[5]

With the Japanese invading parts of Shanghai in August 1937, the Feng family moves from its Avenue Foch home to one of Feng Chong-ching's banks in the central financial district. Given the crisis-driven atmosphere, Gia-fu understands that this emergency situation has everyone tense and anxious, including his father, "who hastily transforms his board room into living quarters for the family." The international security forces, under the jurisdiction of Shanghai's International Settlement, protect the family and others as best they can. This part of Shanghai, under the stipulations of the nineteenth-century unequal treaties, was ceded to the eight conquering foreign nations, with the British as the dominant influence. The Japanese will not invade this part of Shanghai until it attacks Pearl Harbor in 1941 and the United States enters the war.[6]

Despite the country's frightening turn of events and the natural distraction of the situation, Gia-fu still dreads his father's response to his failure. He cannot "imagine what kind of wrath [will] descend." Holding his breath and living scared, Gia-fu awaits his father's fury. Given the dangerous circumstances of the invasion and occupation, Feng Chong-ching, however, is so preoccupied with getting his family moved and cared for, and the bank on an even keel, that he accepts Gia-fu's failure "with a great deal of equanimity." Gia-fu's relief defies description.

In a further surprise, at long last Gia-fu convinces his father to let him study the liberal arts. He enrolls in and attends a joint missionary campus in downtown Shanghai, near the Bund, a major boulevard that runs through the financial district. This campus is run by a combined committee of several universities, made necessary by the invasion and war that has stranded students from many different parts of China occupied by the Japanese. Gia-fu observes the colleges adjusting to the circumstances by allowing students from other universities to *jia tou* (borrow study) and earn credits by transferring their records. The students maintain hope, however, that they will eventually be able to return to their own universities. Unfortunately, this hope will not become reality.

Students are not the only exiles during this tense and terrifying time. Gia-fu knows that "colleges and universities themselves [are] also on the move. [Recently], Peking University had long-marched from the northern capital to southwest Kunming near the border with Vietnam and Burma." Peita or Peking University merges faculties, students, and any equipment it can move with Tsinghua and Nankai Universities to form a "university in exile" in Yunnan, the far western province where Kunming lies. They propose to continue offering excellent advanced education in spite of Japanese efforts to curtail educational development of its "conquered peoples."[7]

But now studying his beloved liberal arts at the local university in Shanghai, Gia-fu is earning straight As, and he is in demand to "ghostwrite other students' papers." His reputation "as a genius" is spreading around the campus where some of his cousins are also enrolled. When Feng Chong-ching hears of these developments, no doubt through the cousins, he finally drops his insistence that Gia-fu become an engineer.

There is an old Chinese proverb, "In every trade, there is a 'Tsuan Yuan,'" which means first in an official examination. Gia-fu's "trade" obviously lies in a different direction than what Feng Chong-ching has sought for him. But after all, hasn't Feng Chong-ching himself whetted his children's appetites for the classics by hiring special tutors for them? Gia-fu, relieved and happy that his father finally sees his true interests and talents, takes a step closer to who he really is, not who his father wants him to be. By acknowledging his son's true gifts and interests, Feng Chong-ching helps restore Gia-fu's self-confidence, and Gia-fu, as he so often does after conflict with his father, breathes a huge sigh of relief.

Gia-fu, at age eighteen, is enjoying academic success, gaining recognition, and taking pleasure in the social aspects of this time and place, which despite the occupation and danger (or perhaps because of it) seem to have intensified the merrymaking. He thrives on the excitement of associating with "the big guys of the campus, the national heroes in athletics." One student in particular seems to assume special significance for Gia-fu, who regards this young man as "extremely handsome, looking like a movie star," with suave manners. About six feet tall with curly hair and round eyes, rare for the Chinese, this friend is a magnet for the young women. Gia-fu is delighted and grateful that this popular young man takes a liking to him and often invites him to his home, only a few blocks from the Fengs. Gia-fu, who thinks himself awkward socially in comparison to his friend, knows he is more proficient academically. He appreciates such a fortunate balance.

Having been in academic environments previously, Gia-fu savors this taste of a more socially oriented school. The experience introduces him to sophisticated social settings and teaches him nuances in "winning friends and influencing people, plus how to be elegant," skills he will draw upon all his life. He sees that how one dresses signals one's importance, making the distinction obvious between rich and poor. Students wear imported Western clothes, some transforming within a matter of months "from country bumpkins into city slickers." Gia-fu cultivates a taste for clothes, enjoying and taking for granted the fact that he can afford them. He also observes students becoming mysteriously rich overnight; he suspects that some of them are involved in "all kinds of monkey business," such as the highly lucrative black market.

While Gia-fu thrives on the academic and social life of the joint university, the KMT Army continues to suffer defeats by the invading Japanese, and ultimately retreats west to Chongqing. By late 1938, the Japanese control much of eastern China, with a goal of commanding most of China's natural resources for Japan's industrial development, thereby extending Japan's cultural leadership in Asia. This "new order," according to historian Jonathan Spence, has been Japan's dream for forty years.[8]

The military situation brings Gia-fu a new internal conflict, this one far beyond Feng Chong-ching's power to control. Shanghai, with so many Chinese living under foreign jurisdiction, has long manifested a hodge-podge of contradictions. Now the Japanese control much of Shanghai, but the International Settlement where Gia-fu lives, studies, and socializes remains under the jurisdiction of foreign powers and enjoys comparative safety. Those Shanghai contradictions now grow even more personal. As a young, strong Chinese man, Gia-fu simultaneously appreciates and resents the protection of foreign powers. He feels he should be doing more to help the country. He should not be protected by foreigners. And he certainly doesn't want to "kowtow to the white people!" Given the larger picture of national defeats, his guilt about being in a relatively safe place—and under foreign protection—grows. He comes to feel that being in this situation is somehow unpatriotic.

Adding to his conflicted feelings, Gia-fu's older siblings have taken on the responsibilities left by their mother's death of looking after the younger ones—Gia-fu, Chao-hua, Lu-tsi, Zhao-shu, and Wan-tsi—and they are taking them quite seriously. They want to know everything, and so question Gia-fu every day when he returns from school. They are friendly and caring about it, but Gia-fu feels he is being watched in every way: how he dresses, who telephones, whom he telephones, the friends he goes out with. He bemoans his situation, thinking, "Nothing [seems] to escape their eyes and ears."

Letters arrive from classmates who have gone to Kunming to study at Southwestern Associated University, the combined universities in exile. Full of "glowing stories of adventures in Southwest China—most of all, that free China was alive and well," these letters help germinate the seeds of restlessness and discontent in Gia-fu's mind. These young Chinese are not living under Japanese threat. They are not living under foreign protection. They are free and studying at a high-quality university far from Shanghai. These classmates show it's possible to live away from threats and restrictions and to prosper.

Sharing the letters with his father, Gia-fu asks permission to go there, to attend Associated University. Feng Chong-ching adamantly refuses. Again, Gia-fu struggles between wanting to please his father and following his own desires. He knows his duty to his father and family, but he wants to be with his classmates in Free China and feels he is being suffocated, watched all the time by his elder siblings. Yes, he is now studying the liberal arts, but it's as if he's "the bird in the cage." His wings are restricted. He wants to leave the cage, use those wings, fly.

Gia-fu determines to fly. In preparation, he takes a job selling advertising space with *The China Press*, an English newspaper. Known by people directing the large banks, Gia-fu succeeds in sales and soon makes enough money to fund his flight. Confident he is doing the right thing and supported by his friends, he begins smuggling his clothes out of his house to that of a friend. He orders new clothes from his tailor because he knows he will be gone when the tailor comes to collect on the bills. He also stashes some of his father's business cards in case he needs help on the trip. He wants to be free, but not necessarily free of the advantages that being his father's son can bring. Within the family, only his next-youngest brother, Chao-hua, and his next-oldest sister, Pei-chi, know of his plans, although second-youngest brother, Zhao-shu, suspects something because he has noticed changes in Gia-fu's wardrobe.

Very early this cold December morning in 1938, three Feng siblings, Gia-fu, nineteen years old, Chao-hua, eighteen, and Pei-chi, twenty, slip silently out of the Feng home and find a taxi to take them to the harbor. Gia-fu has booked a ticket to Hong Kong on the small steamer that departs from the Huangpu River harbor, just off the Bund. Though it seems an adventure, the three realize that for the first time in their lives, they will part for an extended period, an unknown length of time. They do not, in fact, know for sure that they will ever be together again. They stand together in the cold darkness before dawn.

Too soon, the moment comes for Gia-fu to board, and the three say their good-byes as the sky begins to lighten. Pei-chi and Chao-hua, losing their third brother, sob. Gia-fu weeps for the loss of family and home, for the uncertainty this parting brings. Wrenching himself away from his much-loved brother and sister, Gia-fu boards the steamer. It pulls away from the harbor with Gia-fu watching the distance widen and the figures of Chao-hua and Pei-chi and then Shanghai fade into the fog. As the boat steams down the Huangpu to the Yangtze, then down the South China

Sea on that cold December morning, Gia-fu's first trip alone, a notice goes up on the bulletin board at his university campus. A farewell letter from Gia-fu, it draws exclamations of admiration and awe from his contemporaries.

His cage left behind, Gia-fu flies toward freedom and adventure. He's left his younger brother to face their father's wrath. Unleashing his intense anger, Feng Chong-ching whips his son with bamboo branches, forcing him to kneel before Wei Han-chuen's portrait. His fury is such that afterward the boy must see a doctor. For the time being, there is no way for Gia-fu to know.

Gia-fu has bought the least expensive ticket on the small steamer, allowing him a space at the bottom of the vessel, where, in the absence of bunks, he spreads his bedding on the floor. His clothing and general appearance affirm his wealthy background, puzzling his cabin mates about why he is traveling so cheaply. In line with prevailing social customs, deferring to his obvious status, they treat him with reverence.

The neighboring bedding belongs to a tailor, who has brought along several bottles of wine, which he generously shares with his fellow passengers. Gia-fu later learns that the tailor is really a secret policeman, "patrolling traffic between Shanghai and Hong Kong." Another cabin mate, who is also a student, invites Gia-fu to stay with him in Hong Kong.

Gia-fu accepts the invitation. How long he remains in Hong Kong is unknown. He thinks Hong Kong a "very big city... with many sights to see." Now, in late 1938, Hong Kong's population is slightly less than half a million, about a sixth the size of Shanghai, but it is a very different city. Gia-fu finds the weather mild and the streets quiet, and he admires the Hong Kong Chinese for "their ability to speak English, but they [are] shamelessly British." Later in life, Gia-fu will be offended if his American friends ask if he is from Hong Kong.

Soon after Gia-fu's departure, the persistent Feng Chong-ching sends a telegram to a Hong Kong relative in hopes that the relative will find Gia-fu and send him home. Using his connections, the relative learns of Gia-fu's whereabouts through the tailor/secret policeman. Managing to evade the relative, Gia-fu eventually leaves for the Kwang-chou Bay area, near Hainan Island across the South China Sea, adjacent to Indochina.

Gia-fu knows of the military action in that area and worries about trying to cross the front line to get to Kunming. On the move again, he frets in the bottom cabin of the steamer, eventually mustering the courage to go for fresh air and a stroll on deck. There he encounters a general he met at a feast in Hong Kong. Asking about Gia-fu's plans and learning he is headed for Associated University in Kunming, the general offers to help get him there. He invites Gia-fu to move into his cabin, declaring that there is plenty of room. He tells Gia-fu of his friendship with Feng Chong-ching and expresses the wish to have known of Gia-fu's plans in the first place. Gia-fu accepts the invitation and moves into the general's cabin, where he is "treated royally." Additionally, upon landing the general sees that Gia-fu gets safely to Kunming in one of his trucks. Again, like a cat, Gia-fu lands on his feet. He thinks of this meeting as an accident that brings him through safely. For the moment, he doesn't think of the safety net his father brings even to this situation. For the moment, visions of freedom fill his mind.

CHAPTER FOUR

WAR, FREEDOM & GROWING UP

Who can wait quietly while the mud settles?
Who can remain still until the moment of action?

—from Chapter 15, *Tao Te Ching*

A bird out of the cage and testing his wings, Gia-fu lands in Kunming via the general's truck eager to enter the university and live life on his own. At nineteen, he has just made his first trip alone, and he feels ready for more new experiences. Here at the end of 1938, he doesn't know that he will not return home until 1946. While in Kunming, he will complete his bachelor's degree and take his first job as a banker and as manager of a villa owned by the government bank. He will meet intellectuals, American soldiers, the Flying Tigers, and many Chinese and foreign officials. But for now, he, along with the thousands of other refugees who continually flow into the city, knows little about this southwestern region other than that it is part of Free China, largely unhampered by Japanese occupation. Gia-fu has received letters from classmates about the city and the life here, but when he arrives he finds he knows little.

Seeing beauty in this place of mountains and lakes, he appreciates the mild climate, for now even in winter, the temperature averages between forty-five and sixty degrees. Only during the summer rainy season is it uncomfortable. Now having seen firsthand some of the extreme variation in his huge country, he marvels at the difference between this environment and the east coast, but also the difference in the people, who in this much less populated area lack the sophistication of those urbane Shanghaiese. This part of China is home to numerous minority peoples and hill tribes, people who are not culturally, ethnically, or linguistically Chinese. Yunnan Province, with Kunming as its capital, borders Burma and French Indochina, countries that later will be known as Myanmar and Vietnam. Yunnan, about two-thirds the size of France, sees its population grow dramatically during 1937–38. Before the war, about a hundred forty-seven thousand people lived in the whole province. Now in 1938, approximately sixty thousand people have sought refuge here, noticeably changing the dynamics and nature of the place.[1]

While far from the fighting, but not immune to bombs from Japanese aircraft, two of Kunming's distinguishing characteristics keep residents aware of the war. One, it is removed from the main military action and hosts Free China's main air base; flights over the extremely dangerous Hump—the Himalayas—land and take off from here. The other is it is the Chinese terminus of the Burma Road: a rough, treacherous stretch of about 715 miles of dirt and cobbles, built in 1937–38, with 600 miles in China and 115 in Burma. Historian Barbara Tuchman will later describe it as having been "scratched out of the mountainsides by the hand labor of 200,000 men, women and children." Gia-fu sees the dirt road winding through "incredible variations of landscape, from high plateaus to the lush jungles of rain forest." Hairpin turns and slippery conditions contribute to the high number of trucks that go off the cliffs, making the road a veritable death trap. China's only conduit for supplies now that the Japanese have cut off shipping and railroad transport, it also makes smuggling and other corruption possible. It is China's "back door" in many senses and serves a critical purpose during this time of war.[2]

Gia-fu and the thousands of other refugees feel the Yunnanese's ambivalence and resentment toward them as newcomers, invaders themselves, with their different dialects and customs. Almost six decades later, writer Wilma Fairbank will capture the Yunnan natives' feelings in the simple question: "What concern of theirs was Japanese aggression in the remote eastern provinces?" They feel neither humiliation nor pride in this country, which not only amazes those from occupied China but also angers them. They, the refugees, hadn't conspired with the Japanese, and they therefore feel they deserve better treatment.[3]

But Gia-fu has come here to study, to be in Free China, to be free of family obligations and his family's watchful eyes. Free China means free Gia-fu. He also finds himself free of family conveniences, the servants' care and solicitude, but at nineteen his flexibility and sense of adventure help him adjust. Soon he writes to his family to tell them he is safe, and also to ask for money. He may be seeking freedom but not financial independence. Apparently, Feng Chong-ching accepts the reality of his third son's flight, and he begins sending Gia-fu an annual allowance. Because of the war, communication in general and the funds in particular arrive sporadically.

Of the two universities in Kunming, Southwestern Associated University (SAU) and Yunnan University, Gia-fu thinks the latter "far less prestigious" than SAU because of the former's outstanding faculty members. He enrolls in SAU, the university combined of Peita (Peking), Tsinghua, and Nankai Universities, the presidents of which continue to serve collectively as presidents of SAU. Gia-fu thinks these three men "among the most famous educators of the nation" and quite accomplished, as are many of the faculty. He holds the excellent professors in awe and delights in studying under them, contentedly losing himself in his liberal arts studies.

The faculty, indeed, can boast of its quality with professors such as the politically influential Dr. Hu Shih, and Dr. Chen, who receives special favors from Chiang Kai-shek and knows twenty-six languages as well as the original religious literature of each particular language. A particular favorite of Gia-fu's, Dr. Lai is "comparatively young and spirited." Dr. Lai's history lectures attract the largest classes. As did the great storytellers of the old school, he makes history interesting and exciting. His memory of historical incidents amazes his students because he includes specific names, dates, places, and people involved—never using notes. Obviously superior, Dr. Lai will later be mentioned in Joseph Needham's comprehensive, multivolume *Science and Civilization in China*. Smiling and warm, this man contrasts with most of the other professors who, although kind to their students, seem always immersed in their own thoughts.

Another faculty member, the celebrated poet Wen Yidou, has taught classical Chinese literature at Wuhan University in Qingdao, and then at Peking's Tsinghua University. Now he mesmerizes Gia-fu with his focus on the earliest Taoist writings (circa 500 BCE), Tang Dynasty (618–907 CE) poetry, and the "haunting and difficult cycle of poems from the third century BCE written by Qu Yuan." Gia-fu sighs in liberal arts heaven. Finally immersed in classical poetry, religion, and history, he relishes the opportunity to devote his attention to these subjects under such wise and accomplished professors.

He's also aware of political realities of this time and place. Despite the distance to the actual fighting, the Japanese occupation remains a factor in Kunming's life. Many people would not be in the region were it not for the occupation, including the KMT government, which has been pushed west to Chongqing, 392 miles northeast of Kunming in neighboring Szechuan Province where Chiang Kai-shek has set up his wartime capital. Chiang, corrupt and ruthless but supported by the United States and other powerful nations, spends more resources fighting the developing Chinese Communist Party, led by Mao Tse-tung, than fighting the Japanese. Chiang benefits personally a great deal from much of the foreign aid, at various times leaving his soldiers to starve to death. The KMT conscripts poor young Chinese men into military service, a fate Gia-fu escapes, once again due to Feng Chong-ching's wealth and status.

Surrounded by and considerably aware of these circumstances, Gia-fu continues to be immersed in his studies at SAU. The campus, a makeshift affair, lies outside the city walls and reflects the poverty of the times. Having little furniture, Gia-fu and his fellow students stand in the dining room to eat. The roofs, made of tin can scrap iron, leak. When the summer rains hit, Gia-fu and his friends call the loud noise "modern music, drowning out the professors' lectures." Wooden boxes serve as desks and chairs. The public utility, mainly electrical, is mostly out of service because of the daily Japanese bombing. Since no water system except wells exists, students must hike into the city, pay for baths and massages, and then hike back to campus—a trip that takes hours. It is through these massages that Gia-fu discovers structural reintegration or rolfing, although he won't think of this bodywork as associated with these names for another twenty-seven or so years. Now, however, Gia-fu, his fellow students, and the faculty persevere under the most basic conditions.

Because of the air base and the Burma Road, the Japanese regularly bomb Kunming as well as other parts of Free China. Bombings occur almost daily and will continue until the American Volunteer Group (AVG), which will become known as the Flying Tigers, begins highly successful offensive operations against the Japanese air force in 1941, reducing the Japanese bombing threat. But for now the Flying Tigers have yet to be formed and the bombings cause the university students to leave campus every morning for the safer countryside. Then in the afternoon, they walk back to the city to pick up the pieces. Sometimes they help the "save-protect squad" by digging out corpses from the debris, mostly bodies of very old people unable to hike out every day. Gia-fu thinks the corpses "strange to handle. Some [are] very small and light, especially the bound-footed old ladies who had already shrunk to skin and bones before they were suffocated or crushed by the muddy walls."

One afternoon after spending time working with the save-protect squad, Gia-fu returns to his dormitory to see that it too has been a target that day. Rooted to a spot before it, he feels a strange sensation, one mixed of disbelief and horror at the sight of the whole building reduced to rubble. His room, where he slept and studied, has vanished, is destroyed, gone. He thinks of the old people crushed in their own dwellings and feels intensely sad, wondering why he has been spared.

Another morning during his senior year in 1940, in a different dormitory, Gia-fu suffers from a severe toothache; sleeping late, he does not hear the air-raid siren. When he does finally awaken, he discovers that his friends have all left for the countryside. Weary from the pain and longing to stay in bed, his judgment clouded, he decides the Japanese planes won't appear this day and snuggles back down, dozing lightly. But all too soon he sits up, wide awake, realizing his big mistake. In the distance he hears the planes coming. He bolts out of bed and into the yard, taking cover under a tree just in time to see bombs coming down like rain all around him. Huddled under that tree, despite the pain from the toothache, he clamps his jaws and grinds his teeth throughout the seemingly endless explosions all around him.

After what seems an interminable period of time, the explosions stop almost abruptly. Sulfur and dust suffuse the air. Gia-fu cannot breathe; nor can he see through the dust or hear with ears numbed by the thunderous noise. He can, however, feel prickles of pain where debris has showered his body. Feeling lucky not to have been buried by the flying wreckage, he also feels lucky when finally, slowly, he begins to see the sun, which appears as a moon through the dark dust. And at last, the dust settles.

Tentatively, Gia-fu walks around dazed and limping, unsure of whether all parts of his body are still together. Though he's walking, irrationally he fears he's lost a leg or an arm. Blood drips from the top of his head, which seems somehow no longer connected to his neck. He discovers the bleeding wound, but strangely it doesn't hurt. Stupefied by the surrealistic turn of events, his thoughts seem as disconnected as his physical self. He explores the area around the sheltering tree and sees that on all four sides, and within ten feet, there are gaping holes where shells exploded.

Still stunned, he limps to the college's first aid station. As he enters the building, he's comforted by the sight of the college physician, a kindly old man, who speaks words of reassurance while examining Gia-fu's head wound. The doctor, thoroughly probing the area, pronounces the wound superficial, caused by a piece of flying roof tile, not shrapnel. Gia-fu breathes a deep sigh of relief—relief that no shrapnel was involved and that his injury is not serious. He will be fine. After applying a simple dressing of a small patch of gauze and tape, the doctor discharges Gia-fu to return to his studies.

To Gia-fu, however, this opportunity is not to be passed up. After all, he has survived an enemy bombing, and his classmates have already heard of it. Feeling akin to a rugged Western cowboy, back in his room he rummages through his things, pulling out the Stetson hat he brought from Shanghai. Modestly dressed but topped with the big hat, Gia-fu walks around campus "as though I were an instant hero." His classmates are impressed. His professors are not. They ask that he remove the hat during lectures. He balks. The professors insist. Finally he complies. But even with his hat removed, Gia-fu knows his luck is holding.

Fewer than a thousand students attend SAU, and during his two years here, Gia-fu notices that various cliques have formed, primarily based on the students' home provinces. Being extremely status conscious, he observes that the Hunanese students tend to be more affluent, primarily because of their proximity to home and the relative ease with which they can obtain money and treats from their families. Students far from home receive money irregularly, and generally in a lump sum meant to last a year or more. With the arrival of money from home so uncertain, students often have to borrow from each other during their all too frequent money crises.

During his time at SAU, Gia-fu forms many friendships. He considers himself "the life of the party," as well as the negotiator with the local authorities, including the mayor, with whom he claims to have smoked opium and become "fast friends." Considering that Yunnan Province is known as "the land of the poppies," not a few of the local authorities may be engaging in this activity. The mayor prides himself on his friendships with the students from the great university, holding those students from the big cities such as Shanghai—especially Gia-fu—in high regard.

On campus, Gia-fu specifically has made a point of befriending the Hunanese in order to go on their camping trips during the three-month summer vacations. The mild weather at eight-thousand-foot elevation makes for quite pleasant camping. Sometimes the campers stay in old temples, with the young men sleeping in front of the statues and the young women sleeping upstairs in rooms that serve as granaries. The granaries attract rodents, but even the huge rats and other resident vermin don't dampen the students' spirits. Accompanied by a manual phonograph playing Western music, the young people sometimes dance far into the night, enjoying the place, the time, and each other.

The students also go to a lake about a hundred miles from Kunming called Yang-chung Hai, or Sea of the Sun. One night in particular remains in Gia-fu's memory. This night a glacial lake reflects the full moon's beams; its beauty will continue to echo in Gia-fu's life in similar lakes. Five decades later, Jane English will point out one of these, just west of Cottonwood Pass in the Colorado Rockies, as a favorite of Gia-fu's. But now, here at Yang-chung Hai, the lustrous moonlight reveals the glacier's path, moraines and rocks lying in its wake, sentinels of the glacier's magnificent, unhurried journey across this part of the earth. As he absorbs such beauty and grandeur, this moment touches his spirit deeply, causing him to ponder "the insignificance of my brief sojourn on this earth."

In 1940, two years after arriving in Kunming, Gia-fu graduates from SAU. His profound love of learning ensures that history, poetry, literature, world affairs, and other such subjects will always hold a significant place in his life. But with a different focus now that he has earned his degree, he takes a job as a trainee in the Bank of China's auditing department, following in his father's footsteps. The bank has branches all over China, and indeed is the first Chinese bank to have branches in other parts of the world. Feng Chong-ching's connections continue to benefit his sometimes rebellious son, as do the varied experiences Feng Chong-ching provided as his children grew up. Gia-fu recalls an incident when he was very young, before 1928, when each bank in Shanghai issued its own currency or bank notes. He remembers how one day his father had brought home a huge number of bank bills and let Gia-fu sort them out according to the banks. As Gia-fu sorted, Feng Chong-ching would tell Gia-fu each bill's value relative to the Bank of China's bills, which set the standard. Feng Chong-ching, in fact, was the one who set the rate for each bank, since there was no central clearinghouse or coordinating group at that time in Shanghai.

Like Feng Chong-ching's career, Gia-fu's first job requires attention and persistence. He works "the abacus like mad eight hours a day for many months checking the balance sheets." Finally, his fingers achieve a certain degree of dexterity, by which time he gets such a kick out of maneuvering the beads with his fingers that he feels addicted to the abacus.

Mirroring his father's early accomplishments, Gia-fu's dedication and good work bring him recognition within the bank. After training, and barely six months out of college, Gia-fu is sent to take charge of a small office in a town a hundred miles from Kunming. Within the year, this branch bank will serve a "Yankee Air Force base," one of many bases in Free China set up by General Claire Chennault, laying the groundwork for the American Volunteer Group—the Flying Tigers. The AVG will fight extensively in China and Burma before the United States enters the war after Pearl Harbor and will form the basis for the U.S.'s Fourteenth Air Force. Gia-fu's small town lies in the center of a *pan di*, plate-land, a large area of flat, fertile land surrounded by high mountains. Productive, prosperous farming and a booming handicraft industry flourish here aided by the year-round mild climate. The area also serves as a big market for textiles.

During these times, the bank not only deals with financing but also invests in and operates textile factories. The prices of raw materials are controlled at a level only one third of the black market's prices. Price control bureaus are effective in the big cities but do not reach the outlying towns. Gia-fu finds himself in a ticklish situation when his boss decides to ship all the cotton bales outside Kunming so they can be sold for higher prices. This is strictly against the law, but law enforcement agencies turn a blind eye, knowing that the prime minister is chairman of the bank's board. Nonetheless, the transaction is shrouded in secrecy, and those involved know that any mishap will lead to heads rolling. Gia-fu, to his dismay, is chosen to manage this job.

The small office where Gia-fu works has only four employees, plus an assortment of guards, servants, and messenger boys. There are no private telephones, and the only telephone in the whole town shares quarters with the telegraph office situated atop the city wall's western gate. Every day around noon, Gia-fu walks through the main street to the tower to call Mr. Wu, his immediate boss and vice president of the bank, for instructions on whether to sell and, if so, how much. All involved communicate orally, avoiding written contracts that could become evidence of these illegal transactions.

The bank's president, also the president of the textile factory, professes to be an upright Christian and wants nothing to do with these factory transactions for fear of exposure. However, he also realizes the factory cannot survive under the official pricing policy. In this difficult wartime, he allows the transactions to proceed but he doesn't want to know about them. Gia-fu and Mr. Wu become instrumental players in the transactions, the reward for which is a small portion of the profits to keep for themselves. Gia-fu feels this is all done in an atmosphere of trust, with no questions asked.

As with much in Chinese culture, *guanxi* underscores this trust. Guanxi is a concept not easily translated into other languages; Sinologist Boyé Lafayette De Mente will later describe it as *"relationships based on mutual dependence,* with the active element being *feelings* and *emotion."*[4] He will call guanxi "the Chinese Life-Line." Most commonly, albeit simplistically, translated into English as "connections," guanxi grows out of personal relationships. Gia-fu's father has helped people with whom and for whom Gia-fu is now working; therefore they will look out for Gia-fu. The president of the bank began his apprenticeship under Feng Chong-ching; both men were from Chekiang Province. Sharing this history, plus the same customs and dialect, automatically contributes to the bond between Gia-fu and the president.

Guanxi also comes into play in Gia-fu's link to Mr. Chin, the head of the Central Trust Bureau, closely related to the Central Bank of China, the institution handling exchange control operations. Approached by a colleague who is a native of Yunnan Province, Gia-fu discovers his colleague has a source of nearly a quarter million frozen U.S. dollars that can be freed if converted into Burmese rupees. The Chinese foreign exchange is controlled and all private foreign currency accounts are frozen, but through some influence and pull, they can mysteriously be freed. Gia-fu casually mentions that Mr. Chin, an old friend of his father's, can handle this. Sure enough, when the colleague shows up with a huge check for dollars, Gia-fu takes him to bespectacled Mr. Chin.

Everyone benefits, including Gia-fu, who instantly becomes rich by brokering this major transaction. This incident is followed by others, and Gia-fu begins to think that because he continually seems to be in the right place at the right time, the incidents must be divine accidents—accidents that leave Gia-fu with a lot of money.

After living so frugally, especially in the pervasive scarcity of wartime, Gia-fu goes wild with his newfound wealth. He spends money "like a fiend," even returning to campus to find his old friends who have not yet graduated or who have stayed on to become teaching assistants. For friends old and new he throws big parties, and he lends money to anyone who asks. He is particularly keen on lending money to a Dr. Pao; Gia-fu does not consider him a good doctor but has fallen madly in love with his sister, the unofficial queen of the campus.

Gia-fu's assessment of Dr. Pao's abilities springs from an ill-fated experience with the ten-year-old daughter of Gia-fu's maid. The child became very ill, unable to do anything but sit in the kitchen looking half-dazed. The maid couldn't afford a doctor and didn't know what to do. Gia-fu, wanting to help, asked Dr. Pao to examine the girl. Dr. Pao examined her and determined she needed some sort of shot, which he administered. Sadly, the girl died soon after. Gia-fu saw the maid crying a few times but then observed her getting on with life's routine. Puzzling over this mother's seeming acceptance of her child's death, Gia-fu wondered if it came from either weariness and the accompanying inability to expect better, or from a philosophical acceptance of life's ebb and flow.

While struggling to make sense of those dark events and with his esteem for Dr. Pao's medical knowledge and skill ebbing further, Gia-fu's interest in Dr. Pao's sister nonetheless grows deeper. He tries everything, even bribing Dr. Pao, to try to influence her feelings. On one occasion, Dr. Pao allows Gia-fu to stay in his bedroom, which is next to his sister's, hoping that when she comes home the two might get together. Gia-fu sits in the bedroom anxiously awaiting her return. Finally, the door opens and the Pao beauty enters. But she is not alone. Accompanying her is an air force pilot, Captain Wu. Alarmed and brokenhearted, Gia-fu watches through the slightly open door of Dr. Pao's room as the two slip into her room and close the door. Sleepless, Gia-fu remains in the next room listening all night to the two next door. His ear pressed to the wall, he tortures himself with the sounds coming through, but in the end convinces himself that they do not actually make love.

This incident does not alter Gia-fu's feelings, although before too long Miss Pao marries Captain Wu. Gia-fu's feelings for her will remain unrequited, even years later after Captain Wu dies in a midair explosion during the war of liberation and Miss Pao moves to Berkeley, where Gia-fu then resides. While Gia-fu's social contacts with women soon will continue in abundance, more than two decades will pass before, at the age of forty-nine in 1968, he will announce a more significant relationship: his marriage to Paula Jackson.

Now, as the early 1940s edge toward mid-decade, despite his success in banking and finance, Gia-fu feels lost. He has everything he wants materially, but not his would-be girlfriend, Miss Pao. The heartbreak he felt at the loss of his mother returns in another form—this time from feeling that he has lost Miss Pao. And in the midst of war's destruction, everyone, including Gia-fu, feels "life's starkness—death and life, hope and despair." Gia-fu's growing distress leads him to feel that life is meaningless. Abandoned, lonely, empty, and vulnerable, Gia-fu is open to any form of relief. Thus, via his siblings in Shanghai, enters religion.

At the tender age of twelve, Gia-fu's eldest sister had been engaged to a boy, whom she would meet only just prior to their wedding. She is now in her twenties, and her fiancé, having graduated from the Massachusetts Institute of Technology, has returned to China. He is a devout Christian and wishes his prospective wife to become a Christian, too, before they marry. She consents, and she, along with four other Feng siblings, becomes Christian.

In so doing, these Feng brothers and sisters refuse to kneel before the ancestors during the ancestral worship ceremonies, greatly angering Feng Chong-ching. They also write frequently to Gia-fu, urging him to convert, telling him that if he does not "surrender to Jesus, [he will] be in hell." Difficult as it is for Gia-fu to believe in the Christian heaven and hell, he does discern love and joy in their letters. He finds their words more alive than ever before, sounding both serious and happy.

Eldest Sister, having moved from Shanghai and now living with her husband in China's interior, contacts a Christian group member by the name of Chang in Kunming, who also happens to be a prominent banker and friend of their father: yet another in Feng Chong-ching's far-reaching network. Chang invites Gia-fu to his home, providing him a place to go on weekends. Chang nudges Gia-fu toward this religion, and, yielding to the distant and local pressure, Gia-fu decides he will give it a try.

In the backyard of a downtown store owned by one of the church members, Gia-fu and seven others who are to be baptized gather with other members of the church. An unusual assortment, they vary in social class from some who are very poor, working as servants or janitors, to some well off—bankers and other professionals. Gia-fu also notices several foreigners in this assembly, ex-missionaries who have "seen the light and withdrawn from the missions, since the salaries for professional ministry [are] a form of sin. One must live on faith and do exactly what the Holy Spirit [tells] one to do."

Given the belief that professional ministry equals sin, there is no paid minister, so one of the church leaders officiates. Baptizing each of the eight initiates in a broken bathtub in this ramshackle backyard, the church leader and others welcome each new member as "brother" or "sister," titles that will be used from now on irrespective of social standing. Because they are reborn, they truly have become brothers and sisters in the eyes of their Lord.

In this church, everyone lives on faith, and maybe a little charity. Workers devoted to the church travel from home to home, accepting handouts like wandering monks. The group does not have a name, believing that naming it would destroy its ecumenical nature, since all Christians are one.

Nightly prayer meetings are characterized "by loud cries of repentance and vocal petitions. Everyone must pray out loud." Gia-fu discovers that if he attends meetings without raising his voice, he will be buttonholed afterward by someone inquiring about his spiritual well-being. Missing a meeting amounts to a catastrophe, and everyone will come to check on him. "Was [he] sick or sinning?" they'll want to know.

This puritanical group bans smoking, drinking, movies, parties, and associations outside the group unless preaching Jesus Christ's words. One may act only when clear that direction comes from the Holy Spirit. "One's whole life [is] to be a life of prayer, maintaining contact with the Holy Spirit at all times." Gia-fu later likens the aspect of waiting for the inner voice to mystic Quakers, with whom he will begin an association in the next decade in another country.

But now, for one year early in the 1940s, Gia-fu is experiencing a complete turnaround from his former ways. He attends these church meetings regularly for the whole year. He even refuses party invitations, and later in retrospect will refer to himself as a "fanatic Christian." When people ask to see him, he takes them to the meetings rather than see them outside the church. In seeking refuge in the church, he avoids anything that might pull him away. Most who accompany him are taken aback by the crying and loud utterances; they stay through the one meeting, never to return.

Their reactions aren't surprising. Even without the loud voices, China's relationship with Christianity has been mixed, as Gia-fu knows quite well. By the nineteenth century's end, in China as a whole, peasants, besieged and frustrated by aggressive and destructive Christian missionaries and other foreign imperialists, turned to secret societies trying to find some way to revolt. The Boxer Rising, named for a combination of martial arts ("boxing") and shamanistic influence, erupted in the summer of 1900, leaving thousands of Chinese and foreigners dead. The foreign powers reacted brutally and punitively, executing some and imposing other punishments on many, while also requiring China to pay them approximately $333 million, plus exorbitant interest, over a forty-year period. This period is just coming to an end.[5]

On the other hand, Christian missionaries have long been in China establishing health clinics in rural districts and hospitals and colleges in big cities. Taking a broader view, Gia-fu reflects that numbers of Chinese came into contact with Christianity through material benefits such as these. He also knows the Chinese often accept Christianity as one more complementary religion, as they essentially tend to consider religions as all one, perhaps with different functions at different times. After all, Buddhism, Confucianism, and Taoism have coexisted and blended in Chinese lives for centuries. But many Christian missionaries—including, seemingly, members of this church—cannot accept this approach, thinking Christianity the one true religion and considering multireligioned Chinese to be hypocrites.

Eventually, however, his inability to remain a "fanatic Christian" and the demands of his job, added to his disillusionment when a church leader backslides and goes astray, lead Gia-fu to drift away from the group. He has to be out of town much of the time, being always at the beck and call of his superiors. In his situation, private and public life merge; all the bank's workers live in the same compound and everyone knows what's happening with everyone else. If Gia-fu or one of the other employees gets sick, the boss's wife will bring food and take care of him. Gia-fu knows the saying in the bank that "one must love the bank as one loves one's own family." Given these circumstances, he muses, "After all, I could not have given up my career and devoted myself totally to Jesus." To Gia-fu at this point, life's main purpose hinges on "getting along with people and getting ahead in one's career."

Gia-fu's drift from Christianity signals his recovery from the heartbreak of Miss Pao. Yearning to fill the void created by his disappointing attachment, he has found a temporary community of support with unambiguous expectations, providing relief for this lost soul. In the longer run, however, these expectations turn out to be something he cannot share, and he finds that he no longer needs its support. Yet his foray into Christianity points to an intensity and enthusiasm in a search, still to be fulfilled, but with some sense of balance. Christianity does not offer him balanced fulfillment, but his experience with it does not end his search.

By this time in the mid-1940s, Gia-fu feels close to "the pinnacle of [his] power." Managing a villa called Ching-Pi, or Golden Jewel, owned by the bank, the chairman of which is Prime Minister T. V. Soong, Chiang

Kai-shek's brother-in-law, Gia-fu meets many important Chinese and foreign figures. Virtually all foreign dignitaries on their way to the war-time capital, Chongqing, stay overnight at the villa, including American Vice President Henry Wallace and Secretary of State Edward Stettinius, Lady Mountbatten, wife of Admiral Lord Lewis Mountbatten, Claire Chennault, and Chiang Kai-shek himself. Additionally, with other critical operations nearby, such as the Kunming Training Center, formed in 1943 for Americans to train Chinese Army officers, legendary figures such as General Joseph Stilwell travel in and out of the area.[6]

Gia-fu lives in a small room in this villa, which is the only place in the area nice enough to house important guests. His role lies in the public relations realm, devoted mainly to the interests of American soldiers who are arriving by the thousands. By now, 1944, the Chinese and Americans feel they will win the war. The War Area Service Corps, the Chinese agency through which Gia-fu works (while still an employee of the bank), holds the official charge of keeping the Americans happy.

Because Chiang Kai-shek personally benefits so much, a major factor in Gia-fu's job (and in the job of anyone connected to the government in any way) is the Generalissimo's interest in continuing to have the Americans meet his requests and demands for money and other resources. The interaction between Chiang and American officials has seemed a continuous game of cat and mouse, with Chiang always doing what he can to influence American decision makers. Making the GIs as comfortable as possible becomes another of Chiang's tactics, with the War Area Service Corps the means of providing for the Americans. At the Corps' helm sits General J. L. Huang, who also serves as chief of protocol of the Department of Foreign Affairs. Gia-fu thinks Huang heads the list of "brown nosers," this "massive man of six foot four with a round smiling face and erect body." Having met Huang on various occasions, China scholar John King Fairbank will later write descriptions that corroborate Gia-fu's assessment. One in particular, about a lawn party given by Chiang's brother-in-law, Dr. H. H. Kung, for visiting presidential candidate Wendell Willkie finds Huang as master of ceremonies. As usual when Americans are present, Mrs. Chiang presses Huang to "act the court buffoon." Fairbank notes that Huang mixes a combination of Chinese opera dramatics with "the American collegiate style of the 1920s, the result [of which] was pure corn."

Although Gia-fu considers Huang a yes-man, he also knows the general can make things work. But Huang has difficulty with the American know-it-all attitude. Fairbank will observe that Huang suffers incivility from the very officers his corps tries to please, especially if they've been in China for even a short time and, therefore, think they know everything. Huang's response to that attitude, not unreasonably, borders on being anti-American.[7]

In this context, Gia-fu manages the villa and works out logistics for entertaining the American GIs. His own experiences with Americans leave him with mixed feelings. He sees the chaplain having a drink every afternoon, which, ironically, he still can't reconcile with his own foray into Christianity. And while puzzled about the GIs' craziness over pin-up girls and the gamblers who take advantage of others, he feels disquieted by some higher-ups whom he sees drinking and swearing so much of the time. He also encounters the many prejudices, not only of race, but also of differing backgrounds.

One young American intrigues Gia-fu. Shorty assists the base commander adjutant, who does the real work of keeping the base running. Five feet tall and from the South, he tells Gia-fu about how he learned to drive when he was nine. Astonished, Gia-fu tries to imagine this. He cannot drive a car and remembers the calamitous result of his one attempt to learn when still living at his family home. Still fascinated by cars, however, Gia-fu listens to Shorty with a sense of awe and respect.

Gia-fu's responsibilities include arranging dancing parties for the GIs since the villa seems the only place good enough for this kind of occasion. For this first event, he has the setting but wonders what to do about dancing partners. On the scene appears Mrs. Chang Moon-ling, wife of the university president. Mrs. Chang, in her forties, lean and attractive, speaks fluent English and exhibits graceful manners. Gia-fu finds her to be a "ball of fire" when she rounds up coeds from the campus just in time for the party to begin.

Before the party can get under way, however, another logistical challenge arises—how to gather the coeds from across the city and bring them to the villa. With a jeep and driver at his disposal, Gia-fu goes to each one's home or dormitory. Whether at a dorm or private housing, Gia-fu finds himself waiting "many heart pounding minutes" for the young woman to appear. If she appears too soon, she will lose face for seeming to be overly eager, so Gia-fu waits. For those who live off campus on little lanes that won't accommodate a jeep, Gia-fu must walk down the muddy path in his "shiny but delicately soft dancing shoes."

For their part, the young women stand up to the challenge of entertaining the American GIs, although "simply the physical touch by a robust and strange man in uniform was quite an experience for...the shy little coeds." Seeing their role in the dances as their patriotic duty, and bolstered by Mrs. Chang, they learn to deal with even the drunken soldiers. Each experience fuels conversations for days. And the dance parties continue.

Because Gia-fu works for the Bank of China, he works for Chiang Kai-shek's government, the KMT, but his heart and soul are not with the current regime. He knows of too much corruption, too many injustices. He sees how Chiang's policies and denial of any reality beyond his immediate surroundings have led to rampant inflation and extreme scarcity of food and goods among the people. He sees the suffering, which has been going on for some time. People hoard rice and other commodities—anything not perishable, especially foreign medicine. Gia-fu's former professors are incensed, pushed to their limits partly because there is nothing to eat, but more because of the widespread despair and desolation the KMT's actions bring. They speak out in classes and sometimes in campuswide special lectures. And although Yunnan's governor, Long Yun, has all along refused to follow the KMT's rigid censorship laws, thereby making Kunming and SAU what historian Jonathan Spence will later describe as a "vital intellectual center," the professors are closely watched.

Professor Wen Yidou, that extraordinary poet and teacher, delivers searing lectures about the realities, the suffering, and the absurdity of the KMT pursuing civil war against the Chinese Communist Party (CCP), especially when the Japanese were occupying the country. The secret police warn him to stop, threatening his life. He persists, receiving a standing ovation at a special campuswide talk. He announces the threat at the next lecture and dares the secret police to raise their hands and be identified. Then on July 15, 1946, he is gunned down in broad daylight. The whole campus mourns, but not long after the KMT assassinates another outspoken professor, Dr. Li Kun-pu. Most people feel impotent to do anything. Some try to forget. Others go underground to join the CCP. Although by the time of Wen Yidou's killing, Gia-fu has returned to Shanghai and does not take this path, he understands why some of his friends choose this way. The avenues for resistance are few and some students and some faculty, disillusioned by the KMT, turn to the CCP in hopes the Communists can right some of the wrongs of the centuries.

Then a secret police raid with mass arrests of leftist students follows the shootings, but somehow the Communists learn about it and go into hiding beforehand. The secret police make wanton arrests for show and to satisfy their bosses, and tension between the KMT and CCP continues to escalate.[8]

The Japanese, the KMT, the CCP, and the overall circumstances of the war leave indelible impressions on Gia-fu. Among the impressions, those from the Burma Road linger most vividly. For years now, he has seen old women and little children sitting by the roadside pounding rocks into small pieces with some kind of mallet. The smaller pieces help preserve the road because it is not paved, and its 715 miles from China into Burma continue to be a lifeline for supplies into China. Numerous historians will write about the feat of this road, including Jonathan Spence, who will describe how the stereotype of:

> the patient, endlessly hard-working Chinese drew new force from
> the written accounts and photographs showing hundreds of thou-
> sands of Chinese laborers—men, women, and children—work-
> ing by hand in the mountains and gorges, hauling rock and earth
> in baskets, blasting stubborn boulders with bamboo tubes full of
> gunpowder.

Accidents, malaria, and malnutrition take thousands of lives of the primarily conscripted workforce, and the road itself holds numerous problems, such as landslides, narrow tracks, and treacherously slippery mud.[9]

Gia-fu witnesses death from another source on this road. On official business and traveling in a jeep with an American GI, he encounters young men roped one to the next, limping along, all bare skin and bones. Horrified, Gia-fu watches these "little kids in their early teens," who have been conscripted into military service through common brutal means, being marched along the road to a camp some fifty miles away. Completely depleted, one of the boys falls down, mumbling, "Let me die! I cannot take it anymore." Gia-fu sees a fat soldier beat him with his rifle butt until the youth again staggers to his feet. Gia-fu feels nauseated by the sight but is powerless to do anything about it.

He and the GI continue the journey, shocked by more of this horror as they travel the road. By the time they drive the fifty miles to the camp, they have witnessed four deaths. The GI later reports the deaths and the conditions under which they happen. Gia-fu appreciates the effort but knows little will come of the report. The stark injustice rankles, and the brutal images stay with him always.

Then VJ (Victory over Japan) Day comes on August 15, 1945: the unconditional surrender by the Japanese following the American bombing of Hiroshima on August 6 and Nagasaki on August 9. This is a dramatic and deadly climax to the long, horrific Pacific War. More than eight years after the July 7, 1937, incident at Lou Kuo Bridge (Lugouqiao), this war finally ends. Confusion and hardship brought by the war do not evaporate, however, with Japan's surrender. Food remains scarce, inflation out of control, and transportation difficult to come by. Many displaced Chinese seek to reunite with their families, and Gia-fu is among them. He does not secure transportation home until January 1, 1946. He is twenty-seven years old.

During his time in Yunnan Province, Gia-fu has experienced intellectual heights, endured hardship, grown from a student into a self-possessed, successful young man with a banking career, found friends, made money, been heartbroken, and tried religion. These experiences have helped shape and form the person who, on that cold December morning in 1938, unbeknownst to his father, sneaked out of his home.

In 1946, Gia-fu feels confident in who he is, and now this bird can fly home.

CHAPTER FIVE

THE MAN WHO TOUCHED DOWN FROM THE SKY

...having and not having arise together.
Difficult and easy complement each other.
Long and short contrast each other

—from Chapter 2, *Tao Te Ching*

On this cold winter's day, January 1, 1946, one of the ubiquitous silver Douglas C-47 military transports touches down at Shanghai airport bringing more refugees back home from the interior. Among them is a changed Gia-fu, a twenty-seven-year-old who feels a sense of triumph, who feels he has helped win the war because he has been in Free China and not under Japanese occupation. That he was never on the front, nor even in the military, seems irrelevant. His eagerness to join the new power elite to restore prosperity to Shanghai heightens his anticipation of the reunion with his family.

Gia-fu's victorious feelings have solid footing in the Nationalist government's perspective. The KMT, which fled to Chongqing and established the wartime capital there, looks at those who stayed in Shanghai, as well as Nanking and other cities under Japanese occupation, as equal to traitors. Those who fled the occupation are considered loyal. Further, during this year and the following one, many well-to-do Shanghaiese will be executed as traitors, whether they were or not, for Chiang Kai-shek believes that anyone who stayed behind and did well must have worked closely with Japan's puppet regime and collaborated with the enemy.

But Gia-fu's family is safe. Although the Japanese pressured Feng Chong-ching to run the bank for them, he refused. During the occupation years he stayed much to himself, seven years in the second floor of a downtown bank, taking his meals in his bedroom, served by a male servant who knew exactly what he wanted—tea and milk in the morning and a bowl of steaming hot Shanghai noodles topped with a piece of beef or pork for lunch.

It is to his father that Gia-fu first goes. Feng Chong-ching's flat covers the whole second floor and, from below, the bank offices' sounds seep through—muffled voices among the chattering, clattering sounds of the numerous abacuses. Feng Chong-ching waits in the front room, where once the bank's board met. He rarely turns on the lights, and he sits smoking and drinking tea in end-of-the-day shadows, the room illuminated only by the neon lights of the street.

Gia-fu arrives and greets his father with restrained affection. He's glad to be back and see his father again, but still he must act with propriety. He walks to the shuttered French windows and opens them to the fresh air, then steps out onto the little balcony to watch the milling crowd below. Reveling at being in Shanghai, probably the busiest city in the world with its twelve million people, he thinks it almost a nation in itself. He feels proud to have been born here.

But Feng Chong-ching doesn't want to hear the street noise, and he waves at Gia-fu to come in and shut the windows. After these seven years apart he wants to talk with his third son. He tells Gia-fu about the Nationalist government officials who have sent an agent to talk with him about working for them in an important capacity. It is a form of reward for his steadfast refusal to cooperate with the puppet regime during the occupation. Then with a smile and a bit triumphantly, Feng Chong-ching reveals that he has turned down the offer.

"Why not come out to do something for the country?" Gia-fu asks. "It's good for the country as well as for yourself." Dressed in a gray suit with double-breasted jacket, white shirt, and tie, Gia-fu looks the epitome of success. A silk handkerchief tucked just so in his breast jacket pocket completes the picture of a young man eager to take on the world.

In response, Feng Chong-ching only shakes his head, and after a few puffs on his ivory cigarette holder, he sips loud mouthfuls of hot tea and walks out toward the hallway, his place to exercise. This exercise consists of pacing back and forth holding a rubber hot water bag in his hands. Gently and firmly he paces as though lost in thought, and Gia-fu sits, considering thoughts of his own. Years later, after completing translations of ancient Taoist philosopher Chuang Tsu, Gia-fu will think of his father's pacing as reflective of what Chuang Tsu called "mind wandering."

Now Feng Chong-ching returns to his chair, sitting with his right foot over his left and shaking his knees. Gia-fu remembers how his father has always shaken his knees, either sitting up in bed or in a chair, and he considers the habit a way of releasing tension.

Neither Feng Chong-ching nor Gia-fu speaks, both waiting in silence for a long time. Gia-fu knows that his father's main preoccupation in life has been to earn enough money to provide his children the best education possible, and now, he speculates, with all the children grown and through college, perhaps he feels his duty is done. Perhaps, Gia-fu muses, his father has no further ambition. This is common among the Chinese:

the attitude that it is to the family that one has a duty. The idea of working for the people and the nation has no doubt never entered Feng Chong-ching's mind.

In the dusky light of the still room, Gia-fu and his father sit quietly. The silence is profound. It is a new experience to be with his father this way but not an uncomfortable one. Within the next few weeks, he will learn this silence is so characteristic of Feng Chong-ching these days that some of his father's friends wonder whether he has become a monk, whether he has gained some spiritual power. Now, after a few hours together with his father, having talked some, having shared this communal silence, Gia-fu rises and leaves the flat.

An official jeep and driver that remain at Gia-fu's disposal take him to the Feng home on Avenue Foch where the rest of the family waits to greet him. They've convened in the living room to welcome him, no longer the child to be looked after but a young man who has found success. This success of being in Free China, of having a responsible position with the bank and doing well in it, give him great stature and thrust him into the limelight among those who know or know of him. He has become, in the words of the day, "the conqueror, the man who touched down from the sky." Those who stayed behind and did not collaborate with the Japanese are called "people from under the earth." These underground compatriots have worked hard for freedom, but those returning from the interior still consider themselves somewhat superior.

Within a few days of Gia-fu's return, Feng Chong-ching moves back home, pleased that the family is together again. Gia-fu, the prodigal son who went astray but has now returned a success, restores a sense of wholeness to the family, overcoming Feng Chong-ching's reluctance to show approval of a son who has been disobedient. Now that his third son is home and has moved successfully into Feng Chong-ching's own profession, he can show his approval, even his admiration. Gia-fu's uncles reinforce this attitude toward their nephew, and among the fifty-five Feng cousins, Gia-fu shines.

In the course of this next year, Gia-fu receives numerous phone calls from friends, relatives, and even people he doesn't know, asking for jobs, as well as from those seeking a son-in-law. Often he's invited to the homes of rich people he barely knows or hasn't met before. Usually a lavish feast precedes the expectation that Gia-fu will take their daughter out. Gia-fu embraces these opportunities after so many years in the interior when he'd refused to have anything to do with the local girls in the provinces. To him, those young women of the southwestern areas of Yunnan, Szechuan, and Kweichow were unrefined and beneath him. With his unrequited love for Miss Pao some three years back being his only foray into tender matters of the heart, Gia-fu jumps at the chance to socialize with the daughters of these willing capitalists. For now, his interest is directed toward fun, and no relationship of substance comes out of this period.

Delighted to have available the innumerable pleasures Shanghai provides during this time, Gia-fu frequents the expensive foreign cafes that cater to foreigners and upper-class Chinese. These cafes serve coffees from all over the world, along with all kinds of cakes with cream and fruit. One can stay all afternoon listening to Western music, such as orchestral renditions of Strauss waltzes and other classics, sometimes played by live musicians. Other establishments offer floor shows; Gia-fu sees hypnotists and amazing gymnasts and a Hungarian magician who can fly through the air and rest horizontally in midflight for several minutes. Seeing no strings or any other visible means of support, Gia-fu is baffled, never figuring out how the man does this.

Night after night Gia-fu is out on the town, partying and drinking too much but enjoying it all. Returning home in the morning's early hours, he sleeps a little and arises at seven to dress for work at the bank.

Gia-fu usually stops by his father's room after getting dressed, reminiscent of those school-day mornings when Gia-fu and his siblings gathered around their father's bed for their morning greetings and instruction. But now the relationship between Gia-fu and his father has shifted, despite the presence of some of the same trappings. Gia-fu, alone with his father, straightens his necktie while looking in the big mirror. He sees his father either smoking or drinking tea, half sitting up in bed, also looking in the mirror. They often look at each other's images, communicating silently.

One such morning while straightening his tie, Gia-fu finds himself staring at his father's face in the mirror. He seems a completely different man from ten years ago. Then he was the influential banker and everyone had done his bidding. At home he was the powerful patriarch of the Feng family. Now his eyes meet Gia-fu's in the mirror, and reflected there Gia-fu sees his father's utter satisfaction that finally everything has turned out the way it should. He has done his job. His father treats him differently from those earlier times, too, saving him the best cigarettes: Garricks from England.

Within the family, Gia-fu's position has changed significantly, and at one point he finds himself acting as negotiator between Second Sister Pei-chi, and his father, who still holds his last responsibility of seeing his children properly married. Pei-chi wants to marry a young man she has been seeing for several years, but he is from a family in the south and un-known to Feng Chong-ching. To Feng Chong-ching the marriage of his children has to do with relationships between families, and since he does not know this family, he considers the young man an outsider, inappropriate. This despite young Hou's father's kind visit to Feng Chong-ching a few weeks before. After some time the siblings, who all support Pei-chi in her wish to marry Hou, nominate Gia-fu to talk with their father. Eventually he finds the opportunity and does so. Perhaps because of Gia-fu's new stance in the family and the community, he persuades his father, and although Feng Chong-ching's acceptance is grudging, it is nonetheless a signal that wedding plans can proceed.

Feng Chong-ching, Gia-fu, and the rest of the family have seen many changes and, like their countrymen, feel a sense of relief and even hope now that the war has ended. But war's end has failed to bring a sense of order and reason to China in general, especially to Shanghai. One stunning example during the early weeks and months after the Japanese surrender saw Chiang Kai-shek engaging the Japanese military to police the city while he awaited the arrival of his Nationalist army and the U.S. Marines. Journalist Stella Dong, five and a half decades later, will describe how fifteen thousand Japanese soldiers continue to patrol Shanghai's streets, and even as the puppet regime slips out of town, Japanese officials confiscate shiploads of goods from the Chinese.

In addition to Japanese confiscation of Chinese goods, Dong, among other historians and writers, will describe how Chiang and associates divert foreign aid to their private purposes, bringing further deprivation and difficulty to the Chinese people. T. V. Soong, Chiang's brother-in-law, head of finance, and sometimes envoy to the U.S., plays an instrumental role in the diversion by insisting that all relief goods go to a central government-run center, the Chinese National Relief and Rehabilitation Administration (CNRRA). The goods are then stored in private warehouses and sold to the highest bidder, benefiting only the country's so-called leaders.

The multilayered and expansive corruption creates an illusory picture of wealth and prosperity. For many with money, the only option is to spend it on consumer goods. Others suffer terribly as inflation rises uncontrollably and inevitable economic collapse looms. Further, Chiang's reprisals against those who remained in Shanghai during the occupation begin to result, in Dong's words, "in an exodus of wealthy Shanghainese as early as 1946...and by the end of 1948 it had become a well-worn path."[1]

Among those factors contributing to the chaos and economic troubles is Chiang's tremendously expensive, relentless pursuit of war against the Communists. Despite American aid, much of which goes into Chiang and associates' pockets, the Nationalist soldiers are dying of starvation. Chiang rejects the agreement between the Communists and the Kuomintang to share power; a despot cannot share.

So for the Chinese, amid much turmoil, the end of World War II brings the beginnings of an internal civil war between Chiang Kai-shek's corrupt Kuomintang government—and the increasingly strong Communist movement.

In the midst of this jumbled mess, Gia-fu decides to study abroad, in the U.S. He believes he can do more for Shanghai and his country by getting more education, the kind that will serve his distinct purposes—business. He also thinks it a good time to be out of the country for a while. Next youngest brother, Chao-hua, also decides to study in the U.S. They both sign up for the required examination they must pass to get student visas. Despite Gia-fu's boasting to the authorities that they should let him pass because he is so well qualified, he must prepare for the test. Fortunately, a friend from his office lends him her notes with the comment, "Just in case you might have forgotten what you've studied."

The day before Gia-fu is to take the exams, his feet swell up with Hong Kong Foot, an ailment similar to athlete's foot. He lies in the bath soaking his feet, carefully studying his friend's notes. The next day as he takes the exam, he realizes that luckily, everything in the exam was in those notes. He passes, grateful to his friend for lending him her notes and especially for what he deems her devotion to him.

In preparation for his journey, Gia-fu withdraws all his money and, considering the political and economic situation, believes he does so in the nick of time. On yet another cold winter's day, this one in January 1947, Gia-fu again bids good-bye to his family and, with his brother Chao-hua, sails off to the United States aboard the troop transporter USS *General Gordon*. Two young men, off to another country on the other side of the world. Unbeknownst to the brothers and the rest of their family in China, Gia-fu will not return for almost three decades and Chao-hua will never again set foot in the country of their birth.

CHAPTER SIX

THE OTHER SIDE
OF THE WORLD

The Tao of heaven is like the bending of a bow.
The high is lowered, and the low is raised.
If the string is too long, it is shortened;
If there is not enough, it is made longer.

—from Chapter 27, *Tao Te Ching*

A s the bow bends, so the string finds a way to accommodate. This holds in Gia-fu's life, certainly during the years from 1947 into the early 1960s as he encounters unpredictable and volatile environments in which he must function, if not flourish. In parallel, as chronicler of Gia-fu's life and times, I feel the bow's inconstancy as I research and write about this period, seeking a clear picture of what Gia-fu experienced, how he felt, what he really wanted. I know of few photographs of Gia-fu during his early years in the United States; nor have I found many living or written sources from the period. I do know that he came to this strange country a young man trusting in his goal of a master's degree in international banking and economics and believing he would return home to China to use what he learned, only soon to find himself stranded in the alien West.

The knowledge I have and the images I've formed come from scant, random descriptions Gia-fu himself wrote, augmented, though incompletely, by renderings of his friends, family, and acquaintances. Concerning his master's degree, Gia-fu later reinvented his course of study to match the person he came to be, not necessarily who he was in 1947. It wasn't until I questioned two of his brothers about specifics that the original story came to light, later to be confirmed by Lloyd Alexander. Gia-fu's original intent in coming to the U.S. was not to study comparative religion, although in the next decade that's just what he found himself doing.

Much of the story of Gia-fu's first decade in the States, therefore, derives from the context, the times and places in which he found himself, like so many background pieces of a big puzzle. My job has been to gather and arrange those pieces with the hope that the clearer image of the man will emerge. This period of his life, with its gaps and haziness, represents in several ways a lost period. With so few sources to consult, I have often lost my way toward its telling, only to stumble upon a bit of information, a small piece of the puzzle, enough of the picture to show how pivotal these years were to be in the whole of Gia-fu's life. As crucial as this period was, it was also a time when Gia-fu himself came to be lost. Perhaps this is why he wrote so little about parts of it and reinvented others. For this young Chinese man it was a period of expected travel but unexpected dislocation; of confidence in a mission but confidence sluiced away by the strange maneuverings of world powers; of the machinations of politicians on ideological stages creating an international bending of the bow, requiring extensive accommodation.

~

The massive troopship, the USS *General Gordon,* launches this period, steaming its way across the Pacific Ocean carrying Gia-fu and Chao-hua to a new land halfway around the globe. The ship measures 622 feet in length and can accommodate more than four thousand military men.[1] Now, in the aftermath of the war and with the use of warships for civilian purposes, it carries a full load including the two Feng brothers and about three hundred other Chinese students in their mid- to late twenties.

A Chinese-American officer and an American school teacher number among the passengers. Both speak a little Chinese, and they willingly become the students' language teachers and cultural guides. Gia-fu considers this good fortune for, despite years of studying the language, he can hardly understand spoken English. He understands even less about American customs. This listening to and speaking English with the two Americans during the two-week trip across the Pacific helps to offset his dismay about the food he's served. It's flat and dull, and there's no soy sauce to flavor or disguise the bland, dry meat, the overcooked potatoes, the soggy, flavorless vegetables.

Despite the unsatisfactory food, Gia-fu and Chao-hua maintain their optimism in this quest, this mission they are on: seeking Western technical education to take back to their homeland. Gia-fu in banking, economics, and statistics, Chao-hua in mechanical and electrical engineering. Historically, the Chinese made numerous scientific discoveries, some before the rest of the world, among them printing and explosives, including fireworks. But for centuries science was not just neglected; it was rejected as a distraction from the higher ideas expressed in the classics—poetry, music, and philosophy from the likes of Confucius, Lao Tsu, Chuang Tsu, Li Po. The resulting inveterate disdain for things material, however, has left the country behind in developing technical education. Two and a half decades after Gia-fu's trip on the USS *General Gordon*, historian Barbara Tuchman, among others, will note that it wasn't until the end of the nineteenth century that the Chinese began to think that, while remaining true to China's valued ideals, they needed to master Western techniques in order to cope with the threat of the Western world.[2] Gia-fu, Chao-hua, and their three hundred student shipmates' presence on the USS *General Gordon* reflect this view.

It was the Meiji Restoration, opening Japan to the West at the end of the nineteenth century, that helped the Chinese begin to recognize the benefits that mastery of Western education could bring. Well-educated Chinese, however, rarely considered emigrating to the U.S. or any other Western country. To this class of people, who viewed the rest of the world, and particularly the West, as barbaric, less cultured, and less refined, to emigrate would have been degrading. To them, as they might have phrased it, the West was not as close to heaven as was China, the Middle Kingdom. When Chinese students did go to those countries, it was only to get their education to bring home, in hopes of helping China regain its previous glory. And most importantly, because China had been insulted and shamed by imperialist powers, the hope was that it could recover its self-respect. Gia-fu and Chao-hua, well-brought up, well-educated young men of the upper class, saw themselves not as adventurers but as good and dutiful sons of their family and their country.

This attitude contributed to the complexity of students' circumstances abroad. Students honored their heritage and wanted to excel in their studies for their families and for China, but some also wanted to experience the culture in the U.S. while in residence—without losing their own sense of self. Racism in the U.S. against the Chinese further complicated the situation, making it challenging for Chinese students to fit in or be accepted. The history of the Chinese in America is fraught with injustice and horror. Even now, approaching Gia-fu's arrival in the mid-twentieth century, perceptible vestiges endure from the feelings that undergirded late-nineteenth-century actions. The Chinese Exclusion Act of May 6, 1882, had barred Chinese laborers from entering the U.S. and denied citizenship to those who were able to get in anyway, and was not repealed until December 17, 1943, when China was seen as an important ally against the Japanese. It will not be until 1952 that Chinese, whether born in the U.S. or not, will be allowed to become citizens of the U.S.[3]

China scholar Ting Ni will write in 2002 of trials Chinese students faced, one of which was finding housing. She will report some of the excuses Chinese students were hearing:

> I am sorry boys. I do not rent rooms to foreign students because I have a couple of American boys here. If I take you, I am afraid that the American boys would want to move. So far I have not taken any foreign students.

> "What kind of rooms do you want," ask the landladies. "We want single rooms," reply the Chinese students. In reply the landlady says that they have only double rooms. Later, other Chinese students inquire, asking for double rooms. In reply, the landlady says, "Sorry, we have only single rooms."

> Chinese students tell the lady that they are interested in looking at her rooms. "Sorry," shaking her head, "we have no rooms available."[4]

The complex relationship between China and the West, a century after the Meiji Restoration and twenty-one years after Gia-fu and Chao-hua sail to the U.S., will be summed up by poet and literary critic Yang Lian: "There are complications in the particular circumstances of China in the twentieth century...Wounded national pride, a vanished cultural superiority complex, the humiliation of defeat in war, and the sincerity of youth are all components of a love-hate relationship with the West..."[5]

And now, in 1947, within these contradictions, people in a turbulent world are trying to recover from a major war and incorporate the scientific advances and social permutations that accompanied that major military conflict. All over the globe people are piecing their lives back together. War-torn countries such as Poland, France, and Germany are dealing with masses of people returning to their respective homelands. In other places people like Gia-fu, after a brief return to his home and family, seek opportunity elsewhere. Many, the two brothers among them, gravitate to American soil where, with the single exception of the attack on

Pearl Harbor, no bombs have fallen, no rockets have exploded, no guns have been fired. They're heading to join the four to five thousand other idealistic Chinese who have come temporarily and with a specific purpose to the prospering U.S.

The United States that Gia-fu and Chao-hua are entering is seeing huge social changes intertwine inevitably with scientific advances, as technology begins to enter family and work life at an unprecedented rate. The last years of the forties and the beginning of the fifties will see the growth of television and the enormous social changes it will bring. Two years from now, in 1949, there will be slightly more than a million television sets in American homes. In just another four years, there will be nineteen million. Just now, in 1947, McDonald's is born and motels are beginning to spring up. By 1951 Holiday Inns will arrive. These and other concepts contribute to the changing social landscape in the U.S.; many of these won't find their way to China for at least four more decades. As the U.S. explodes with possibilities, ideas, and advances, both social and technological, China will soon be closing down—and being closed off from the rest of the world.

Yet even with the explosive growth and changes in the U.S., the social injustice of racism and its accompanying discriminatory practices are not yet among the more public national issues. Overt discrimination—segregated seating on buses and trains, segregated schools, and separate water fountains and facilities in general for black Americans—are accepted practices in the South, with marginally less overt expressions of racism in other parts of the country. Within a few years, in his search for self, Gia-fu will find himself drawn into attempts to address such injustices.

Now with next year's 1948 presidential elections in sight, national politics are heating up. Harry Truman, as sitting president, will become the Democratic candidate and Thomas Dewey the Republican Party's choice. Searching for a foothold to end the Democrats' almost sixteen-year hold on the presidency, some Republicans turn to the tactic of anti-Communist red-baiting as a sure winner. Honorably, the Republican candidate Dewey refuses to use this as a political weapon; however, his reluctance does not deter others for long.[6]

U.S.-China relations are playing a prominent role in the political scene, especially given America's misguided support of Chiang Kai-shek and the KMT party in the civil war against the Chinese Communist Party. Chiang has been fighting the Communists in various ways since 1927, even when efforts could have been directed toward the Japanese, and most recently fighting an all-out civil war since 1945. He has rejected any cooperation with the Communists, while the Communists are gaining ground in the hearts and minds of the many Chinese who have been undermined and betrayed by the corrupt, power-hungry Chiang and the KMT. While Gia-fu and Chao-hua are sailing to the U.S., George Marshall is returning from his mediation assignment in China where he has been trying to assist in resolving the Communist-Nationalist KMT conflict. Marshall blames both sides for failing to reach an agreement, but particularly the KMT.

U.S. election issues begin to boil, isolationism versus internationalism prominent among them. Internationalism, which some regard as socially responsible action in an increasingly interdependent world, instead takes on a patriarchical tone and will become cast as a single-minded fight against Communism, with profound consequences for Gia-fu and Chao-hua. Perhaps because using the atom bomb has given the U.S an unprecedented sense of power, the U.S. begins to see itself as guardian—just as some others see it as dominator—of the world.

This sense of power will play out in a very messy way in Korea, further alienating China and the U.S. and affecting the plans of many Chinese students, including Gia-fu and Chao-hua, in the next few years. In his memoirs, China scholar John King Fairbank will later note, "Within twenty-four hours of Hiroshima, planners in Washington were redefining America's position in Korea" countering the growing Chinese and Soviet Communist influence in that country. Through other eyes, the U.S.S.R. and China were intent on countering the growing U.S. influence in Korea.[7]

As events unfold over the next few years, Gia-fu and Chao-hua have no inkling of how profound an effect these political machinations will have on their future. For now, in late January 1947, the two brothers have arrived in San Francisco and, after checking into the YMCA, the first thing on their minds is finding decent food.

The two head for Chinatown and settle on one of the many restaurants they find on Grant Avenue. In the brightly lit room decorated in red and gold and surrounded by the chatter of a familiar language, although a dialect of Canton in the south, they eagerly feast their eyes on the menu, which is of course written in Chinese and contains names of delicacies they have been deprived of on their long sea journey. Crab, shrimp, eel, jellyfish, whole fish—steamed or fried—chicken, pork, steamed dumplings, fried dumplings—savory and sweet—soups, and innumerable other delights. Nearly wild with hunger and anticipation, they make their selections and await their banquet. In that noisy, crowded restaurant far from home, they happily sample multiple dishes, dousing them in soy sauce and slurping an unending supply of fragrant tea. For the first time since leaving Shanghai, amid sights, sounds, and tastes reminiscent of home, the brothers set aside that little gnawing feeling of apprehension that accompanies their curiosity about what the next year or two in this new country will bring. Even their sense of purpose and their imminent parting are forgotten as they lose themselves in the spread before them.[8]

Throughout their years in the U.S., the brothers will find numerous Chinese restaurants in small and large American cities, many of which are run by husband, wife, and children. Most of these establishments have tailored their food to please American palates while still knowing how to cook for their countrymen. Gia-fu and Chao-hua have never encountered chow mein or fried noodles or fortune cookies, for example, because these dishes originated in the U.S. Chow mein, they learn, was born of a mishap when a Chinese cook accidentally dropped some noodles in hot oil. The result was a hit with his customers, so became part of his regular offerings. Fortune cookies, it turns out, were an American intimation of the comingling of the two cultures.[9]

After several days at the San Francisco YMCA, the two move for a short time to the Cornell Hotel at the corner of Bush and Powell streets, right next to Chinatown. More than fifty years later, Chao-hua will return to this hotel to talk about a book being written about Gia-fu, a startling coincidence to all concerned.

Gia-fu finds the people of Chinatown very kind. It comforts him enormously to find people who appreciate and accept his being Chinese. But at the same time, most of these people are from the laboring class and many come from the south of China; these are not the Chinese he has grown up with and known. As with every culture, distinctions based on differences in ethnicity, geography, education, and social class can, and often have, created barriers among the Chinese. From farther north and from a wealthy family, Gia-fu knows that the daughters and sons of the elite expect, and are expected, to return to the homeland to take important business positions and political posts. These elites number few and live lives apart from those in the Chinatowns of the U.S. As Professor William Wei of the University of Colorado will observe in 1999, Gia-fu's being Chinese in the U.S. at this time, but from farther north and of a class that did not easily fit in with the vast majority of Chinese, resulted in a double and more complicated dilemma for him.[10] As he did in Kunming, he takes the circumstances as they are for the moment, adjusting as well as he can with so many new experiences bombarding him at every turn.

Although the exact times and dates remain unclear, soon the brothers go their separate ways—Gia-fu most likely by train to Philadelphia to begin his master's program at the Wharton School of the University of Pennsylvania. He's interested in attending the world's first collegiate business school, founded in 1881 and enjoying a strong reputation in international banking.[11] Eager as always to gain as much knowledge as possible, Gia-fu looks forward to his new studies. Chao-hua heads south and east to begin his master's program in electrical engineering at the University of Texas at Austin. Though saddened by the parting, Gia-fu's optimism and eagerness to get on with his goal carry him through the emotion of their separation. He will complete his program at the Wharton School in a year and a half, but Chao-hua, a self-described restless student, will move to various universities over the next several years, including Stanford, Yale, then Cornell, and on to postgraduate work at the University of Wisconsin, Madison.

Some scattered facts illumine the haziness of this time. In Philadelphia, Gia-fu lives in the International House with other foreign students, including other Chinese. Always social, always open to new experiences and meeting new people, he establishes a sense of camaraderie with his fellow international students and engages in an active social life. Finally indulging his desire to drive, he buys a 1947 Kaiser, having apparently overcome the trauma of crashing his father's car more than a decade before. The car comes in handy with his schedule jammed full of classes during the day—more than the normal load so that he can complete his degree in as short a time as possible—and dancing every evening.

With this ambitious schedule of classes and no time to go home to change into evening dress, his custom is to leave his fancy dancing suit and shoes in his car and find some place to change after classes. This arrangement works well for some time until calamity strikes. Someone breaks a car window and steals his dancing clothes. Only temporarily distressed by this turn of events and recognizing his luck in having some depth to his wardrobe, Gia-fu finds another suit and pair of shoes to wear. But the car window poses a different problem. With no extra money to have it repaired, he has to drive with it broken until his next allowance arrives. He may have worked in banking and is now studying this subject, but his studies and experience don't necessarily equate prudence in managing his own limited funds.

While he's studying again, Gia-fu receives an allowance from his father. Feng Chong-ching supports his third and fourth sons' desires for advanced degrees and education and this includes a financial arrangement. That Gia-fu studies at the Wharton School and Chao-hua pursues engineering pleases their father. He also counts on his two sons' return within two years, bringing home to China the benefits of the knowledge acquired abroad.

Living at the International House creates a web of friendships and opportunities for Gia-fu, as do good relationships with key professors. His finance professor, Dr. John Whittlesey, who is associated with Pendle Hill, the Quaker study center just outside Philadelphia, invites Gia-fu to accompany him there. There Gia-fu meets people to whom he finds himself drawn by their varying interests. Some of them are deeply involved in prayer and meditation, some determined pacifists who have resisted the draft, even serving jail terms for their beliefs, and some are interested in Oriental culture. Unlike his experience with the Christians in Kunming, Gia-fu feels no pressure to be or act a certain way; he only feels acceptance.

The simplicity of the place, the quiet, the calm of the people and their deep beliefs offer a refuge, an alternative to his busy university life.

From its beginning in 1930, Pendle Hill would be described, even on its website in 2006, as an "educational experiment, grounded in the spiritual and social principles of Friends—a community centered in the daily meeting for worship and sharing a common life of study, work, recreation, and mutual care and concern for one another." Thus it is a teaching and learning community without degrees, prerequisites, or defined courses of study, and consists of a barn and several outbuildings. Gia-fu finds the mix of people and interests intriguing and enormously compelling. He also finds himself drawn to a number of aspects of Quaker philosophy, in particular that of direct, immediate experience.[12] Some of the principles and ideas he encounters will find expression throughout much of the rest of his life, first in his direct association with the Quakers and later in reflections of these ideas at Esalen and Stillpoint.

The Quaker emphasis on peace, both in promoting nonviolence in the world and deep within oneself—an inner peace—also draws Gia-fu. His experiences in Kunming as well as Shanghai, of seeing the destruction and devastation war brings, remain with him, and finding an alternative appeals to something deep within. Howard Brinton, Pendle Hill's codirector from 1936 to the early 1950s, will aptly describe the essence of what now attracts Gia-fu:

> The first answer which we propose to the problem: so to order the inner life that outer pressures can be adequately met and dealt with. This is not the method of the ascetic who conquers his sensual desires by violence toward himself, nor of the hermit who avoids his fellow men, nor of the stoic who makes himself independent and indifferent to the world around him. It is rather an ordering of the inner life, so that there will be a proper balance of inner and outer, inner holding first place. In one sense we become independent of outer tumults and conflicts, but in another sense we are not independent because we must seek to reproduce in the world around us the inner peace created within ourselves. If we do not seek to reproduce our inner peace it will become lifeless and static.[13]

Gia-fu seeks peace and he seeks purpose. He still plans to return to China, but his plans are delayed by a dramatic change in his homeland. The war between the Kuomintang and the Communists finally ends in the KMT's defeat on October 1, 1949, and the consequent establishment of the People's Republic of China. Because of the unpredictable situation with the new Communist government, many parents of students of the propertied classes urge their children to continue their studies in the U.S. and wait to see what direction China will take in the future. Not knowing what opportunities, if any, his sons will have under the Communists' rule, Gia-fu's father is among those who counsel their children to stay. In light of his father's advice and having completed his master's degree in banking and economics at Wharton, Gia-fu enrolls in a PhD program in statistics at New York University. But still he finds opportunities to return to Pendle Hill on weekends.

For his part at home in China, Feng Chong-ching sees rampant inflation and the rapid decline of his assets. But he also sees a confusing situation, one that's difficult for him to read. In an effort to maintain some sense of stability, the CCP, recognizing that Party members are much more experienced in rural and village affairs than in urban operations, keep many officials and foreigners in their posts for the time being, while at the same time loudly condemning imperialists—that is, any foreigner—and also bureaucrats. It decries the elite, the educated. It launches a massive propaganda campaign in support of its new policies and organizes citizen study groups to learn the teachings of Chairman Mao Tse-tung, emphasizing the power of the new order—the proletariat. No one knows what direction this new regime will take and what it will mean on a personal level.[14] This is what concerns Feng Chong-ching. What would his sons be returning to?

And yet another complicating factor arises. Within a year of the founding of the People's Republic of China, the Korean War begins in June 1950. This war will later be described as a "proxy war" between the U.S. and the Communist governments of China and the Soviet Union.[15] Because of this war, under the authority of the Passport Control Act, the U.S. bars many Chinese students, including Gia-fu and Chao-hua, from returning to their homeland. Now the brothers are stranded, legally.

They can't go home, even if the climate, situation, and parental opinion in China are favorable. Gia-fu begins to feel the effects. He finds himself in another cage, unable to go where he wants, unable to do what he's ready to do. There's no place for him in China at present, and he has little desire to remain in the U.S. where there's no possibility to realize his hopes. He feels the U.S. considers him an enemy.

China scholar Ting Ni will later describe the situation for Chinese students in the U.S., writing that "With the continuing deterioration of the relationship between [China and the U.S.], legislation changed from legality of residence to illegality of departure."[16] The U.S. government fears the students will aid the enemy with knowledge of important Western technology, in engineering, any of the hard sciences, and even economics. Some students, faced with the prospect of living indefinitely in a strange land, are overwhelmed by feelings of isolation and despair and commit suicide. Gia-fu, though dispirited and somewhat homesick, tries to make the best of the situation, thinking things may stabilize before long. Somehow, he knows, he has to survive until that stability is achieved.

During his time in New York in 1949 and the early 1950s, Gia-fu attends his classes at the university and, interestingly, works on Wall Street. There probably aren't many other Wall Street employees who live in a hostel with other international students. But it's through his web of relationships from the International House while at the Wharton School and his involvement in the hostel in New York that Gia-fu finds himself absorbed in a project: a film about youth in America. One of the Rockefellers, most likely through John D. Rockefeller's foundation, wants to show that, contrary to popular opinion in Europe, American youth and the youth hostel movement in this country include serious-minded young people. The film is to have some interracial aspect, with intermingling among white and minority groups—a cause championed by American liberals. Gia-fu is selected to, in his words, "represent the yellow race." Probably because he understands that Americans are generally not very sophisticated in their understanding of race and culture, he agrees to participate. He's proud to represent his countrymen and he does it with aplomb.

On the appointed afternoon, a limousine arrives to drive Gia-fu to the wilderness location for the filming. Here, in the gently rolling hills, among the fragrant pines and persistent chirping of myriad birds, for the first time, he meets an American millionaire, who isn't as awful as Gia-fu expected. In fact, this Mr. Rockefeller treats Gia-fu very kindly, as an equal. These circumstances are vastly different, Gia-fu thinks, from the way the British behaved toward the Chinese in Shanghai and some Americans behaved in Kunming. Moved by this encounter, he resolves to get to know Americans better and expand his friendships beyond the international student groups. And although he may not consider this meeting a divine accident, as he did think of meeting the general on his way to Kunming, it may be. This meeting broadens Gia-fu's perceptions and helps him begin to move beyond the limitations his wealth and his background, as well as British discrimination toward Chinese, have created. It encourages him to be less distrustful of Westerners and more open to possibilities for relationships with them. The irony lies in an American millionaire serving as impetus. Quite possibly the experience helps him reflect on his own discrimination as an elite against the provincial girls in Kunming.

Yet despite this positive encounter and the widening of his circle and the loosening of his views, he begins to feel trapped, out of place. Despite his studies and his job, he feels lost. Typical of many students from Third World countries, his illusions about a hundred Wall Street families controlling the U.S. and its streets being paved with gold have long faded. Now working on Wall Street, he finds the American economic system much more complex than he originally thought. He also finds himself stuck at his current job level because of his visa status.[17] Finally, his interest in his work and studies wanes. He feels at loose ends.

This dislocation he feels is amplified by the way people stare at him, no matter if it's in subway cars or in the elevators of skyscrapers, and it perplexes him. When he considers that only two or three years earlier he was working in Shanghai's financial district where he was not a stranger, he comes to see himself as a stranger in a strange place. In China he was master of his land, his own home. Having come so far, having done so much, now that he is only a guest, a captive guest confronting suspicious-looking hosts at every turn, he is unsettled and depressed.

He tries to calm down. He tries to understand his feelings, his reactions to his circumstances of being out of place and seemingly out of time. He tries not to let these feelings overwhelm him, but he finds it difficult to see things otherwise. Seeking something beyond himself, he begins to wander, going from place to place looking for some semblance of a supportive environment. He attends an array of Christian retreats, even some for Chinese. The latter make him feel even worse because of the prejudices between the various Chinese groups, be they provincial or class oriented.[18] His awareness grows as he experiences prejudice himself, sees it in his countrymen, and begins casting back over his own values and behavior in China. He didn't see it then, as he acted out his own prejudices by avoiding the local provincial girls, but he sees it now for what it clearly was. Eventually he moves into a cooperative house, run by a Quaker group, which he finds much less dogmatic and freer than others he's encountered. The Quakers offer acceptance, room to think, a modicum of peace.

Returning to Pendle Hill one weekend, Gia-fu meets a young woman named Margaret Olney and they strike up a friendship. Decades later, recalling their meeting during the time he learned he could not return to China, Margaret will comment on how unhappy Gia-fu seemed. He told her he had to adjust to life in this country but the worst part was being barred from returning to his homeland. He was so lonely.[19]

His options severely limited, mixed up, confused about who he is and what his underlying values are, Gia-fu senses he is trying to behave in a Western way. He sees himself suppressing his Eastern heritage, and simply does not know who he is anymore.

Around this time, his second-younger brother, Zhao-shu, completes his master of science degree in mechanical engineering at England's Birmingham University. Although he has been accepted for a doctoral program at Michigan State University, he is unable to obtain a U.S. visa. His interest in remaining in England is low and options are narrow, but with no U.S. visa, Zhao-shu responds to China's campaign urging Chinese students studying abroad to return home and prepares to do so. The prospect of being with family again is an added incentive for Zhao-shu. But going home still isn't an option for Gia-fu or Chao-hua, who have held hopes that Zhao-shu would join them in the U.S. That he cannot join them and chooses to return to China further disappoints Gia-fu. Once again, international politics play heavily in the lives of the Feng family.

Searching for a way of life that might bring him some peace, some sense of self, some understanding of his place in this country and in this world, over the next year or two Gia-fu drives what he calls his jalopy from one interracial intentional community to another, including Macedonia, Koinonia in Americus, Georgia (where Habitat for Humanity will later be created), and the Tuolumne in California. Looking for his identity, looking for appreciation and acceptance, he is mostly looking to find his own physical rhythm and a way of life through which he can develop his potential.

The communes focus on farming and hard labor, and Gia-fu, with his slight build, finds the emphasis on physical labor difficult. He works along with all the other residents and by day's end he's completely exhausted. Evenings, he attends group meetings, but his fatigue and the warmth of the room conspire, lulling him to sleep almost every time. After a time he finds himself frustrated by these rural, agrarian circumstances; to him, it seems that American intellectuals are rotting away on farms, not cultivating or applying their abilities as he feels they should be doing. This is not what he wants to do; he has other talents to develop.

Though he came to the U.S. seeking to grow intellectually and obtain the kind of knowledge that can help China, now it's unclear whether or not he'll be able to apply his talents in his home country. And it's most difficult for him to apply them in this country, with its ambivalence toward anyone outside the mainstream. He's plagued with uncertainty and a multitude of questions. What are his abilities? How can he contribute, and toward what? What place can he find to open his heart, to find some sense of fulfillment?

While Gia-fu seeks his identity in these alien circumstances, the U.S. struggles to face up to its own identity. As he seeks workable interracial settings and his place in this country, the country itself is quickly coming face to face with the hypocrisy found between its proclamations of freedom for all and its actual practices. The question is whether to make good on its constitutional promise for all Americans or to continue affording, or denying, citizens their rights based on their skin color.

Forcing the issue, a courageous black welder in Topeka, Kansas, brings a direct challenge to the discrepancy between the Constitution and practice. Not a radical but a mild, religious man, Oliver Brown objects to his daughter having to travel far to attend a black school when a white school sits near their home. He files suit against the Topeka Board of Education in 1951. On May 17, 1954, Chief Justice Earl Warren reads the Supreme Court's unanimous decision: "We conclude that in the field of public opinion the doctrine of 'separate but equal' has no place. Separate educational facilities are inherently unequal." Chief Justice Warren demonstrates leadership based on a strong sense of moral purpose, and he does so in the face of great difficulty, including a Court wracked with long-standing divisions among its members, strong opposition from the South, and even covert support of segregation by President Eisenhower. Reaction to the Supreme Court ruling is sadly predictable. Billboards and signposts sprout like mushrooms across the country, and especially in the South, screaming, "Impeach Earl Warren!" Tension between the races becomes more palpable, and racist violence remains a threat.[20]

Still, the first of the three branches of government has acted. The judicial branch leads in the struggle for equal rights. The nation's newspapers and then the television networks begin to educate Americans about the struggle, and both black and white Americans push for greater equality and equity—as the civil rights movement becomes a force for freedom in this country.

Not surprisingly, the immediate aftershocks of the 1957 integration of Central High School in Little Rock produce some unexpected but devastating consequences for Gia-fu and his peers at Koinonia. A white backlash erupts in the community toward this interracial Christian commune, a commune that considers all races equal. Prior to the Supreme Court decision, very few hostile acts were directed toward the commune members by the people in and around Americus, Georgia. In fact, their neighbors had been very friendly. But now they boycott the little farm.

The supermarkets refuse to buy the eggs laid by its four thousand chickens. The insurance companies cancel its insurance, and the bank refuses to extend its mortgage.

One Sunday morning, one of the black male teenage commune members drives to church with one of the white girls. They arrive to find many of the white male teenagers from the town sitting on the front steps of the church—with shotguns. A neighbor of the farm, Mr. Hamilton, calls the sheriff to disarm the angry boys. This situation passes but problems continue, heightening Gia-fu's dismay, deepening his understanding of U.S. culture and its contradictions. And perhaps his own.

Hostility resulting in boycotts and refusal of normal services to the farm bring the thousand-acre operation to its knees. The only remaining possibility is to sell the pecans and peanuts grown on its acreage, because nuts can be packed and mailed outside the state. Gia-fu sees this as the economics of racial confrontation. Trapped as he is, he can see the mirror it holds up for himself: he is from the elite class of China but is caught in a place whose majority accord privilege only to those who look like them, whose majority won't let others live with the respect they demand for themselves, who won't allow them fiscal independence and certainly not prosperity. Again, he casts back over his own life of privilege, opportunity, and possibility, now recognizing what he could not catch clear sight of before—what it means to be the underdog, or worse, the detested. Difficult as it is, it pushes him to continue broadening his perspective and examining his values.

Gia-fu respects the brave fight of the commune founder, Clarence Jordan: how he stands up for what he believes, what he considers Christian beliefs. He regrets the irony that Jordon's taking black youths to Sunday morning worship services is not acceptable to other Christians in the churches. Jordan's commitment to justice and to the ideas that people can choose to live together peacefully, honestly, and connected to the land are seeds that have now been further nurtured in Gia-fu. Years later in 1969, he will be greatly saddened to learn that Clarence Jordan has died of a heart attack.

Acknowledging to himself that what he seeks is not in Georgia, Gia-fu heads west, or more specifically, northwest, to attend two months of seminars with international students on Orcas Island in the San Juans just off Seattle. These seminars sponsored by the American Friends Service Committee, his continuing Quaker connection, focus on civil rights and international harmony. And Gia-fu, still his old self in some ways, finds the coed nature of the seminars a special attraction; his social self still quite robust, he delights in interacting with the young women there. He admits that he's interested in both the local women and the foreign students, although other than his interest, little is recorded, remembered, or known about Gia-fu's romantic life. But the two months pass, and Gia-fu is on the road again.

Gia-fu's wandering takes him briefly to Tuolumne, a California commune, but then subsides with his next move, this time to San Francisco. Here, whether by fate, divine accident, or happenstance, he lands in a place where he can begin to develop the potential he knows he has but hasn't exactly defined. Here, he finally finds a niche for his talents to be used and for his inner self to find nourishment.

His sojourn in the Bay Area begins on a spiritual note in reconnecting with an old friend. Arriving in the city, Gia-fu looks up Pendle Hill friend Margaret Olney in Berkeley. Margaret lives with her grandmother in a big old home, complete with a cook. Grandmother is quite proper, and she and "Jeff," as Gia-fu is called by most American acquaintances and friends, get along quite well. Gia-fu thinks Grandmother is very much like Chinese ladies, which surprises Margaret.

Margaret is truly Gia-fu's friend, and her willingness to let him drive her, her grandmother, and sister to Thanksgiving dinner attests to her loyalty. Margaret's sister pronounces Gia-fu the worst driver she has ever encountered and refuses ever to ride with him again, although reportedly she is more amused than terrified. Margaret's friendship provides a welcome anchor for this wandering soul, and Gia-fu values being treated almost as one of the family. For her part, Margaret appreciates Gia-fu and respects his search for something meaningful. This friendship and fond memories will never waver.

In his search for self, here in San Francisco in the mid-fifties, Gia-fu finds himself in a time and place, and soon in a circle of friends, that will point him in an unexpected and definitive direction. The bowstring begins to vibrate with possibility.

He hears a program featuring Alan Watts, philosopher, writer, erstwhile clergyman, who is credited with being the first person to bring Eastern thought to the West in ways that people can understand. A regular on radio and television, Watts also teaches at the Academy of Asian Studies, where from 1952 to 1956 he serves as its administrator. Two decades later, the Academy will be known as the California Institute of Asian Studies, and in this place, Margaret Susan Wilson will earn her master's degree in Far Eastern studies. Now at the Academy, Alan Watts, a key figure to writers and artists on the West Coast, is on his way to gaining national visibility.[21] In early 1954 Gia-fu attends a lecture by Watts, hearing for the first time from a Westerner the original texts of Taoism, Zen, and other Eastern philosophies used as a basis for reflecting on ordinary problems, daily existence. Touching understandings deep in the recesses of Gia-fu's memory and in his heart, Watts's lecture strikes an inner chord for Gia-fu; it changes the course of Gia-fu's life. The string assumes its appropriate length, finding a way to accommodate the bow.

CHAPTER SEVEN

EAST MEETS WEST

In the pursuit of learning, every day something is acquired.
In the pursuit of Tao, every day something is dropped.

—from Chapter 48, *Tao Te Ching*

So captivated is Gia-fu by his study of comparative religion that it's no wonder he later tells people the reason he came to the U.S. was to study just that—comparative religion. Despite his master's degree from the Wharton School and his original intention of returning to China, here in San Francisco in 1954 he cannot believe anything else could be possible right now. He's discovered a way to develop his potential, to mine his talents. Through Alan Watts, he has found the perfect place for himself, translating his beloved Chinese classics and studying the religions and arts of China and other cultures at the American Academy of Asian Studies.

The classes he's enrolled in, one of which is taught by Alan Watts, prove a gold mine for this seeker, as do Watts and the Academy itself. Gia-fu can hardly believe the wealth of riches arrayed here, the brilliance of the international stars that have been part of the Academy and those here now: Dr. Haridas Chaudhuri, former head of the philosophy department at Krishnagar College in Bengal, associate of Sri Aurobindo—and future mentor of Susan Wilson; Sir C. P. Ramaswamy Aiyar, formerly Diwan (head official) of India's State of Travancore and then Chancellor at the University of Banaras; Judith Tyberg, teaching Sanskrit and yoga; Polish-born Rom Landau, head of the Islamic program and author of books on Morocco and Arab mentality; Sabro Hasegawa, father of the Japanese School of Modern Painting; Dr. Malalasekhara, president of the World Buddhist Association and former Ceylon ambassador to the Soviet Union; and of course, Frederic Spiegelberg, recently returned to Stanford University as professor of Indic and Slavic studies, but who served as the Academy's director of studies from its inception in 1951, creating much of the breadth and depth of the Academy's program.[1]

At present, Watts serves as the Academy's administrator, continuing his teaching, radio broadcasts, and writing as well. He finds Gia-fu fascinating, too, and the two men learn they have much to contribute to each other's pursuits. Watts, with his wide-ranging knowledge of wisdom traditions from Taoism, Buddhism, Christianity, and Islam, and his ability to help others see how such teachings can enrich life, is intrigued by Gia-fu's classical Chinese education. He immediately sees that Gia-fu's knowledge of significant Chinese works and language skills in Chinese and English can be put to use translating important texts, and he engages Gia-fu in these efforts. Gia-fu finds great joy applying his talents as he immerses himself in translating the classics he loves—Chuang Tsu, Lao Tsu, the *I Ching*—many of which his father ensured that he study as a child, and those he reveled in at Southwestern Associated University in Kunming.

And there is Alan Watts himself. Watts intrigues. Anglican priest, broadcaster, author (of what will be more than twenty-five books before his death), lecturer, interpreter of Eastern thought to the West, Watts has come to the Academy most recently from Northwestern University, where he was the chaplain. Almost two decades later in his autobiography, Watts will describe himself as a person who welcomes, encourages, promotes naturalness and spontaneity, who resonates to his own rhythms, not the prescribed rhythms of others. He will write, "The spirit in which I was working at the Academy of Asian Studies to start something which—based primarily on Lao-tzu and Chuang-tzu—would counterbalance, out-fox, soften, and ally the martial, mechanically marching, tick-tock, and saw-toothed jagged life-rhythm which has been rattling the world at least since the Caesar's legionnaires stamped out of Rome."[2]

Through wisdom and skills inherent in the arts, philosophy, the body, exploration of one's mind, through flower arranging, judo, archery, and myriad other means, Watts seeks a state of consciousness free from ego-centric desire; he also seeks to provide the means for others to experience this state. His attitude, his interests, his unorthodox approach to life capture Gia-fu's imagination. Gia-fu sees a place for himself, a path for learning, but perhaps most importantly, also a way to put to use what he studies and to contribute.

Finding this niche comes at a critical time, a point at which Gia-fu must decide whether to return to China or to stay in the U.S. The recently passed Refugee Relief Act of 1953 now allows Chinese who entered the U.S. before July 1, 1953, one year to apply to adjust their immigration status.[3] Deportation is the highly likely alternative. Given this law, Gia-fu has been considering returning to China despite the fact that under the Communist regime, the Feng family has lost most of its fortune. Several of his brothers and sisters remain in Shanghai, as does his father, but the future in China for them and for him, people with their privileged background, is uncertain.

And by no means would he be returning to the China he left. The current China has just come through two mass campaigns against what the Chinese Communist Party calls counter-revolutionaries, meaning anyone even slightly suspected of not supporting the revolution or of engaging in some form of corruption. Even though there's been a general shift in the government's former military approach to one using more persuasive means—study groups, propaganda, brainwashing—public executions are still part of the campaigns. Widespread public struggle meetings and sundry humiliations targeting intellectuals now seem to be the norm,[4] leaving Feng Chong-ching wary of asking his sons to return.

Gia-fu does stay in the U.S., but he cannot know that within the decade he will again be barred from going back, this time by his mother country. He chooses, for now, to remain in San Francisco, immersed in the ideas, the people, the intensity of the Academy and San Francisco of the 1950s.

The Academy in particular seems a vortex as energy emanates from the mix of ideas and people. In retrospect, Watts will describe it as "one of the principal roots of what later came to be known, in the early Sixties, as the San Francisco Renaissance...that huge tide of spiritual energy in the form of poetry, music, philosophy, painting...and general life-style [that] swept out of this city and its environs to affect America and the whole world..."[5]

Louis Gainsborough, the Academy's founder, was a San Francisco businessman whose company, Login Corporation, had trading ventures all over the world. He had a particular fondness for Asia and wanted to create a different kind of school. It was to be a graduate school, not limited by the usual disciplinary boundaries that existed in colleges and universities at the time. He wanted to do something to help people really understand each other. He had, in his words, "dealt with these [Asian] people and...understood that you don't divorce business, politics, and religion in the countries of Asia. If you want to understand those people you've got to understand the way they think: their philosophies and their religions and so forth." So he set out to create a new, more integrated approach to educating, with heads of major universities and the ambassadors of most of the Asian countries serving on his advisory board. And what he created was the American Academy of Asian Studies.[6]

Through the Academy, Gia-fu sees a way to honor and bring together the different parts of himself. He doesn't have to disavow who he is. His background in business and banking isn't a detriment; his knowledge of the classics is most definitely an asset, as is his ability to translate. His experiences with the Quakers and the intentional communities are also pluses. And at long last in his time in the U.S., being Chinese holds special value in this place that appreciates, even seeks out, different cultures. Equally important, he sees a way to continue learning and developing through his work and studies at the Academy. The people he meets, some in the vanguard of social experimentation, also help extend his world. Writer Jack Kerouac is one of these.

Gia-fu thinks of Kerouac as the father of the Beat generation. Kerouac is, indeed, a key part of its genesis, although he will later distance himself from some of the other central figures. Warm memories will stay with Gia-fu from this association, memories of sipping wine with Kerouac in the basement of the rambling old mansion housing the Academy on Broadway in Pacific Heights. He and Kerouac have some things in common: their interest in Eastern thought and the fact that English is their second language. Kerouac is French-Canadian.

One exchange in particular will stay with him, one that takes place in the cool wee hours of the morning. After a long discussion while drinking wine with others from the Academy, Gia-fu and Kerouac opt for some fresh air. Strolling leisurely along the empty sidewalk, they continue talking at an equally leisurely pace. They've been considering what it really means to be enlightened, and they look at this state of mind from various angles, as if looking at and commenting on a precious stone being held up to the light. Coming to a nearby park they find plenty of vacant benches, since it will be hours before the regular occupants, elderly retired bench-sitters, show up. Choosing the closest one, they sit down on either end of the bench, Kerouac reclining back and stretching his long legs in front of him, Gia-fu sitting more upright with his arm over the back of bench, and angled toward Kerouac. He can see Kerouac's handsome face profiled in the light from the nearby streetlamp as Kerouac leans back, folding his hands behind his head and looking up at night sky that's ever so slowly beginning to lighten.

Despite the amused look on his face, Kerouac nonetheless speaks earnestly. "One of my favorite images, one that seems the very essence of enlightenment, comes from Chinatown."

Gia-fu is captivated by Kerouac's tone as well as his topic. "What is this special image? Tell me."

Anticipating profound wisdom, a startling insight, a revelation, Gia-fu leans his slight frame toward Kerouac. Tilting his head slightly to the left, he awaits this special moment. Kerouac, as if lost in the memory of that image, sighs, and after what seems to Gia-fu an interminable pause, speaks.

"It's child, a little boy, in everyday shirt and trousers." Gia-fu leans closer, his head tilting a fraction more. Kerouac speaks again. "He's laughing and running down the pavement with his fly wide open, and he's urinating all over the place."

Gia-fu erupts with laughter—at the scene, his friend, and his own expectations. He sees this, indeed, sums up Kerouac's idea of enlightenment. He seems to think of it as total self-abandonment, the realization of self-nature without even being conscious of it: an idea that sometimes gets interpreted as doing whatever one wants. Alan Watts would call it Beat Zen, which he contrasts with Square Zen and Zen; the difference being that Square Zen is a more traditional, disciplined approach to enlightenment. And summing up the relationship between Beat Zen, Square Zen, and Zen, Watts will write in a 1958 article in the *Chicago Review*, "For Zen is above all the Liberation of the mind from conventional thought, and this is something utterly different from rebellion against convention, on the one hand, or adopting foreign conventions, on the other."[7] Realization of self-nature—touching something deeper than momentary gratification or justification, something much more profound than rebellion. Self-nature—that multifaceted gem, that sense of emptiness that isn't really empty or blank. It's just not captured by assertions such as "I am this" or "I am that."

In those early dawn hours, there on that park bench with Kerouac, Gia-fu recognizes that this is the search he has longed for, and that he has found a place where he can begin it in earnest. A solid base has formed from which he can explore, to further realize his own self-nature; he's begun the integration of where he's come from and where he now finds himself.

Here at the Academy, he sees more broadly the possibility of the integration of Eastern and Western cultures, and this perception informs his own self-integration. He himself becomes more interested in the old Chinese religion of Taoism, studying with Gi-ming Shien, who has studied with some of the Taoist hermits living in caves in China. More than two decades later, in a 1977 New Dimensions Radio interview of his own, Gia-fu will talk about how it took Westerners to bring out his deeper Eastern self: Westerners such as Watts, and later Dick Price and others.

Becoming involved with Alan Watts and the Academy and its circle is something Gia-fu considers in the realm of divine accident. He pursues an interest, awakened by Watts, in putting spiritual teachings to work in everyday, pragmatic life. He also explores the relationship between physical and emotional well-being, between muscle and mind, as well as spirit, through tai chi, acupressure, and other kinds of traditional Chinese bodywork. Now he is pursuing his own life. Later he will write:

> Perhaps it is more important to see all things as they are, which is the Buddhist concept of "suchness." The Taoist went a little further also accepting the self-nature of each individual, sentient being. Like Chuang [Tsu] said, "When the wind blows through the ten thousand different hollows, they all make their own sounds. Why should there be anything else that causes the sound?" As it was in the beginning of the second inner chapter of Chuang Tsu, the autonomous nature of all things is like the ghost of a machine. Each machine has its own life and spirit, but then the Taoist also emphasized perfect quietude through total acceptance of the universal order, such as the grains in a rock.

In the universal order, the relationships among the grains in a rock become increasingly evident now and in later years as the enormous influence of Watts, Kerouac, and others play out in Gia-fu's life. They become apparent in the interests he pursues and also stylistically, in the stream-of-consciousness, free-association, hip way he sometimes talks and later in the way he will write. These individuals are the mirrors through which Gia-fu sees himself, but the wind that blows through the hollow that is Gia-fu makes its own unique sound.

Three decades later, Gia-fu will reflect these central thoughts in his writings:

> As I looked upon the past, many, many of the incidents that happened, which influenced or changed the direction of my life, were those "divine" accidents. One can argue endlessly about the existence of God or predestination and free will, just like the chicken and egg argument. The Taoist had a better way of disposing it saying both "and," and "either or" and "yes no." It is paradoxical. There are no arguments with a Taoist.

~

Forty-four years after their initial meeting, on a warm July afternoon, Robert Breckenridge will sit on a deck in Boulder, Colorado, and talk to me about the Gia-fu of those days in San Francisco. The July 1998 visit will be one of many seemingly serendipitous encounters, amazing coincidences, synchronistic incidents in my retracing Gia-fu's life. It will hand me another lens through which to see Gia-fu's progression from student and translator at the Academy to teacher and head of the Stillpoint community, where Robert also spent time with him.

Robert, on his return from a driving trip to San Francisco from the remote Guatemalan village where he has lived for many years, will stop by Stillpoint, accompanied by his Mayan assistant, Carlos, and his dog, Lovely. Stopping at Stillpoint in hopes of bunking there for the night, he learns from Lloyd Alexander, there for a few weeks' stay, that David and I have just left only a few hours earlier. We were headed back to Boulder with our friends and visitors, Feng Zhao-shu and Du Chong-hui, Gia-fu's youngest brother and sister-in-law, from Tai'an in Shandong Province.

A few hours later Robert will sit on the deck in Boulder under a shady crabapple tree, sipping wine and talking for hours with Chong-hui, Zhao-shu, Carlos, David, and me. Robert will impress us with his stories and storytelling skill and, most importantly, provide us other insights, contacts, and clues to Gia-fu's life at the Academy and beyond, including his first meeting with Gia-fu in San Francisco in 1954.

Fresh from a BA degree in psychology from the University of Colorado at Boulder, Robert decides to attend the Academy for graduate study, despite the fact that he knows nothing about Zen, Taoism, or any other Eastern philosophy or religion. Driving the eleven hundred miles to San Francisco, where he's never been before, he heads straight to the old Victorian mansion that houses the Academy, overlooking the Golden Gate, the hills of Marin County, and Angel Island. His knock on the door is greeted by a woman in a sari, who takes him upstairs to talk with Alan Watts. Watts sets aside what he's doing and welcomes Robert. They talk for some time, Watts learning about Robert and his undefined interest in the Academy and Robert learning more about the Academy. At the end of their conversation, Watts says, "Stay for dinner," and Robert does.

Entering the basement dining room that adjoins the kitchen, Robert sees a table with about fifteen chairs around it. Watts takes a seat at one end, next to a gallon each of red and white wine, and invites Robert to sit wherever he likes. In the next moment, a group of people deep in conversation come into the room and sit down at the table, Gia-fu among them. To Robert listening to their conversation, the intensity with which they respond to each other, and the depth of their comments, these people seem brilliant and very well educated. In contrast, he feels insecure and out of place, even though Watts has introduced him to the group.

Sitting quietly, Robert toys with his food, sips his wine, until finally someone asks, "Well, what did you study at the university, Robert?"

"Psychology, but I didn't learn much about it except for statistics and experimental methods. But I studied Freud a little bit," he tells them.

Robert's response spurs more discussion, and then dinner is finally over. Gia-fu walks over to Robert. "Come to my room and we will talk."

The two climb the stairs to Gia-fu's tiny third-floor room, which holds a single cot-like bed and chair. Gia-fu offers Robert the chair, and he sits on the bed. Leaning back a little, he looks at Robert and sighs, "Ah, yes. Sigmund Freud. He knew it all."

Robert's first encounter with a Chinese person finds him absorbed by their conversation. They talk for hours, plumbing layers of their curiosity about psychology, religion, spirituality, life. This is the first of many times they will be together. In varying circumstances their association will continue off and on until Gia-fu's death a little more than three decades later.

Circumstances do, indeed, vary; things change. By 1956, while successful in generating new energy and ways of thinking by creatively bringing people, ideas, and cultures together, the Academy encounters a conflict with the oversight institution. Earlier, for accreditation purposes, the Academy had negotiated an agreement with the College of the Pacific to be its off-campus graduate school of Asian studies. Now the college's administration is not pleased with Watts's approach to running things. In Robert's eyes, the conflict rests in the college administration's perspective that Watts was "leading [the students] astray, perhaps as Socrates allegedly did the youth of Athens. [The conflict was also] a result of Alan's lack of interest/expertise in administrative duties, as well as the financial difficulties of the school."[8] Watts's interest does indeed lie in helping students in their search for wisdom and enlightenment, not in the boring administrative and financial details so unfortunately necessary to any institution's operation.[9]

With Watts's departure looming, Ananda Claude Dalenberg, a big, deeply reflective, gentle man, leads Gia-fu, Robert, and three others in starting a cooperative called the East-West House on San Francisco's California Street.[10] They, Gi-ming Shien, and several others move into the large, multistoried Victorian row house to continue their own East-meeting-West tradition. They invite Watts to continue teaching there, and although he doesn't do this, he does occasionally visit.

The East-West House attracts individuals from many walks, other students of Asian studies, poets, and artists. It will become so popular that in 1958 another house will be started only a few blocks away, this one called the Hyphen House, thus named for the hyphen between East and West.[11] Visitors and residents of the two houses will include writers Alan Watts, Jack Kerouac; poets Lew Welch, Gary Snyder, Joanne Kyger, Philip Whalen, and Lawrence Ferlinghetti; and other seekers, among them fellow student at the Academy and future cofounder of Esalen Institute, Dick Price.

For a couple of years only men live at the East-West House. This changes in 1958 when Mertis Shekeloff moves in. Mertis had come from Louisiana to Oakland with her family at the age of twelve. After high school she enrolled in the University of California at Berkeley, graduating in 1957. Forty years later she will describe the times, recalling two memorable events—Sputnik and the Emmett Till tragedy. The latter has particularly deep and disturbing significance for her. "Emmett Till was a young [fourteen-year-old], black kid in Chicago who went to Mississippi. They said that he whistled at this white woman, and he was lynched. Well, when that happened, I had had it with this country. So that's when I left for Mexico."

As an African-American who has spent her early years in Louisiana, Mertis knows the struggles between the equal rights promise and the reality in the U.S. of the 1950s. But after living in Mexico about six months, she decides to return to the Bay Area. Two big events, this time both of which are positive, await her—meeting Brian Shekeloff, her future husband, and moving into the East-West House.

Tall and stunning, Mertis is an artist's model. She often poses for painter Peter Blass. Through Mertis, Peter and his wife, May, befriend and essentially adopt the residents of the East-West House. Peter and May enjoy having these lively, interesting people around, and they provide money for bus or cab fares so they all can come to their home in Berkeley. They all feel on the edge of something novel, some fresh sense of being, some new sense of freedom, and they want to drink it in and enjoy it with each other. And so the web of these friendships extends ever wider.

They are part of the generation coming of age just after World War II, part of the generation of the Beats, perhaps resulting, as Jack Kerouac later put it, from "disillusionment stemming from the Cold War, [and espousing] mystical detachment and relaxation of social and sexual tensions."[12] Gia-fu, Mertis, and friends share an interest in spiritual liberation, and they share their personal thoughts and feelings freely, in everyday exchanges, in prose and poetry.

And they even share the cooking. When it's Gia-fu's turn, he often cooks one of his favorite dishes. He calls it simply pork butts. In preparation, he makes a special trip to the Chinese market on lively Polk Street for high-quality pork. He also insists on watching the butcher cut the meat to ensure it's done just right. With pork selected and correctly cut, he returns home to prepare this delicacy performance-style for anyone who happens to be there.

Pulling out the big iron skillet, Gia-fu places it over a high fire. He adds the pork, enjoying the sound of the sizzle. After it's cooked a bit, he tosses in whole peeled garlic, and a mouth-watering fragrance permeates the kitchen. As the garlic browns, he seems to instantly whip up a kind of sweet and sour sauce, grabbing bottles, jars, and fresh spices, mixing the ingredients with rapid movements. For the finale, he pours the sauce over the meat, container held high in the air, the liquid slowly trickling out, around, and over the pork. Exaggerating all his motions, he gives his onlookers a Chinese-opera-style performance, as well as a sumptuous dish.

Others in the house draw on their talents to provide special meals, too. One meal remembered by many is poet Lew Welch's inspired all-white dinner. The thought of such a lovely dinner (potatoes, turnips, fish, white wine, and bread served on white dishes) touched the sensitive Lew, bringing tears to his eyes. The meal itself proved memorable in its uniqueness.[13]

This unusual, close-knit family of friends even talks openly about personal hygiene and what it means. Poet and friend Joanne Kyger will later recall the joke in the East-West House about "clean asshole." She will write in a letter forty years later:

This was a very important part of human hygiene often overlooked by Americans. Later when I visited India, I realized that it was an important and fastidious part of keeping one's body clean there too. Gia Fu would offer to demonstrate on how to practice this aspect of body hygiene to anyone that was interested. It was a funny and light-hearted suggestion but earthy and sincere. The inference was if you couldn't keep your asshole clean forget about your spirit and soul.[14]

Shunning complacency, defying prudishness, and deploring the hypocrisy of racist attitudes and practices in the country, they create a world for themselves in the East-West House that extends ever outward, challenging the status quo. And the country as a whole is being pushed to look seriously at the status quo as a new awareness fuels serious questions about it. Rosa Parks, Emmett Till, Martin Luther King Jr., and any number of unknown leaders provide critical impetus for deep social change, change with repercussions such as Gia-fu saw in the Georgia commune, and that continues to spread throughout the country. But now, in San Francisco, Gia-fu finds himself in a place where the very flavor, the taste, the aroma of change differs from that of Americus, Georgia, where the ugliness of fear and hate dominated the scene. All around him in this city by the bay, life veritably explodes with the fusion of art forms, life perspectives, and all manner of possibilities.

Being in San Francisco and the Bay Area, the East-West House circle find themselves part of a primary center for poets and movements of all sorts. San Francisco in the late 1950s proves "a period of mixing it up, of bringing ideas and epiphanies from one medium to another, a period when not only jazz (and later, rhythm and blues and rock and roll), but esoteric and occult traditions, contemporary politics, popular culture, mass media, drugs, sex, and non-European traditions..." characterize life. The Beats and other harbingers of social experimentation are part of Gia-fu's life. Many were part of the Academy, and they are now woven into the very fabric of the East-West House, underlying the increasingly buzzing innovation and excitement of San Francisco.[15]

The East-West House circle includes poets Joanne Kyger and Gary Snyder, who later will marry, and whom Gia-fu, with Mertis and Brian Shekeloff, will visit in Japan within the decade. Gia-fu knows Gary through the Academy, but he and Joanne first meet when he and some other members of the East-West House visit her in her apartment on

Columbus Avenue over La Rocca's bar in North Beach, prior to her move to the East-West House. There in her apartment they strike up a conversation, and Joanne decides to show Gia-fu a poem she is writing. The poem is, in Joanne's words, "about the house of the dying; where people go to die in Shanghai." The poem will later be published in 1965 in Joanne's first book of poetry.

Joanne tells Gia-fu about living in Peking, Shanghai, and other places for the first two and a half years of her life. Thus they discover a mutual interest, a tie that is Gia-fu's hometown, his home country. Joanne thinks Gia-fu is "very out going and easy to get along with." He also seems kind and genuinely interested in others. Even in this first meeting, he encourages her about her writing, which she appreciates. She doesn't know about his background in American poetry, but she does feel sure about his sincerity and his interest in what she writes. This begins a friendship of long standing.[16]

May 1959 finds an eclectic and harmonious group of friends and family, among them Joanne, Gary Snyder, Lew Welch, Ananda Claude Dalenberg, and other East-West House residents, at Mertis and Brian Shekeloff's wedding. Gia-fu is present, looking young for his forty years and handsomely dressed in a suit and tie. The festive occasion brings friends and family together, some meeting for the first time; others are friends and acquaintances of many years. Mertis's mother and grandmother look elegant and proud as Zen Abbot Shunryu Suzuki performs the ceremony in an impromptu fashion in San Francisco's Buddhist temple.

After the ceremony, Mertis and Brian ask Gia-fu to sign the wedding certificate as a witness. He signs in Chinese. Then Abbot Suzuki, as the official performing the ceremony, signs, also in Chinese. Mertis's mother examines the signatures for several minutes. Looking up, with a puzzled look on her face, she asks her daughter, "Is this legal?"

Gia-fu feels stimulated and content in his San Francisco setting. He's now studying banking at San Francisco State University and earning money walking dogs for older rich ladies, somehow managing to survive. Earlier he worked for a while as an accountant in Chinatown, and he sometimes substitute teaches in middle schools in the Bay Area. At one point he fills in as an alternative source teacher at Peninsula School, a Quaker-inspired school in Menlo Park.

His brother Chao-hua, now called C.H., is in the Bay Area, too, drawn here by Gia-fu. He stays for a few weeks at the East-West House, and he will remember this time always. He is especially fond of Lew Welch. Years later, on May 23, 1971, C.H. will be greatly saddened when he learns Lew has walked off from friend Gary Snyder's mountain home carrying his .30-30 rifle, never to be seen again. C.H. will tell this story when walking in San Francisco with David and me, pointing out where the East-West House was once inhabited by so many vibrant, free souls.

The combination of people, time, and place feels singular. Forty years later Mertis will confirm this feeling. "God, we had great times! I was working at the Coffee Gallery in North Beach, and sometimes I'd come home around two [a.m.] and say, 'Let's go to Big Sur... or Let's go sleep on the beach in San Francisco.' The response was always, Okay! We had great fun!" Great fun, perhaps even profound fun, for spontaneity, living in the moment, living life fully, characterizes these times.[17]

These days and years in San Francisco contrast starkly with the situation Gia-fu's family in China is experiencing. There, Head of State and Communist Party (CCP) Chairman Mao Tse-tung and the Party have launched the second five-year plan, these five years extending from 1958 to 1962. The plan brings yet another campaign reflecting Mao's philosophy, which he writes about in an internal document circulated to senior CCP members:

> Continuing revolution. Our revolutions come one after another...
> Our revolutions are like battle. After a victory, we must at once put forward a new task. In this way, cadres and the masses will forever be filled with revolutionary fervour, instead of conceit...

This plan is called the Great Leap Forward. Because the first five-year plan was so successful, Mao wants to push even harder, to accelerate agricultural and industrial development. Under this plan, China rapidly reforms into communes of approximately five thousand members each. Individuals give up ownership of everything—tools, farm animals, their homes. They no longer work for themselves but for the commune. By the end of 1958, seven hundred million people live in approximately 23,500 communes.

Requiring high production, Mao forces peasants to dig up the soil by hand, turning every field over, and while he also requires excessively close planting, he won't invest in fertilizer. He promotes scheme after scheme, none thoughtful or based on facts or knowledge, all destined to destroy the land and deplete the workforce.

Mao demands that citizens build backyard production plants to make iron and steel at home so China won't have to import heavy machinery. This effort goes to the extreme, with people melting down cooking pots and everything else made of metal to produce for Mao and for China. In some cases, people are left without anything to cook their food in—what food there is—and the metal is such poor quality that the machinery made from it easily breaks. Metal production, which requires enormous time and energy, particularly at the pace the government is demanding, takes workers away from the fields. Ultimately, there's not enough food being produced and food shortages begin to take their toll on the populace—certainly in rural China, and even in the urban areas.

The urban areas, where Gia-fu's father, Feng Chong-ching, and siblings live, also feel the effects of the commune effort. Mao's plan is to organize urban communes and put an end to wages. He wants "to put the whole society on a non-cash barracks system." Again his plan doesn't work, but it does wreak havoc on the cities. And although the death tolls in the cities are lower than in rural areas, they're still plenty high.

By late 1960, with millions of Chinese dead from starvation—some estimate thirty million or more—Mao finally admits the failure of the Great Leap Forward. He steps down as head of state, although he still maintains the Party chairman role, a powerful position in itself. And then, between 1959 and 1962, the combination of these poor policies and rainfall patterns bring a time called Three Bitter Years. Famine continues, and so does its high death toll. But with Mao out of the lead, the three men, Lui Shaoqi, Deng Xiaoping, and Zhou Enlai, who take charge bring more sane policies and instill some slight sense of stability to the country. It's too late to undo the harsh effects of the Great Leap Forward, but at least the Leap doesn't continue. The madness slows for a few short years, until Mao's next campaign hits in the mid-sixties.[18]

And the contrast with the U.S., especially with San Francisco, couldn't be greater. The turmoil brewing in San Francisco is social change of a different nature and a wholly different magnitude. It's not surprising that Feng Chong-ching advises Gia-fu and C.H. to stay put, and not surprising at all that Gia-fu and C.H. want to.

With its boldly experimental artists, spiritual seekers, and political activists, San Francisco is, indeed, the antithesis of China. From 1958 to 1961, writer and later artist Pierre DeLattre runs a spiritual coffee house that's a gathering place on San Francisco's upper Grant Avenue, which offers opportunity for him to get to know Gia-fu and his friends. A San Francisco resident from 1955 to 1963, he serves dinner with bread and wine, so his place gets dubbed the Bread and Wine Mission. An ordained minister outside the organized church, and soon to leave Christianity altogether, Pierre's interest has turned to the Academy, Taoism, Buddhism, and the East-West House, so it seems natural that the East-West House circle frequents his place.

Nightly, beginning at four in the afternoon and going until two or three in the morning, people gather at the Bread and Wine Mission to, as Pierre will later describe it, "recite poetry to jazz, do improvised theatre, work on peace and civil rights projects, talk." And every Saturday there are poetry readings. Ferlinghetti, Ginsberg, Brautigan, Snyder, Whalen, and sometimes English poets such as Thom Gunn and Stephen Spender come to read their latest work to crowds of four hundred. Then on Sunday nights people bring their guitars and banjos, often numbering thirty or forty instruments, and along with the drummers, they make music.

Gia-fu comes in, sometimes with Gary Snyder or Joanne Kyger (who doesn't really like the place) or Lew Welch, Pierre's favorite reading poet. To Pierre, it seems everyone loves Gia-fu, that his relaxed, winning presence expresses "the Tao entirely in its delight, an acquiescence...to the 'suchness' of others." These friends laugh together, enjoying the creative games they play with each other and the spontaneity that is the essence of this time. They delight in the flashes of insight that take precedence over reasoned argument, and they value the silence and attention that preclude dogma or preaching.

Pierre notices how Gia-fu's exotic presence and the radiance he exudes in his own unique way create a sense of awe among others. And his playing of the er-hu, or what his friends call the Chinese fiddle, at the musical sessions is memorable. In fact, more than forty years later, Pierre DeLattre will write:

> When he played it for us my sensibilities were opened precisely to what I would now call the Tao. His playing released a kind of swimming feeling inside the body, a wiggling and a flowing, a jiggling loose of tight spots…I would have to say that Gia-fu's Chinese fiddle music seemed to locate the stopped up places in the psycho-physical medium of the body, and break them loose. So, of course, we found ourselves giggling a lot, feeling strangely released after he played. And that laughing of ours caused him to laugh. So he brought the laughter of flowing music into the body. That's what I remember of him.[19]

To Gia-fu, to be in a place where he can experience the various dimensions of himself and be accepted for who he is by people who are doing creative things in the world nurture his own creativity and sense of peace. For this moment, he has found a satisfying place to be, and he chooses to stay in it. He also understands that now there is nothing beyond his family to return to in China. There would be no way to support himself, economically, emotionally, or spiritually. In the pursuit of the Tao, as something is acquired, so also is something dropped. On September 4, 1962, giving up his legal ties to China, Gia-fu will become a citizen of the United States of America. In him, East meets West. But before he takes this official step, he will begin yet another phase of his life in the U.S.[20]

CHAPTER EIGHT

ENCOUNTERING ESALEN

The Tao is an empty vessel; it is used, but never filled. Oh, unfathomable source of ten thousand things!

—from Chapter 4, *Tao Te Ching*

Like the vessel that is used but never filled, life brims with possibility as Gia-fu again finds himself on the brink of something new. These years in the early 1960s abound with friends, intriguing ideas, promising opportunities, flowing from that unfathomable source of ten thousand things. And Gia-fu, ever thirsting for learning, for growth, is often attracted to new experiences by friends. For Gia-fu, friends and friendship carry great importance, time and again influencing the course of his life: friends attracted him to Kunming; Margaret Olney helped anchor him in San Francisco; Alan Watts befriended him, which led him to stay in the U.S. Now friendship brings him to his next adventure and quite literally to the next chapter of his life.

A friend from the early days at the Academy, Dick Price has returned to the Bay Area after a rough several years back in his home state of Illinois. The two, always appreciating their time together, see each other often. At one get-together Dick tells Gia-fu about a new venture, a venue for exploring philosophy, psychology, and more esoteric disciplines, which he and Michael Murphy are starting south of Monterey in Big Sur on the beautiful Murphy family property. Dick's enthusiasm for this undertaking they will eventually call Esalen attracts Gia-fu's attention, as well as that of others at the East-West House.

Michael and Dick come from similar backgrounds but are two very different personalities. A native Californian, Michael grew up in Salinas where his grandfather was a prominent physician. Dr. Murphy built two hospitals in Salinas and delivered many of the babies born there, including John Steinbeck, who would become a close friend of Michael's family. Based on how personality differences in Michael and his brother Dennis matched differences in the two Salinas brothers in Steinbeck's *East of Eden*, many people thought Steinbeck used Michael and Dennis as real-life models for the archetype brothers Cain and Abel. True or not, Dennis and Michael, respectively called the Devil and the Saint, undoubtedly enjoyed the comparison.

Michael, always a voracious reader, nurtured a taste for authors of substance, even reading Emerson, Jung, and Will Durant in high school. He was also an avid golfer, as well as student body president. His interest in religion, Eastern and Western, was piqued during his sophomore year at Stanford, where he stumbled onto Frederic Spiegelberg, the celebrated Asian scholar and later a major figure at the Academy of Asian Studies. Michael became deeply interested in Aurobindo Ghose (Sri Aurobindo), the Indian political activist against British rule, who became a spiritual teacher and who so influenced the founders and many faculty at the Academy.

Recruited into the army in 1952 during the Korean War, Michael was stationed in Puerto Rico where his job was interviewing draftees. Given his degree in psychology from Stanford, the army thought he would be able to determine whether Puerto Ricans who failed the exams did so honestly. Discharged from the army, he returned to Stanford for graduate studies in philosophy but was unhappy with how the program was conducted. After two years of discontented study, he decided to go to India where he spent a year and a half at the Aurobindo ashram in Pondicherry. Upon his return to San Francisco, he went to the Academy to study with Haridas Chaudhuri, who had been one of Aurobindo's leading disciples. He also took Spiegelberg's course on Indian religion at the Academy. Michael was living at the Academy when he met Dick Price. A mutual friend had suggested that Dick look him up.[1]

Dick grew up in a well-off Illinois family. He and Michael attended Stanford at the same time in the early 1950s, but despite the likelihood they had been in the same psychology classes, they hadn't known each other. In 1952, Dick earned a degree in psychology, while also maintaining an interest in social anthropology. Afterward he attended graduate school at Harvard for a year, studying clinical psychology. He then joined the air force and after a short time in Colorado was stationed at Parks Air Force Base, about forty miles east of San Francisco. Married to Bonnie, to whom Gia-fu had introduced him, Dick occasionally showed up at the base while allowing others to cover for his many absences, studied at the Academy and, as Walter Truett Anderson would later describe it, slowly was "going crazy."[2] He had what the air force called a nervous breakdown, and he, at the time, called an ecstatic experience. Anderson later wrote that Dick "experienced wild ideas, a sense of vast possibilities, and a constant stream of almost uncontainable energy."

First put in an army hospital, he was subsequently transferred to a hospital on the air force base, where he was kept for about three months, receiving electroshock treatments and medication. When he was finally able "to burn out all the strange energy coursing through him," he felt he was finished with the episode. But unfortunately, his father, who had never before given Dick much attention, stepped in to pull strings and have him transferred to an air force hospital in Illinois. He then convinced Dick to admit himself to a private clinic, the Institute of Living in Connecticut. Dick did this but got very little attention there and tried to check himself out. Upon hearing of Dick's wish to leave, his father had him committed. He was trapped until others decided he could go. Thirty-plus years later, in an interview only months before his death in 1985, Dick would describe his experience this way:

> Very much of my own experience…was quite brutalizing. Rather than seeing someone through a particular type of experience, it was an effort to suppress and negate in every possible way what I was going through. There was a fundamental mistake being made and that mistake was supposing that the healing process was the disease, rather than the process whereby the disease is healed. The disease, if any, was the state previous to the "psychosis." The so-called "psychosis" was an attempt toward spontaneous healing, and it was a movement toward health, not a movement toward disease.[3]

Finally released after almost a year, about fifty-nine insulin treatments and ten electroshocks later, Dick, a beaten man, lived at home going through the motions of daily life. He worked as an assistant purchasing agent for an uncle whose company manufactured illuminated beer signs. But he was saving his money and trying to restore himself emotionally so he could do something with his life besides work in business. He intended to find a place where people who were going through what he'd been through would get better treatment. He wanted to learn from such a place and use that knowledge to help others. After about three years' soulless existence in Illinois, he heard about Gia-fu and others' East-West House cooperative. In May 1960 he returned to San Francisco and his friends.

Now in the spring of 1961, Dick and Michael have moved south and are living at the Murphy family property in the Big House at Big Sur Hot Springs. A few other people live in various buildings on the property. But here Dick and Michael can spend the time they want meditating, reading, and enjoying the beauty surrounding them. Gradually, the setting and the fact that these two have such stimulating common interests, plus events such as Alan Watts's talks in the area, begin to spark conceptions of creating something new right here in Big Sur. Ideas for a center begin to take hold and develop. As they plan how their dreams might unfold, they agree that their programs will be open and flexible and not restricted to a particular school of thought. Two decades later, Walter Truett Anderson will describe their vision in *The Upstart Spring: Esalen and the American Awakening:* "They would establish a center for the exploration of new ideas. The guiding principle would be synthesis: the flowing-together of East and West, the ancient and the modern, science and religion, scholarship and art."[4]

It's an apt description, and it's not surprising that the two would come to this idea, for in a way, it's a logical step from the Academy. Or perhaps, more fully, it was a natural extension of the whole of Dick and Michael's combined experiences, the Academy being an important part. Given the way Alan Watts would later describe it, the Academy would seem to have served as a developmental step in Dick and Michael's vision: "In retrospect one can see that the Academy of Asian Studies was a transitional institution emerging from the failure of universities and churches to satisfy important spiritual needs. It was a bridge between the idea of a graduate school and the idea of a 'growth center.'"[5] Dick and Michael imagine a growth center that integrates a wide range of ways to explore who and what we humans are and what we're capable of.

The spectacular Murphy family property in Big Sur, a couple hours' drive south of San Francisco down Highway 1, is the perfect location for this center. Encompassing 375 rugged acres of spectacularly beautiful land along the coast, the property comprises cliffs, majestic trees, a waterfall, and the hot mineral springs called Big Sur Hot Springs.

For some time the property has been known as Slate's Hot Springs, but after Michael develops an agreement with his grandmother to use the land, he and Dick call the whole place Big Sur Hot Springs. By 1964 it will be called Esalen, after the Indian tribe that lived in the area until the eighteenth century, when they were ultimately extinguished by newcomers to the area.[6] But the springs will retain the official name of Big Sur Hot Springs. Now, some transitions need to be set in motion.

For some time the property and especially the hot springs have attracted numerous individuals and groups. Michael discovers a varied and colorful assortment of folks using the place, including rough people camping in the mountains, possibly involved in drug dealing, numbers of homosexual men from San Francisco, and an evangelical Christian sect called the First Church of God of Prophecy. The latter group has been invited there for meetings by Mrs. Webb, a friend of Michael's grandmother who has been serving as caretaker of the property.

During the several months' transition from his grandmother's stewardship to Michael and Dick formally taking it on, there are confrontations with all of the groups. In one of these, Hunter Thompson, now security guard and future "gonzo journalist," is badly beaten by a group of men at the baths.

Finally deciding it's time for a showdown, Michael and Dick find support in Thompson and some of the other folks living there, including the soon-to-be-famous folk singer Joan Baez and her boyfriend and two other couples. The crux of the incident takes place at the hot springs baths, the same baths of which Gia-fu would soon become "the keeper."

New Yorker writer Calvin Tomkins fifteen years later will capture the essence of the incident in an article about Michael and Esalen, also illustrating the unusual kinds of things that would continue to happen there—the quirky, the dramatic, the unexpected:

> On what came to be known as the Night of the Dobermans, Murphy and Price locked themselves in at the baths and sat down to wait. Almost immediately, they heard a thunderous commotion on the path leading down to the hot springs, and moments later they were joined by about a dozen young males in T-shirts and blue jeans. A retreat seemed advisable at this point. Murphy and Price walked back up the hill, to the accompaniment of loud taunts and

jeers, and set out to round up their cohorts. Murphy went to where Joan Baez and her friends were living, and got the men to come out and bring their dogs—three young Doberman pinschers on short leashes. The assembled home forces then headed back toward the baths. On the way, the two male Dobermans got into a vicious battle over the female. Dobermans are noisy fighters—no silent bulldog grips for them. The owners finally got the dogs apart and continued down to the baths, but nobody was there. They came back up the hill to find the invaders regrouped in the main parking lot. They were about thirty strong by then, menacing but dogless. The male Dobermans had another set-to at the edge of the parking lot, and again the night air was rent by sounds of unimaginable savagery. The owners got them separated again just in time to see the last of the enemy jumping into cars and lamming it up the road.[7]

Michael and Dick have lots of connections, and through them they find encouragement for their plans. Writers Aldous Huxley and Gerald Heard are both interested in how unused or latent human potential can be actualized. Huxley is a profoundly curious man, and his curiosity leads him into many realms, among them education, psychotherapy, physical development, and Gestalt therapy. His thinking is that some organization should conduct a comprehensive research effort into all the ways of actualizing human potential and how these methods could be developed for lifelong education.

Heard, who also has a deeply inquiring mind, believes humankind to be at a crossroads and needs something to push it forward. He thinks the research Huxley describes is absolutely necessary to move things in a productive direction. Michael and Dick get encouragement from both of these forward-looking thinkers.

Dick and Michael also talk with Frederic Spiegelberg, Alan Watts, Gregory Bateson, and others. Walter Truett Anderson will later describe the contacts the two have as "the beginning of what was to become a formidable cadre of philosophers, psychologists, artists, writers, theologians, and wise souls" who have deep interest in what they are proposing, provide suggestions, and agree to lead seminars at the new center. As the two talk to each icon, they mention other well-known names, thereby continually widening the circle.[8]

Dick and Michael begin to pull together a staff for their center, and Gia-fu is among the first to join. Gia-fu, perpetually interested in developing himself, also feels the magnetic pull of this groundbreaking effort to bring together different disciplines, cultures, and philosophies to bear directly on how we live our lives. His own life reflects the intimate, fertile connections between Eastern thought and that of the West, and he finds the idea of delving ever more deeply into these connections in this beautiful, natural setting irresistible. And there is his good friend Dick Price at the center of it.

Around the end of 1961, Gia-fu joins Dick, Michael, and others at Big Sur Hot Springs. Armed with his own abacus, Gia-fu fills the role of accountant in addition to keeper of the baths, as well as what some describe as resident Oriental mystic.

Gia-fu's use of an abacus to keep the accounts is not the only thing that's different at this place, as the first IRS audit will illustrate. The IRS accountant arrives on the appointed morning, turns in at the Big Sur Hot Springs entrance, drives down the long, narrow, curving lane, through the towering evergreens, and parks in a place designated for visitors. As he walks away from the car, he looks around and notices a group standing near the swimming pool, chatting. They're not wearing clothes. He pauses for a moment, seemingly considering the scenery. Then he moves toward the office door and passes a couple of men in loincloths. As he looks around, he sees other people wearing feathers. Some are playing volleyball.

The Bohemian, wild appearance of the people somehow seems to mirror the wildness of Big Sur, the cliffs, the ocean, this particular property. The accountant suspects that life here is conducted with considerable abandon. Continuing toward the office, he opens the door and enters. A slight, smiling Chinese man greets him, bowing repeatedly. It is Gia-fu serving in his role as accountant.

As for the accounting, during his brief stay, the IRS representative observes Gia-fu's system of bookkeeping using his treasured abacus. He examines the numerous small, varying-sized pieces of paper on which

Gia-fu records information. And after vigilantly auditing "the books," with deliberation and great care, he pronounces to the assembled Gia-fu, Michael, and Dick, "Gentlemen, your situation is not only unusual. It's unique." But they pass the audit. More than thirty-five years later, Michael will laughingly recount this incident, cherishing the times, the people, the place.[9]

Uniqueness. The auditor's word defines this Institute: not only its bookkeeping system and the way its programs unfold, but also the seemingly serendipitous way people and place come together. Serendipity, synchronicity, divine accidents? Gia-fu's life seems filled with these, however termed—a life populated by auspicious times and illustrious people.

Summer 1962. Psychologist Abraham Maslow and his wife, Bertha, come upon the Hot Springs during a vacation along the coast. Seeing the Hot Springs sign, they turn into the entrance thinking to spend the night. They know neither Michael nor Dick and are completely unaware of what is developing on this property. They find Gia-fu on desk duty, and they ask for a room. When the man signs the register, Gia-fu looks at the signature and recognizes the name. He looks up at Maslow, then abruptly dashes out of the room, leaving the couple confused and wondering. But he is absent for only a moment, only long enough to retrieve his copy of *Toward a Psychology of Being*. Clearly elated, holding out the book, Gia-fu asks if he is *this* Abraham Maslow. The man affirms that he is, and Gia-fu begins bowing, crying out, "Maslow! Maslow! Maslow!"

Michael is away from the Springs for the day, but Dick appears, introduces himself, and spends some time with the Maslows telling them about the plans. Maslow finds the ideas fascinating. His long-standing fascination with the potential in human beings will lead him to be a strong supporter during the Institute's early days. Believing that the dominant schools of psychology focus too much on mental illness rather than mental health, he wants to explore the principles of health and understand how people fulfill their potential, how they self-actualize. To him models of health are intellectuals in some way, which means using one's mental abilities toward a social purpose, a social good.[10] Some will think it unfortunate that as the growth and self-potential aspect blossom here, attention to the intellect will wane.

"The Human Potentiality"—this becomes the first program series at Big Sur Hot Springs. Willis Harman, a Stanford engineering professor whose interests range far beyond engineering, leads the first seminar of the series, "The Expanding Vision." Participants in this program and other early activities engage in intellectual discussion and multidisciplinary explorations of psychology, described by writer Walter Truett Anderson as "psychology mixed with philosophy, evolutionary theory, religions Eastern and Western."[11]

Soon, however, participants want to move beyond the intellectual, expressing the desire to experience what's being discussed. They want to experience Watts's descriptions of satori, the Zen concept of instantaneous spiritual awakening or enlightenment, or Maslow's exploration of peak experiences. Hearing and talking about these phenomena are not enough, and Michael and Dick come to realize this. The center they've envisioned, with specific plans continuing to unfold, offers a vast array of programs and presenters from holistic depth psychology, ecology, democracy, kundalini power of Indian yoga, Zen, photography, research on peace. Adding to its menu of intellectual pursuits, their center soon becomes a place to explore these areas experientially.

These are the dawning years of the sixties, and given the growing interest in psychedelic drugs, it seems inevitable that exploration of drugs and their potential in self-actualization will become part of the scene at Big Sur Hot Springs, at least for a time. It seems possible such drugs may aid in the pursuit of opening and deepening one's experiences and in the understanding of self. Then, during the winter of 1962 and spring of 1963, the second Human Potentiality series does see the effect of growing curiosity and interest in drugs.

Michael himself experiments with hallucinogens, but in a limited way. His first hallucinogenic trip in 1962 in the Big House, which sits in a stunning spot on a cliff overlooking the Pacific, is memorable.

A young man who had experienced the peyote rites of the Southwestern Indians has given Michael some dry, old peyote buttons. Curious about what experience they can induce, Michael ingests the buttons. At first he feels that nothing is happening and goes upstairs to his room. He sits all alone, feeling a little funny, a little queasy. He lies down. Suddenly hearing some noise, he realizes Gia-fu is looking for him. Gia-fu has come up the stairs and is knocking on the door. He's come to tell Michael that a group of ladies awaits downstairs, a seemingly strongly Christian group.

Not knowing that Michael has taken peyote, Gia-fu has come in thinking Michael's taking a nap or just resting. He leans down to get close to Michael's ear, intent on delivering his message, and forcefully enunciates, "Michael! I have many heavy Christian ladies, led by Mrs. Lightfoot!"

Gia-fu's manner, his words, and the hilarity of the situation hit Michael like a sudden flash, a thunderbolt, and he starts to laugh. Gia-fu, looking at Michael but still unaware of the peyote, also starts to laugh. They laugh louder, the two fueling each other's glee. Gia-fu, always given to merriment and laughing, doubles over, guffawing convulsively. He finally staggers from the room, hearing Michael's hooting laughter behind him. Several minutes later, Michael looks out a window only to see Gia-fu down below, all by himself against a tree, awash in gales of laughter.

Michael's solo peyote trip lasts about six hours. Separately Dick and Michael's brother, Dennis, stop by to see how he's doing, but he's on to other visions now, the heavy Christian ladies and the associated mirth already in the past.[12]

But drugs are not the centerpiece here. Curiosity about them and their usefulness for gaining insight somewhat affects programming, with a few seminars on psychedelics included. Some participants use their own psychedelics in these sessions, though none are ever provided by the Institute. But more importantly for the program, the 1962–63 series offers more variety, a reflection of the interests of both participants and those in charge of programming. Seminars exploring Great Ideas such as those of Aurobindo, prayer and meditation retreats, and sessions incorporating music, art, and poetry expand the offerings. And it is in this program series that one can see the genesis of what will become the three major program strands: encounter, Gestalt therapy, and bodywork.

Gia-fu helps establish the bodywork strand through tai chi chu'an and shiatsu therapy. He teaches tai chi in the mornings, often on the deck of the swimming pool on a cliff overlooking the vast Pacific Ocean. A photograph captures a serene Gia-fu standing by the pool teaching tai chi to five students. The students are dressed in conventional clothes, some in tailored dresses with just-below-the-knee hemlines, others in slacks and sweaters. Gia-fu himself wears a dark cardigan over a white turtleneck and sports very short hair as he leads the students through the tai chi sequence. The photograph belies the perception that people wear only scant or unusual clothing here. Many seem to be very much in the mainstream, dressing pretty conventionally.

Gia-fu's tai chi classes are something new, and they are popular with participants. Anderson will later recount an anonymous comment about Gia-fu. "I remember…that there was either a guy there named Gia-fu who taught Tai Chi or a guy named Tai chi who taught Gia-fu."[13]

Gia-fu has refreshed and extended his childhood and later knowledge and skill in these traditional arts while at the Academy for Asian Studies, and he will study them further while in Japan in 1963 and '64. Ultimately, he will be greatly influenced by the program's other two strands: encounter, an outgrowth of management and group dynamics that comes to Esalen early in 1963, and Gestalt therapy, which arrives a little later in 1963. Both of these are anchored firmly in early twentieth-century Europe but were undeveloped there, possibly because of the war.[14] Gia-fu will come to believe that Westerners can most easily understand Taoism and Eastern thought through connections with psychotherapy. Gestalt, with its emphasis on being in the present and the mind-body as a complete whole, will become Gia-fu's preferred style of psychotherapy. He gets ample opportunity to understand and work with Gestalt at Esalen from the very beginning.

Wilson Van Dusen, chief clinical psychologist at Mendocino State Hospital, and Eugene Sagan, a psychologist in private practice and father of the future scientist Carl Sagan, lead the first Gestalt therapy seminar held at Big Sur Hot Springs. Both have direct experience with Fritz Perls who, with wife Laura Perls, is the founder of Gestalt therapy. Beginning the weekend workshop with a description of key principles of the approach, they explain that the German word *Gestalt* has no direct translation to a single English term, that *Gestalt* means a whole that is more than the sum of its parts. It involves being in the present, working in the here and now with a goal of integrating all aspects of the personality, including a heightened awareness of sensory experience. Body and mind affect each other. They are parts of the whole being—an idea that proves a veritable magnet for Gia-fu.

The work involves the therapist observing what a person is doing while she is doing it: how she acts, what words she uses, what mannerisms she displays. Guiding her attention to what she is doing, the therapist thereby directs her to the emotional reality of her life.

Given the program's experimental spirit and Gestalt's bias toward the experiential rather than the theoretical, Van Dusen and Sagan propose to demonstrate. They ask for volunteers. Quiet descends on the group. Patiently, the seminar leaders wait. Finally, a hand goes up and the volunteer, the first patient, steps forward. It is Gia-fu. Gestalt therapy arrives at Big Sur and unretractably in the life of Gia-fu Feng.

Gia-fu finds Gestalt therapy's attraction multidimensional. First, much in the style of the late 1950s and now in the 1960s, it challenges the status quo—it challenges existing and often unexamined ways of thinking. Second, focusing on the here and now, the present, one can burrow ever deeper into one's own awareness. And third, by promoting awareness of self, it helps one recognize choices that bring freedom, that allow a person to be a responsible participant in his own life. More than three decades later in *Completing the Circle: Taking Gestalt to Asia,* writer Paula Bottome will describe the life one can achieve through Gestalt therapy: "Lived in this way, life takes on a clarity and intensity that enhance experience and satisfy our deepest longings for integrity, meaning, and authenticity."[15] Gia-fu's search for self-awareness, for developing his own potential, has uncovered a powerful catalyst in helping him understand more fully who he is and how he will direct his life. The method's impact on Gia-fu's thinking will be matched by the impact of its cofounder, Fritz Perls, whom he will meet within the year.

In the interim, friends Mertis Shekeloff and her husband, Brian, who works for the university museum in Berkeley, decide to go to Japan after a lawsuit settlement from an accident in which Brian was injured. Gia-fu, who has lived with them at various times, says, "Okay. I'll come, too."

Mertis is delighted that she'll have another adult to help her with lively, active Peter, their young son. So in October 1963, Mertis, Brian, Peter, and Gia-fu travel by steamer to Japan. Another steamer trip for Gia-fu, but in yet another set of circumstances. This time he travels not to seek a university degree or to be free of Japanese occupation but, ironically, to visit the country itself and gain education that comes of world travel. This trip's purpose lies in integrating and expanding his experiences of Big Sur Hot Springs. And it's his first trip out of the country as a U.S. citizen.

These few months become another shadowy period in Gia-fu's life. Even Mertis knows little of his activity on this trip when he isn't with them. What is known from stamps on his passports, his friends' memories, and what he will later write about, provides some clues. He'll note, ever so briefly, that while in Japan, he studies shiatsu with Mani-koshi, an expert in this Japanese form of physiotherapy that originated in China more than two thousand years ago. Sadly, he travels very near China and his family but he cannot see them. His U.S. passport clearly states:

> This passport is not valid for travel to or in communist controlled portions of China, Korea, Viet-Nam, or to or in Albania [and] Cuba. A person who travels to or in the listed countries or areas may be liable for prosecution under Section 1185, Title 8, US Code.

While the U.S. restricts his travel, so do the continuing difficult circumstances in China. Still recovering from the Great Leap Forward, which broke the spirit and ended the lives of millions of Chinese, China struggles to feed its people as it increasingly holds itself apart from the rest of the world. And despite Mao's not being the official head of state, he still wields incredible power as Communist Party chairman. The September 13, 1963, issue of *Time* magazine, featuring China on its cover, reports in its feature article that:

> ... Mao finds little sympathy anywhere in the world today... In fact, he has plunged China into an isolation so complete that he can count as certain allies only tiny North Korea in Asia and even tinier Albania in Europe.[16]

This view of China is promoted especially strongly by conservatives such as Henry Luce, owner of *Time*. But in the eyes of other individuals and groups, the Committee of Concerned Asian Scholars, for one, China's responses to others are exacerbated in part by U.S. policies and positions.[17] A prominent example is the policy of containment, prompted by the U.S.'s great fear that Communism would be spread beyond China when in fact there was never an attempt to do so. Nonetheless, the U.S. plays a role in helping to isolate China from the rest of the world.

Gia-fu can't feel very good about the overall situation, but he says little about it. However, he's upset that while he's in Japan, people think he's Japanese and speak to him in their language, expecting him to respond. He doesn't know Japanese, so when he doesn't respond—can't respond—he receives cool treatment.

The travelers stay for a short while with Joanne Kyger and Gary Snyder, who have been in Kyoto for a while studying Zen Buddhism. The Shekeloffs get their own place, and Gia-fu stays with them before he sets out on travels of his own. Mertis and Brian teach English and have a beautiful house and an exceedingly nice life. Brian collects for the university museum, and Gia-fu, while there and not studying shiatsu, sometimes accompanies him.

On a visit one day, Joanne shows them some woven mats she's just bought. Curious, Mertis asks how much Joanne paid for them. Joanne tells her, and Mertis's reaction comes quickly, "That's way too much!"

A sinking feeling hits Joanne as she thinks she's been too extravagant. Gia-fu, examining the mats closely, chimes in, saying, "No, no. Look! This is a very special plant fiber, and see, they are woven very finely."

Joanne feels redeemed by Gia-fu's observations, his attention to the mats and to her. She will continue to appreciate his comment and the person she knew forty years later, when she will still be using those mats.[18]

Gia-fu travels out of Japan, visiting Hong Kong, Macao, and Taipei from late December 1963, returning to Japan on February 25, 1964. While in Hong Kong he visits his sister Wan-tsi, or Ellen, the Western name she has taken. Other than Chao-hua, Ellen is the only family member he has seen since he left China in 1947. Soon after he returns to the U.S., he will see Eldest Sister Mei-chi, who, having been widowed, will move to the U.S. with her little boy, Peter.

Gia-fu returns from Japan in June 1964. Fritz Perls arrives at Big Sur Hot Springs, now called Esalen, shortly after. Perls's influence on Esalen will be deep and wide, and on Gia-fu, profound indeed.

Some background on Perls, how he came to be in the U.S. and developed the ideas that so capture Gia-fu, helps explain Gia-fu's interest in him as a person and the ideas he promotes. That he was also from a country to which he could not return for many years gives Gia-fu another reason for interest and empathy. Born to a Berlin wine merchant and his wife in 1893, Perls came of age in an anti-Semitic Germany, a situation he deeply resented. He attended medical school, interrupting his education for World War I military service, during which he was wounded. He completed his medical degree in 1921, after which he set up practice as a neuropsychiatrist.

When Perls moved from Berlin to Frankfurt in 1926, he met Lore Posner, a psychology student. The two later married. They fled Nazi Germany in 1933 with their two-year-old daughter, staying in Amsterdam for a very difficult time, until Fritz secured an analyst's position in South Africa, where they stayed for twelve years. During this time they had a son and Fritz founded the South African Institute for Psychoanalysis, published his first book, *Ego, Hunger and Aggression*, and for four years served as a psychiatrist with the South African army.

In 1946, one year before Gia-fu came to the U.S., Fritz moved there via Canada. He first settled in New Haven but was encouraged by Erich Fromm to move to New York. In 1950, he published *Gestalt Therapy*, a book that in time would become exceedingly popular. Fritz never gave Lore, or Laura as she called herself after coming to the U.S., the credit due her for her role in contributing to and helping develop the ideas in the book, or in the Gestalt therapy movement itself. Laura would continue working with the ideas, but Fritz would never acknowledge her work.

Eventually, Fritz left New York and his family and moved to Florida, then to the West Coast. In 1964 he arrives at Esalen, an increasingly popular figure, considered by many to be the father of Gestalt therapy.

Perls's complex and exceptionally strong personality can dominate most situations. He's a man of contradictions, on the one hand not caring what people think and often behaving outrageously, violating rules, insulting others. But on the other hand he seeks approval, wanting love and attention. His enormously popular poem (often seen without the last line) will later in the 1960s express the "do-your-own-thing" attitude so popular at the time and contribute to his becoming a pop hero. The poem reflects his worldview in all its existential bleakness:

> I do my thing, and you do your thing.
> I am not in this world to live up to your expectations
> And you are not in this world to live up to mine.
> You are you and I am I,
> And if by chance we find each other, it's beautiful
> If not, it can't be helped.

Doing his thing, Perls is known for his fights and conflicts with others. As Jack Gaines would write in his biography some fifteen years later, citing a friend of Perls, "Fritz loved some types—open bastard-bitch—open defenses, that type. He didn't like anyone who would placate him or be too good to him or used good-girl or good-boy defenses—that drove him up the wall."[19]

Despite the influence they ultimately have on each other—with Fritz's influence on Gia-fu most profound—it seems that Gia-fu and Fritz don't often "find each other," for conflicts frequently arise between them. Michael Murphy observes their arguments and will reflect thirty-five years later about "an antipathy between them. Of course, there was a lot of antipathy between Fritz and a lot of people," but he doesn't know exactly what it is between Fritz and Gia-fu.[20] Difficult as it is to imagine anyone not liking the good-natured Gia-fu, Perls does seem to have it in for him. Some hypothesize it's Perls's distrust of anything hinting at mysticism, which he must somehow associate with Gia-fu. On Gia-fu's part, some speculate that some of the friction could stem from Perls's domineering manner and Gia-fu's reaction to an overbearing patriarchal figure. Shades of his father.

But whereas Perls is often viewed as being rude and impatient, Gia-fu is seen as lighthearted, sometimes unpredictable although not destructive in any way. Michael thinks him a very sweet-tempered, well-bred man. He figures Gia-fu's unpredictability may come from the spirit, the spontaneity of the times, and from having been at the East-West House with the Beats. But really, Gia-fu has always had the actor, the ham, in him; it just hasn't always had the opportunity to come out. Occasionally in the dining room, when Fritz is sitting near, Gia-fu takes center stage, and declaims in a loud voice some great truth from the *Tao Te Ching* or other classic. In a commanding voice, he pronounces wisdom or insights, such as, "What others teach, I also teach; that is: 'A violent man will die a violent death!' This will be the essence of my teaching." Or perhaps, "The sage stays behind, thus he is ahead. He is detached, thus at one with all."[21]

His pronouncements come as the truth, but because they come from left field, out of the blue, everyone understands that he is mocking—mocking self, mocking philosophy, mocking everything, as a kind of court jester causing people to step back and be less serious, even about things that are important.

The antagonism between Perls and Gia-fu isn't evident at first, although Perls's temper is, and he shows it not long after Gia-fu returns from Japan. Perls comes to the front desk where Gia-fu is on duty. He complains loudly that his workshops haven't filled. He says this is probably because the publicity was inadequate. Swearing and ranting, Perls asserts that his workshops always fill, so someone obviously screwed up—possibly implying it's Gia-fu. Gia-fu quietly lets him rave for half an hour but nothing changes. Some of the workshops have to be canceled anyway.

Gia-fu learns from Fritz himself that he's had some interest in Oriental religion, and that he went to a Zen monastery in Japan back in the early 1960s. He's also interested in getting some bodywork for his breathing, with which, along with other health conditions, he's having problems. One day he stops in at one of Gia-fu's workshops and corners him. "What do you know?" he asks. Without waiting for a response he says, "Try it on me."

Gia-fu feels he isn't very far into bodywork for Perls's type of breathing problems, which are related to a weak heart, but he gives him shiatsu treatments. Perls is very prompt for five sessions in a row. Then someone in the office makes a mistake and charges Perls fifty dollars for Gia-fu's bodywork. Custom dictates that because Gia-fu attends his workshops, he should have the work free. But the mistake causes Perls, to whom money is a big issue, to be furious at Gia-fu. Eventually Perls advises people not to go to Gia-fu. Then when Ida Rolf, another kind of body-work practitioner, arrives at Esalen, he tells people to go to Ida Rolf and "forget this Chinaman."

Fifteen years later, Perls's biographer, Jack Gaines, will observe that some saw Gia-fu as "both an admirer and rival of Fritz Perls." The antagonism may be interpreted as rivalry, or perhaps Perls really considers Gia-fu a competitor. For Gia-fu's part, he has reached a point in his own development at which he will not back down, in no small part because of his work with Gestalt. And his admiration of Perls is clear in his later reflections:

> I don't feel bitter. I took him as he was because I understood his background so well. His parents and brothers were all burned to death [in the Holocaust] and he was still able to come out of it. I'm a member of a minority myself, so I can understand. I think he had guts and he was honest; that besides, because he forced the group not to come to me, and sort of kicked me out, I moved out and got my own center in Los Gatos Hills. So he actually helped me to have my own trip.

Fritz Perls and Gestalt therapy provide a key to the question Ananda Claude Dalenberg will pose in the Cornell Hotel interview some thirty years later. What changed Gia-fu from the quiet, Quaker-like person he was to the outspoken teacher he became? What happened at Esalen? Those near Gia-fu later in his life will observe that he seems sometimes to embody Perls's confrontive, combative approach, but unlike Perls, Gia-fu also reveals his tenderness, his compassion.

And Gia-fu doesn't miss the similarity between Perls's ideal and Zen Buddhism. He considers this another example of how Eastern religions have crept into the West through the back door of psychotherapy. Later he will recall that in 1965, before each session, Perls would say, "What I'm going to do here is to assist you to have a sudden awakening." A sudden awakening, satori, lies at the heart of Zen Buddhism. But although Gia-fu could see similarities, Perls thought his approach differed from the meditative Zen. Perls saw that as another "trip" and pushed his students and patients to work, to "get off your fanny." More contradictions.

After Perls's death in 1970, Gia-fu will acknowledge their strange, contradictory relationship, their unlikely bond, admitting that he misses Fritz. And besides missing Fritz, Gia-fu will think that at Esalen in the late 1970s, people don't do the hard work that Perls required. He will think they are just "groovy tripping," not critiquing, not pushing each other.

Despite all the contrariness, Gia-fu will understand Fritz's gift, his way of working with people. "[Fritz] contributed to me. He was a true revolutionary. Nobody can imitate his way of digging into people. And I have seen maybe one hundred Gestalt therapists after him, and nobody is like him."[22]

And by now, in 1966, no one is like Perls in helping Gia-fu move to the next phase of his life. Perls's continued animosity toward him makes it difficult for Gia-fu to remain at Esalen. Paradoxically, this hostility, this antagonism, only serves, as Gia-fu himself will say, to help him take the next step, to begin to actualize his own dream—a dream that has slowly taken shape over the past decade at Big Sur and in San Francisco, and perhaps from a seed planted at Pendle Hill. The dream brings religion and psychotherapy together. In Gia-fu's mind religion is to be seen not as myth, superstition, and worship, but as something that takes life and death seriously. This sense of religion focuses on the here and now, where one's behavior reflects what one really feels in an integration of mind, body, and spirit.

He began a key chapter of his life with Dick and Michael's vision and their dream. Now he has his own dream in which he establishes a community, living close to nature in a community of individuals desiring to get closer to their inner nature and to live together differently. His vision is of a Taoist utopia, ultimately a hundred-family village in the mountains. Inspired and fortified by all he has seen, learned, and done at Esalen, Gia-fu leaves this place of possibility and moves on to manifest the possibilities of his own dream, drawing on that unfathomable source of ten thousand things.

Gia-fu's mother, Wei Han-chuen,
circa 1933. Courtesy Sue Bailey

Gia-fu's father, Feng Chong-ching,
circa 1933. Courtesy Sue Bailey

Gia-fu's father, Feng Chong-ching,
Shanghai, circa 1930.
Courtesy Dexter Woo

Gia-fu, circa 1924.
Courtesy Sue Bailey

*Gia-fu Feng,
Philadelphia, 1949.
Courtesy Dexter Woo*

*Gia-fu Feng and Mertis Shekeloff, East-West House,
San Francisco, 1958. Courtesy Mertis Shekeloff*

*At the Skekeloff wedding, from left, unnamed priest, Gia-fu Feng,
Brian and Mertis Shekeloff, Gladys Southall—Mertis's mother,
and Raylene Albert at the Zen Temple, San Francisco, 1959.
Courtesy Mertis Shekeloff*

*Party after the Shekeloff
wedding at the East-West
House. Back row: Jay
Blaise, Raylene Albert,
Mertis and Brian Shekeloff;
middle row center: Lew
Welch; front row center:
Gia-fu Feng; right: Joanne
Kyger, 1959. Courtesy
Mertis Shekeloff*

Gia-fu, circa 1962.
Courtesy Sue Bailey

Gia-fu teaching tai chi
on the swimming pool
deck at Esalen, Big Sur,
California, May 1965.
Courtesy Sue Bailey

*Gia-fu in his
infamous bathrobe,
Los Gatos, 1971.
Photograph by
Jane English*

*Gia-fu and Jane English, wedding in Yosemite, 1971.
Courtesy Jane English*

*Gia-fu's nephew Dexter Woo,
Gia-fu and Jane, San Francisco, 1970.
Courtesy Dexter Woo*

*Gia-fu on Chocorua Lake, New Hampshire, 1973.
Photograph by Jane English*

Gia-fu playing the er-hu, Esalen, circa 1973.
Photograph by Jane English

Gia-fu, center, with niece Feng Yun ke, left, China, 1975.
Courtesy Sue Bailey

Calligraphy at tai chi camps in Europe, circa 1978.
Courtesy Jane English

Gia-fu with Richard Hoffman, Manitou Springs Stillpoint, circa 1977. Courtesy Richard Hoffman

Tai chi camps in Europe, circa 1980. Courtesy Jane English

Tai Chi camp poster, 1982. Courtesy Carmen Baehr

Sue Bailey and Gia-fu, Wetmore Stillpoint, circa 1983.
Courtesy Richard Hoffman

Tai chi in Australia, circa 1983. From the author's collection

Carmen Baehr and Gia-fu, Wetmore Stillpoint, 1984.
Courtesy Richard Hoffman

Gia-fu's hermitage at Wetmore Stillpoint. From the author's collection

Margaret Susan Wilson, Wetmore Stillpoint, 1990.
From the author's collection

Gia-fu's father, Feng Chong-ching, in later years, undated. Courtesy Dexter Woo

Shi Tao, Ken Cohen and Shi Jing (Alan Redman), Colorado, 2001. Courtesy Ken Cohen

Gia-fu on beach, Maine, circa 1971. Photograph by Jane English

CHAPTER NINE

THE SETTLED HEART

If the sage would guide the people, he must serve with humility.
If he would lead them, he must follow behind.

—from Chapter 66, *Tao Te Ching*

The year is 1966, and high in the hills above Los Gatos, California, Gia-fu finds the place. Here his dream can unfold; here he can start his own community.

Stillpoint. This is the name he chooses. The point in meditation between the in-breath and the out-breath; the point that is still—and empty. It's also an old Chinese expression, translated in English as "settled heart." "We may wander, but we take our settled heart with us." [1] Gia-fu has wandered, and his heart has now become settled enough to find and name this place. And those who live in this community will be called Stillpointers. Even after they leave they will still be referred to in this way.

In one form or another Stillpoint will be part of Gia-fu's life for almost two decades, in California, briefly in Vermont, and then Colorado, until the very end. Now, his first Stillpoint, which he calls Stillpoint Foundation, becomes a reality on this leased mountain property at 20300 Bear Creek Road. Steep terrain, close enough to the ocean to be engulfed in the morning fog, several buildings for group meetings, meditation, cooking, sleeping, a sauna, hot tub, and lots of trees. A beautiful place, and its beauty will work on those who live here.

Gia-fu wants to put to use what the ancient Taoists learned: that healthy human life flourishes in nature, in simplicity, therein letting one's own true nature come forth. [2] For many, this reflects the idyllic; for some, it's a way to help heal their deepest wounds. Taoists understand that no successful approach to life can go against nature, and therefore a central Taoist premise is that of *wu wei*, meaning no action contrary to nature, or authentic action. Sometimes interpreted as simply "nonaction," it gets misunderstood as not doing anything, or even worse, as the simplistic "go with the flow" idea so popular these days.

The importance of nature to Gia-fu can't be summed up in that Western notion of pantheism—*pan* meaning "all," and *theism* meaning "god," so that God and the universe are the same—for pantheism names God, which Taoists do not. Nor does pantheism take into account the Taoist view of emptiness, the lack of preconceptions about emptiness, and the usefulness of it. [3] Six years later, in their translation of the *Tao Te Ching*, Gia-fu and Jane English will provide this insight about emptiness:

Shape clay into a vessel;
It is the space within that makes it useful.[4]

There's another dimension to this way of life, this utopia, for as a Taoist, Gia-fu knows that utopia comes from understanding the balance of yin *and* yang. This balance is difficult for Westerners to grasp, given the tendency to makes things conceptual, dualistic, one or the other. Gia-fu knows that whatever it is, it's not just a *this*-or-*that* dichotomy; it is, in fact, *both*. Good and evil, positive and negative, masculine and feminine—all have some aspect of the other in them. Can't have one without the other. That's why in the round black-and-white tai chi symbol, sometimes called the yin and yang symbol, each contains a circle of the other's color. Each is part of the whole, and the other part is reflected within it.

Nature reflects yin and yang, if we only look at the whole of it. Beautiful wildflowers, rain, grasses, trees, ducks, deer, lightning storms, fire, thunder, earthquakes, lions feasting on gazelles, wolves eating lambs. It's not a simple matter of good and bad; it's a simple and not-so-simple matter of nature. Nature just is, and when we think of it only in terms of our reactions to it, our descriptions of beauty, terror, and all, we're forgetting that those are only our reactions and not the whole of nature.

People have forever sought utopia and so now does Gia-fu. But Taoists understand utopia can't be found in the external world; it must come from within, from calmness of mind, an internal attitude. Gia-fu firmly believes this state can be cultivated through meditation, walking and, of course, being in nature. And for health and vitality, tai chi and massage play a vital role, as does a healthful diet. As a community there must be a means for deciding how best to proceed as a group, for working out differences and truly being honest with oneself and each other. Daily group meetings, daily Gestalt sessions work best here.

Committed to these ideas of living communally, simply, honestly in nature, Gia-fu invites others to join him. People are drawn to him and Stillpoint for various reasons; some because they know Gia-fu from Esalen and resonate to who he is and what he's trying to do; some primarily to learn tai chi; others hear about him and come to check out the situation. Some come for short periods, others stay on.

Even with his own community now started, during the first few years Gia-fu continues teaching tai chi at Esalen. He travels the two-hundred-mile round trip on the narrow, winding, spectacular coastal route from Los Gatos to Esalen once a week. The classes tend to stay at an introductory level because new Esalen guests attend each time. But then a young couple comes along. Anne and John Heider are participants in Esalen's nine-month program for encounter group training led by Will Schutz and Ed Maupin, and Anne will soon become a continuing student of Gia-fu's. Regarding their encounter group training, the leaders' expertise clearly match Anne and John's interests: Schutz in groups and training new group leaders; Maupin more in meditation and Eastern philosophy. The combination also mirrors Gia-fu's interests and experience, but at this point he's not involved in the leader training, only the tai chi classes.

Anne has not done tai chi before and she loves it. She and another student, Jill, show up every week for class ready to learn more. Gia-fu sees this thread of continuity as an opportunity to move the two beyond the introductory to increasingly more complex and difficult movements. He teaches on the deck by the swimming pool, where he usually holds his classes, sometimes in sunshine and sometimes in the wind and billowing fog—and always with the sound of waves crashing below, filling their ears as they move slowly, deliberately through the tai chi forms.

To Anne, Gia-fu appears short and skinny, with a ragged mustache—and a most engaging presence. Striding around, everything he does, he does wholeheartedly, whether it's tai chi or walking meditation—walking, walking, walking, right there on the deck. To her, he's a "benign rascal, a little bit of the Robin Hood…kind and generous with people he respects," and definitely not with those he doesn't.

In tai chi, when an older person does the form, the younger person copies it. Gia-fu leads his classes this way, sometimes stopping to show how to do something in detail. He asks a student to stand on one foot for an extended period. Watching, he comments, "Do not wobble." Then, seeing the student wobble and try not to, he shouts, "If wobble, wobble!"[5] His message to be wholehearted about whatever you do comes through loudly and clearly.

Later, when Anne studies with a traditional tai chi master, a Mr. Wu, she'll realize just how nontraditional Gia-fu's approach was. She will recall, "Gia-fu had been playing [the tai chi master] role in a very Puckish, buccaneer manner...very entrepreneurial. There was a big contrast between the way Gia-fu and Mr. Wu taught tai chi. I never would have found out that he was an 'instant master' had I not studied with Mr. Wu." Even so, given his ability to help Westerners understand this ancient Chinese art and tailor the forms toward that end, Anne will feel Gia-fu had the knowledge and background to offer something important, recognizing that he must have had traditional training at some point.

Gia-fu seems especially confident in Anne's interest and progress, a confidence revealed one week when a severe rainstorm prevents his travel to Esalen and he asks Anne to lead the class. This she does, and she does it well. When he decides to create an illustrated book on tai chi and the *I Ching*, he invites Anne to be the model.

The inspiration to create the book comes from publications on a wide variety of topics related to the pioneering human potential work at Esalen. One of these publications is Bernard (Bernie) Gunther's book on massage, and it sells very well, a fact not lost on Gia-fu. And after translating so many works, he'd like to produce books of his own.

Through his web of relationships at Esalen, Gia-fu joins with Jerome Kirk, professor at the University of California at Irvine's Program in Language and Development. Since tai chi consists of a long series of movements, Gia-fu wants to have photographs illustrating the movements from beginning to end. Gia-fu and Jerome ask West Coast photographer Hugh Wilkerson to join in the project, and the three develop a plan for the book.

Anne does say yes to Gia-fu's invitation to model the movements, but she has a stipulation. She candidly tells him, "I want to be paid up front." Although he huffs and puffs about it, he finally agrees to do so.

The shooting begins. Hugh chooses locations in the Big Sur countryside, and the three of them troop to the designated spot for each session. Sometimes they're on the beach, waves crashing in the background, sometimes by a stream or on a hillside—always a natural, beautiful setting. Varying from the traditional tai chi dress of black cotton jacket and blue cotton pants, Anne wears a green tunic Hugh's wife has made, some-times with tights, other times not. In some shots her loose long hair flows down her back; in others it hangs in a single long braid over her right shoulder, or is caught up in a simple band at the nape of her neck. And with Anne still a relative newcomer to tai chi, Gia-fu teaches her some of the moves on the spot.

Anne's slender figure, long dark hair, and look of complete absorp-tion in the tai chi movements, from Opening Position Hands, through Wild Horse Ruffling Mane, Right Frog Kick, and all the way to Closing Position, make her an apt model for the project. Gia-fu wants Anne's pic-ture on the front and consistent with the illustrations inside. But later when the cover photo is to be shot, Anne is several months pregnant. They decide the photo should reveal her head, outstretched arms, and upper body only, and that is what appears on the cover.[6]

The book includes both tai chi instructions and a translation of the ancient *I Ching, the Book of Changes*. Gia-fu, in his wholeheartedness, lightheartedness, and sense of experimentation, translates the *I Ching* in the popular vernacular of the day. So, contrasting Gia-fu's approach to another, classic translation, the 1899 Christian missionary James Legge version, which reads:

> *Khien* indicates progress and success. The superior man,
> (being humble as it implies), will have a (good) issue
> (to his undertakings).

This first translation of Gia-fu's says:

> Humility is groovy.
> The Superior Man sees things through to completion.[7]

And so, Gia-fu now sees his first book completed. Groovy.

Also seeing things through to completion, Anne and John study and lead groups themselves at Esalen until 1971, and Esalen's influences, including Will Schutz and Gia-fu, will be with them long after that. Together they start the Human Potential School of Mendocino, where Jane English, a former fellow Girl Scout and private school student with Anne, is involved. Anne and John later divorce, going their separate ways.

John, a clinical psychologist, will teach at the Menninger Foundation School of Psychiatry and will serve as a staff psychologist at the Veterans Administration hospital in Topeka, Kansas. In 1985, he will publish *The Tao of Leadership*, an adaptation of the *Tao Te Ching* that will draw upon Gia-fu and Jane English's 1972 translation, among others.

Anne's path will lead her to Stanford to earn a doctorate and to study with traditional tai chi master Mr. Wu in Palo Alto. A professor of choral music, she will become director of choral activities at Chicago's Roosevelt University and, as a conductor and teacher of conducting, she will notice herself using tai chi. More than three decades later she will observe:

> A conductor has to move slowly, but with energy, using graceful, rounded movements. One does different things simultaneously with the two hands, and all of this is found in tai chi. Those early tai chi lessons from Gia-fu definitely make me a more nuanced conductor, and that has to be a connection to my professional success.[8]

Gia-fu influences and inspires others just as others affect his life. Through Esalen's network of relationships and connections, through Stillpoint, and his work in Gestalt and tai chi, people come to know about him. Lloyd Alexander is one of these. Some time in the late 1960s, Lloyd reads in a Gestalt publication a commentary by Gia-fu, which he finds intriguing in its unique perspective, but which he also questions. He sends a note to Gia-fu along with a catalog of his Syria, Virginia, Gestalt center. Soon Lloyd receives Gia-fu's response: "Well, maybe you have something there. But, this kind of philosophy we can't discuss in letters. Please come out here. We have a place for you. Let me know when you can get here."[9]

Several months later, on a trip to California, Lloyd arranges to go to Stillpoint and the two finally meet face to face. Lloyd sees a slender man—not as small as he will seem a decade or so later—with longish hair and sporting "a very suitable beard for a Taoist sage." Gia-fu, dressed in loose-hanging clothes—a light-colored cotton jacket and drawstring pants—studies the also slender Lloyd, who is maybe seven or eight inches taller than he. Lloyd's long, graying hair is pulled back in a ponytail, his beard falls to belly-button level, and he wears the ubiquitous Birkenstocks of the day with his bright blue jumpsuit. The jumpsuit, Fritz Perls's signature outfit, reminds Gia-fu of his two-in-one nemesis and mentor.

It's a beautiful, warm day, and the two stand outside the main house, surrounded by tall oak trees, exchanging initial greetings. They talk for a few minutes before Gia-fu, in his loud voice, insists, "You must stay for at least a week or two. We have much to discuss!" Lloyd does stay and thus begins an enduring friendship, one which will later lead the two to take a vow of brotherhood, another way in which Gia-fu re-creates family for himself. Now they enjoy their time together, sitting on the deck of the house, looking out over the valley below and the forested hills beyond, leisurely sharing insights about their mutual interests and learning about each other. Beyond their current interests, they're surprised to learn they both attended the Wharton School and both had earlier careers in banking. They had some of the same professors there, Dr. Whittlesey, for one; even more compelling to them is the fact that they'd both spent time at Pendle Hill.

The next morning Lloyd joins the predawn meditation, part of the Stillpoint routine. The meditation room is all glass, and through it Lloyd sees the fog pressing in, obscuring the already dim view of valley and hills. It's around four a.m., an hour Lloyd thinks ungodly. The burning incense produces a raw, acrid smell, unlike some of the more refined incense he's encountered. The meditation itself seems chaotic with the fifteen or so Stillpointers, dressed in loose, comfortable clothing, sitting on the floor on cushions around the large room, doing whatever kind of meditation they want and making whatever sound they want to make. Some do zazen—Zen whole-hearted sitting; some follow a simple mindfulness breathing meditation; some chant. Every now and then the group coalesces in their various sounds, producing something harmonious, something that seems to vibrate. That it's a chaotic meditation will later cause Lloyd to think that guru Rajneesh, because of the similarities in approach, takes his meditation from Gia-fu. For this moment, sitting until five thirty or so, these meditators see the sky gradually lighten, then the sun rise over the mountain, dissipating the fog. It's an unbelievably beautiful sight, one that Lloyd likens to the opening scene of the movie

2001: A Space Odyssey—primal earth, unspoiled, ancient, magnificent. And it's like this every unspeakably beautiful morning.

Lloyd also detects a Quaker influence in the morning sessions, nothing expressly labeled such, but if one has experienced this, which he has, it's evident in all that's going on. There is about it a kind of quiet, waiting-for-the-spirit-to-appear ambience.

A group meeting follows meditation, some of which concerns logistics for the day, but mostly it is devoted to group dynamics and issues within the group. Fritz Perls's influence can be felt here, as well as Esalen-like encounter group techniques. Group participation and continual feedback, Gia-fu believes, will increase the group's ability to analyze and interpret their behavior and their problems. And using the Gestalt technique of the "hot seat," in which all the attention focuses on one person, promotes his or her awareness of self in the moment. At some point, and more than once, everyone gets to experience the hot seat. If anyone has a problem or concern, this is where it comes out—directly, face-to-face, and, most often, emotionally.

Gia-fu leads these meetings, sometimes asking if anyone has an issue to bring up, sometimes just telling people what they are like, what their hang-ups are. His voice often hoarse, intense, he sets the stage for others to do the same. He makes sure everything gets put on the table and that whatever comes up gets resolved. Still somewhat fresh from Esalen, Gia-fu capitalizes on the intensity of this approach, which seems to match his own inner intensity. Although it will always remain a part of how he works with groups, the encounter group approach will soften in the years to come.[10]

After the meeting, people have the day to soak in the hot tub, take hikes, talk with each other. Gia-fu encourages people to walk, walking himself every day, usually ten miles or more. The group comes together for dinner, and everyone takes turns preparing the meal, this part not unlike the East-West House arrangement.

And what about women in Gia-fu's life? Certainly, he's always expressed a natural, healthy interest. In Shanghai, young women numbered among his friends, some perhaps more than friends, especially during his highly social times—university life and his return from Kunming. And while in Kunming, there was Miss Pao, for whom he had strong feelings, unrequited though they were. While at the Wharton School, he enjoyed dancing and, though specific details are sketchy at best, probably other social occasions there and in New York. In San Francisco and Esalen he certainly had women friends. But so far, no evidence has come to light of anything more or stronger.

I know of no relationship Gia-fu forms until he has his own home, a home for his heart as well as his physical being, in his own community, his Stillpoint. But here he does enter into public, important relationships. He envisions a community of families. Perhaps he reasons that if there are to be families, if he is to be the community's spiritual father-head, then he should have a partner, a mate. Perhaps he also thinks the East-meeting-West theme should be reflected in that partnership, though it's also quite possible that Western women are the only ones he meets in his particular circumstances. Whatever the reasons, over the next two decades, Gia-fu will be involved with a series of women, and Paula Jackson, a young woman who was at Esalen and now lives at Stillpoint, is the first.

As other aspects of Gia-fu's life remain vague or shadowy, so does his relationship with Paula. I was already well into my research when I came across their wedding announcement in one of the many boxes stuffed away in the corners of the Wetmore barn. Until then I knew nothing of this young woman's existence. The announcement, a three-and-a-half-by-six-inch folded piece of paper, features a sepia-tone photograph of Gia-fu and Paula on the front. Gia-fu is looking at her while his right hand is reaching behind and around her head, pulling back her medium-length, dark hair. She faces him, but her eyes are cast downward. Her left arm encircles Gia-fu's waist and he has placed his left hand over her left hand at his side. She wears a simple sundress; he nattily wears a loose white turtleneck sweater, sleeves pushed up to his elbow. Judging from the photo, they are about the same height, both slender, if not thin, both healthy and fit. The bride is twenty-six years old; the groom, forty-nine. He exudes an air of satisfaction, perhaps affection, a slight contrast to her indeterminate look.

Inside, the announcement reads:

On August 24, 1968
Paula Jackson &
Gia-fu Feng
were married at
Stillpoint Foundation
20300 Bear Creek Road
Los Gatos, California 95030
Te. (408) 354-6739
Reception continuously
at your convenience

The marriage, not a formal one in terms of license and registering—
and California isn't a common-law state—lasts only a few months. Just
as there's no evidence of the marriage having been legally recorded, so is
there no evidence of its termination. And there's no information about
what transpired during those "married" months.

And then, two years later, there is Jane. Jane English has just completed
her PhD in physics at the University of Wisconsin. Now she has a one-
year postdoctoral appointment, which has taken her to the University of
California at Berkeley to work on a collaborative physics project. She's
at the renowned Lawrence Laboratory's particle accelerator as part of a
collaborative project among UC Berkeley, the University of Hawaii, and
the University of Wisconsin.

Jane, now age twenty-eight in 1970, lives with other graduate students
but stays on longer than the rest, moving in with another young woman
by the name of Katie Marks. Katie invites her to Stillpoint, describing it
as "a meditation place in Los Gatos." She doesn't say much about Gia-fu.
Attracted by the idea of a sauna and the opportunity to escape the city,
Jane decides to go, and it becomes a decision that will affect her life
enormously.

Here in the Los Gatos hills, Jane discovers a different and very unin-
hibited lifestyle, which she takes in stride despite her strict New England
upbringing. She and Katie drive to Stillpoint's entrance, turning off Bear
Creek Road and through the Chinese-style red gate, and driving up to

the unpaved parking lot. As they walk from the parking area down to the low, woodsy-looking two-story house, her photographer's eye takes in the huge California live oaks, the madrone trees, and the poison oak, as well as the spectacular panorama of the hills and valley. They near the house, observing people lounging around on the deck in various states of dress, or undress. Some have been taking advantage of the hot tub, some the sauna, both of which are right off the deck, and they are now enjoying the late afternoon sunshine.

Availing themselves of the hot tub, Jane and Katie join in the easy camaraderie and peacefulness in the final rays of an ending day. As a few Stillpointers prepare dinner, Jane notes their ability to work unharmed, sans clothing, around the hot stove. She worries a little that one of them might get burned, but they skillfully avoid any such calamity. Standing near the stove, appreciating its warmth, Jane is a little surprised when Gia-fu comes up behind her and strikes up a conversation.

They talk for a bit, Jane thinking Gia-fu quite worldly with his ability to discuss a wide range of subjects—physics, photography, literature, and current events. She also thinks he emanates an "ancient-guru quality." There's a quietness to him, depth, and a sense of vitality and humor. Their conversation flows easily, as does conversation with others here. Jane enjoys this visit, the people, the place, causing her to return occasionally on weekends while she continues her work in the Berkeley lab.

One morning as she's finishing a midnight to eight a.m. shift at the particle accelerator, a colleague tells her she has a phone call. It's Rutgers University offering her another postdoctoral position. Standing at the outdoor phone booth, basking in the soft morning sunlight and looking out across the bay to the Golden Gate Bridge reflecting the sun's rays, she responds viscerally to the thought of leaving this warmth for cold, gray New Jersey. She declines the offer. But the phone call provokes her to think about what she really wants to do and what she really cares about. Although she's never had formal training in it, she realizes her love of photography rivals her interest in physics, and she knows she's taken some pretty good photographs. It does, after all, run in the family. Her grandfather, Walter H. James, was a very accomplished nature photographer. After considering the options and coming to terms with what she really holds dear, she decides to turn more to photography and try making a living at it.

Jane returns to Wisconsin to clear out her belongings from the house she's been sharing with her physicist boyfriend and assesses her financial situation. She knows she must be frugal with the nest egg she's saved from pay increases accompanying her upward movement from teaching assistant to research assistant to research associate. With the opportunity to stay at Stillpoint for three dollars a day, she figures she can live a couple of years on her savings. Equally important, Stillpoint would be a good place to continue working on her photography. So, in August 1970, just two months after her first visit there, she moves to Stillpoint. Looking back two and a half decades, Jane won't be able to recall just how it came about that she and Gia-fu became partners.

She knows Gia-fu's attracted to her, and the two simply fall into doing things together. He often accompanies her when she's out photographing. He walks, enjoying whatever place they're in, as she wanders off shooting rolls and rolls of film. It's obvious he takes pleasure in the easy companionship and sense of camaraderie, each absorbed in his and her own activity, engaged in it wholeheartedly, individually, together.[11]

Judith Bolinger, a soon-to-be Stillpointer, will describe some twenty-six years later how she saw them:

> He liked her because she was a PhD in physics. He thought that was the cat's pajamas, and he liked that she was extremely quick and smart. And he loved talking with her. It was that kind of stuff... whatever she was into, particle physics, he loved those conversations. And also they really grew to appreciate each other's artistic side. Her photography and his calligraphy.[12]

They have adventures, and one begins with a plan to visit Sequoia and King's Canyon national parks in the southern Sierra Nevada, just about a month after Jane has come to Stillpoint to stay. Knowing the Sacramento Valley can get pretty hot in September, the two plan an early morning start to miss the hottest part of the day. Driving Gia-fu's beat-up old 1953 Mercedes down Bear Creek Road and off across the valley, they anticipate the wonders, the beauty they'll see. What they don't anticipate, however, defines the day. Out in the middle of the valley, around Los Banos, the old car breaks down. Here in the middle of nowhere there's nothing to do except try to wave down a passing motorist to send help.

They climb out of the car and stand watching for approaching vehicles—the proper New England girl, PhD in physics, wearing jeans and T-shirt, and the long-haired, bearded Chinese man, still in his blue-and-white-flowered terry cloth bathrobe—shirt on top and pants on under the robe, waving frantically as several cars pass them by. Finally, someone stops to see what's wrong and agrees to send a mechanic and tow truck from town.

In addition to Jane's enjoyment of nature, her wide-ranging interests, and her photography, Gia-fu appreciates her organizational skills, skills he either lacks or simply neglects. Growing up, he had little need to develop them, with a maid taking care of him most of the time. And he's somehow managed to get by without paying too much attention to organization since then, even at Esalen with the bookkeeping. At his various Stillpoints, he will always designate someone as manager, and Jane will soon take on this role.

At some point after Jane moves to Stillpoint to stay, Gia-fu invites her to his little cabin atop a hill off from the main house. There she sees enormous disarray, especially in one huge cubed box containing everything from ten-year-old phone messages to photographs and letters to his naturalization papers. She takes on the task of sorting the stuff in the box, gaining Gia-fu's deep appreciation for the result and for her skills. He begins to see how Jane's skills can complement his, fill in where he is lacking. But his fifty-one years of life experiences bring him something that Jane, at twenty-eight, has yet to live through. He's been through war, separation from family, dislocation in a foreign land, and loss of and search for his identity. He's also reaped the richness of experiences in his search for self at the Academy, the East-West House, Esalen, and for a few years now, his own community. With all this has come an acknowledgment of his true nature, a ripening of who he is, some wisdom gained that he can share with others at Stillpoint—for isn't that the point? That they learn from and with each other in this community?

From the perspective gained over two and a half decades, Jane will look back and describe her experience this way:

> You know, I was just following something. We had a good time up in the national parks. We rented a little cabin, and we hiked. He was the first person I'd go photographing with because when I'd be photographing trees or grass or something, I'd get totally into it, and I didn't feel hurried by him. He'd just walk back and forth along the trail, perfectly happy to be walking. He didn't care whether he was walking with any destination in mind. He just liked walking. So, I could sit there and do my stuff, and he'd go along.

The two enjoy talking about all kinds of things and, despite their very different backgrounds and upbringings, they find they have much in common, not the least of which is a sense of propriety and doing things right.

Gia-fu confides in Jane. He tells her about his guilt over not going to his mother until she died, how he still dreams about her, how somehow he cannot resolve his feelings of loss and remorse about her. And something he will never write about, something that haunts him, are images that remain with him from Shanghai of Japanese soldiers torturing a young woman, burning her genitals with a candle. These memories, the remorse, the horror, Jane feels, affect him deeply and compromise his physical relationships with women.

Their relationship grows and deepens over the months. On Christmas Day 1970, Gia-fu and Jane visit Gia-fu's friend Bob Shapiro in Mill Valley, Jane meeting Bob for the first time. In the course of their conversation, Bob suggests that the couple have Alan Watts, who lives just up the hill, perform a Buddhist wedding ceremony for them. They've already had their own informal wedding ceremony, this one in Yosemite National Park in October just a couple of months ago. A simple ceremony: in the presence of a few other Stillpointers, in the moonlight they walked toward each other, saying, "Now we are married." And that was it. Nonetheless, they resonate to Bob's idea. He calls Alan and learns Alan's having a big party that evening. Alan thinks it a perfect opportunity to have the ceremony, and he's delighted to perform it.

Gia-fu, Jane, and Bob arrive at Alan's at the designated hour. At Alan's direction the bride, groom, and guests arrange themselves in the beautifully appointed room, a room filled with paintings, carpets, and religious artifacts from all over the world. On the spur of the moment another couple decides they want to get married, too, so Alan performs the ceremony in duplicate. Jane doesn't know anyone there besides Gia-fu and Bob, whom she's known only a few hours. But Alan performs the ceremony with aplomb, reflecting his experience as Anglican priest as well as scholar, teacher, practitioner of Buddhism and other religions, and good friend of Gia-fu's.

It's the only time Jane will meet Watts but she will long remember the room, and especially the piano built into the wall—the strings vertical and played like a harp, with none of the rest of the piano there, or at least not visible. She'll also remember talking with Watts afterward about modern physics and Zen koans. It will stick in her mind that when Watts becomes very intellectual on the relationship between physics and Zen, she stifles the urge to tickle his stomach "just to get him out of his head!"

Word about Stillpoint spreads in varied ways and new faces continue to appear there, just as old friends and acquaintances stop by when passing through. In the summer of 1970, before Jane comes to Stillpoint, Judith Bolinger and Chris Fessenden, who later marry, fall into the new-faces category. Judith recently earned a master's degree and taught high school in Philadelphia for a year. After that year, she realized it wasn't what she wanted to do, so became a self-proclaimed "dropout from teaching." For the last two weeks of July, Judith and Chris have been hiking around California, a time Chris will later describe as "flirting with the area." While at Midpeninusla Free University in Palo Alto, they hear about Stillpoint where tai chi and other courses are taught. Wanting to check it out, they hitch a ride with someone who's headed there.

They arrive about dinnertime and proceed down to the main house. Entering through the front door, they hear voices and follow them farther into the house. Judith will long remember her first impression, and twenty-seven years later she'll describe it. "I'll never forget walking into the place and into the room where everybody would gather to eat. They were all sitting naked around a couple of roasted chickens."

Quickly assessing the situation, Judith says, "Hi. Where do we register?"

Judith and Chris stay the night and then the next day travel back up to San Francisco with their ride. But after they arrive in San Francisco, Judith discovers she's left her purse, money and all, in the car, which has now returned to Stillpoint. They borrow a car and drive back to Stillpoint. Parking the car, Chris takes the precaution of leaving it in gear while they go to fetch Judith's purse. Sadly, the car isn't one that will stay in gear, and during Judith and Chris's brief absence, it rolls down an embankment. They return to find the car wedged in bushes and trees some thirty feet down the bank. The mininightmare, as Chris will later call it, progresses, and they have to call someone to come tow the car out. The upshot of the experience is that with the time needed to repair the car, Chris and Judith end up staying at Stillpoint for two weeks.

Given this longer stay, Judith and Chris, along with the others there, experience the daily group sessions with all of Gia-fu's intensity and his extremely gracious side. In the group meetings it may not always seem so, but mostly he does "serve the community with humility." Chris thinks of his style as sometimes elliptical and sometimes direct. He sees Gia-fu as the "ringmaster of this floating circus." Gia-fu wants everyone to be happy, and he wants everyone to be healthy. He teaches them tai chi, and he goes even more seriously into diet. He reads Henry Bieler's *Food Is Your Best Medicine* and becomes a convert. With typical convert zeal, he gets the others to join him, particularly eating yeast and lots of zucchini. Every morning there's yeast in the tea. Every day there is zucchini. Soon, because of the alkalizing effect on the system, the women start getting yeast infections. And even though they taper off the yeast, Gia-fu still insists it's the answer for getting B vitamins and healthy living. It's possible Gia-fu may now be battling the onset of type 2 diabetes: another reason to be very careful about his diet.[13]

It's a community of a wide range of ages and a wide range of perspectives, including an osteopath, a firefighter, a couple who had been in a kibbutz in Israel, a very young woman thought of as a "cute little kid, but a whiner," another young woman considered a "professional victim," a few writers-to-be. But besides Gia-fu there's only one other non-Caucasian, an African-American man. During the week, there are generally twenty to thirty people. Weekends bring more, including men looking for women, a circumstance that doesn't exactly thrill most of the regulars. After a while this kind of "seeker" is discouraged from visits there. Through it all, the people there are in their own way trying for some sort of emotional honesty and find that being at Stillpoint with Gia-fu and others supports that quest.[14]

Although Stillpoint does attract numerous and varied people, it's not everyone's cup of tea. And while dropped inhibitions and experimentation pervade the times, not everyone moves in this direction, or even if they do, not at the same pace. Natalie Ednie, for example. Married to an air force lieutenant colonel and psychiatrist, Natalie has been looking into this new therapy, Gestalt therapy, for her husband, who can't get away long enough to check it out himself. Natalie, who has six children but who thinks it important to investigate Gestalt, takes the time and makes several trips to Esalen where she participates in Gestalt therapy workshops. She's just getting to know about the counterculture and has had only a little contact with it. At Esalen she hears about Stillpoint and decides on one of her trips through Los Gatos to stop by.

Driving her car, which has been giving her trouble lately, to the road where she thinks Stillpoint is, she stops off to check directions at the Catholic seminary at the bottom of the mountain where Bear Creek Road begins. A priest in a plaid shirt, probably on retreat, tells her how to find Stillpoint. He says some of the people there come down to the seminary occasionally and the folks at the seminary sometimes go to Stillpoint.

Following the priest's directions, she drives across a bridge over a small gully, parks her car by the road, and walks to the house. Seeing many shoes at the door, she takes her own shoes off and enters the house. There, in a big room, on the floor where sun is streaming through the windows, lies a woman, completely naked except for a pair of sunglasses covering her eyes.

A startled Natalie utters something and, at the sound, the woman sits up, takes off the sunglasses, and hangs them over her nipple. By now Natalie's doing some strong, albeit silent, self-talk, "There is nothing here to be afraid of. You are not in danger. This is just an unusual situation.

You're not accustomed to this sort of thing. But you are not in danger. There's nothing to be afraid of."

The woman greets Natalie and they talk for a short time. She learns that both Gia-fu and Jane are traveling and she's invited to have dinner, to stay. She's very uncertain about it, but continues to tell herself it's okay.

Natalie helps prepare dinner, chopping all kinds of vegetables and various strange foods, one of which she'll later come to know as tofu. A couple of people spread a bedsheet on the floor and put plates and the necessary utensils out. When everything's ready, the fifteen or so people, Natalie among them, all sit on the floor around the bedsheet-cum-tablecloth. Holding hands, they express appreciation for the food. Natalie feels the strong energy in the room. She also notices that every-one's wearing clothes except for the woman she first met. It's not clear where the sunglasses are.

Wanting to contribute something, especially since she feels she's crashing, not necessarily intruding, Natalie offers to do the dishes. There are lots of dishes and, her offer accepted, she prepares the water and starts in. People drift away, much to Natalie's relief because she prefers to be alone. And although everyone has been extremely nice, she doesn't know how to connect with these people.

But then, just as she's settling in washing the dishes, a young man comes through. He's wearing only a long robe, open in the front. He walks up behind her, wraps the robe around her, too, and gives her a hug, asking, "Aren't you coming out to 'turn on'? We 'turn on' at sunset."

Disentangling herself, she murmurs some reply and the young man goes away. By now she's very upset. Although she knows how to say no gracefully to high-ranking air force officers, she's had no experience fend-ing off what she'll later describe as a "counter-culture hit."

Now she knows she can't stay here. She can't wait to get away. She flees. Running to her car, she hopes with every cell of her body that her car starts, that she can get away. Thank goodness, it does start. Careening down the mountain, sobbing from the fright of it all, sobbing because she's upset with herself for being upset, she reaches the seminary.

She knows she's in no shape to drive very far, so she goes in and asks if there's a place where she can be alone. She's shown to a room, and she sits, crying for some time. But then a man enters. He asks if he can say mass. Although she's not Catholic, she says yes and stays in the room. The man puts on the vestments and gets out all of the necessary ceremonial objects. As he holds the communion tray, a paten, and says a blessing for it, the last rays of the sun come through the window and catch the golden tray, burnishing the entire room in its reflection. The priest's soft chanting sounds, the last light of the day reflected on the paten, and the surrounding quiet produce an oddly settling feeling in Natalie. She's just experienced two very different, very strange situations. She knows she belongs in neither milieu—not Stillpoint and not the Catholic tradition. Yet she feels herself on a spiritual path. She feels she's on it alone. Everything seems okay. And thirty-six years later, Natalie will look back on this experience, understanding that she would handle it all very differently with what she's learned over the years, and also understanding that that experience taught her something very important about herself.

Eventually, Natalie will encounter Gia-fu and Jane. Gia-fu she had seen at Esalen some time ago, although she can't recall exactly when. She remembers him in the dining room sitting quietly, eating his dinner, a turban on his head. The turban pulls her to go sit with him. She remembers how quiet he was, how he wasn't easily drawn into conversation, not by her shy self or by others. Jane she will later meet in Charlotte Selver's physical trainings called sensory awareness in 1975. She will observe how Jane asks questions that seem to displease Charlotte and the group, which puzzles Natalie. But she'll come to learn that Jane voices questions that others either can't or won't, and because of this she serves as the alternative voice, the lightning rod of the group. Questioning, pushing, wanting to know, wanting to put the puzzle together, and sooner than others feel it is time to do so. After all, she's a physicist; she has a scientifically inquiring mind.[15]

For those who do find in Stillpoint a sense of community, a good place to be for now, there are various ways to stretch themselves without going beyond their limits. The whole community takes monthly full-moon camping trips. It makes sense, with such a range of people and experiences in the community, that some people feel more comfortable than others camping out in the wilderness. For some it's a great adventure. For others it's something to endure, maybe learn from, grow from. Trusty is one of these. He's a very large, strong man, a firefighter from San Jose, a street-smart city guy, and very much out of his element in the wilds of Yosemite. The group camps on Tioga Road, up toward Tioga Pass, the terrain dotted with glaciated lakes, the air thin, cold, crisp. Gia-fu thinks back to those camping trips in Kunming, seemingly in another lifetime. Jane thinks of trips with her parents and brother, so many fun adventures. Sitting around the campfire under the stars, paled somewhat by the brilliance of the full moon, everyone appreciates the stillness, the quiet. But when they go to their tents and sleeping bags for the night, Trusty takes an ax with him, just in case a bear or other wild animal gets too close.

During January 1971, in search of something more to do in the daily meetings, Gia-fu thinks of translating the *Tao Te Ching*, that ancient Chinese classic thought to be written in the sixth century BCE by Lao Tsu. Though historians are uncertain whether Lao Tsu really existed and, therefore, whether the journey that resulted in the *Tao Te Ching* took place, legend has it that Lao Tsu was keeper of the imperial archives in Honan. Further, he taught, "The Tao that can be told is not the eternal Tao." This is the very essence of Taoism. But as the story goes, Lao Tsu became sickened at heart by mankind's ways and rode to the desert to die. As he passed through the gates of northwestern China, the gatekeeper talked Lao Tsu into writing down his teachings for others. The resulting eighty-one chapters have been a major influence on Chinese thought and culture for more than two and a half millennia. It's a classic dear to Gia-fu's heart.[16]

The community will work on it together, a chapter a day. The project begins, Gia-fu reading a chapter and then translating it into very rough English. The group then takes it up, considering the meaning, discussing it in depth, and figuring out the best way to express it. Within a couple of months, they work through the full eighty-one chapters two or three times. Gradually the idea of the translation becoming a book evolves, and Gia-fu realizes that this, again approached in a collaborative way, can be his second book.

Spring of 1971 brings change. It's been brewing for a while but now reaches a point at which the Stillpointers must make a decision. The ferment grows out of the neighbors' dissatisfaction with the unusual Stillpoint community itself and the "un–building-permit buildings" that have sprouted on the land. To show their displeasure, the neighbors put up barbed-wire fences so the Stillpointers can't go onto their property, greatly curtailing access to good walks. They register complaints with the county about the buildings, and they just generally shun the community—echoes of the farm commune in Georgia.

Gia-fu is the one to attend to these matters with county officials, and he addresses questions and concerns as best he can. But it becomes increasingly clear that it's time to move on. Heeding the wisdom of the *Tao Te Ching*, "Yield and overcome," Gia-fu and the others pack up their belongings and prepare to leave. Taking their settled hearts with them, the Stillpoint community begins its trek across the country, leaving the Los Gatos hills behind.

CHAPTER TEN

HAPPY
WANDERING

The sky is blue. Is that really so?
Or does it only look blue because it stretches off into infinity?

—from Chapter 1, *Chuang Tsu: Inner Chapters*

A caravan of two vans and three sedans wends its way up through the Sierras, carrying fifteen or so Stillpointers on their pilgrimage across the country. A few stay behind in various parts of California, drawn by other places to be, other interests to explore. The caravan's stalwart travelers stop on snowy Donner Pass for lunch this first day, a crisp, cobalt-blue-sky day in May 1971. On their way east, they'll journey on to Yellowstone National Park and across the Dakotas to Wisconsin, stopping for a short visit with friends of Jane's. Then they'll keep going, taking turns driving—except for Gia-fu, much to everyone's relief—all the way to Vermont, to Jane's beloved New England.

This journey marks another new phase for Gia-fu, for within the next year he will, in collaboration with Jane and other Stillpointers, see his second book published, a book that will bring him more recognition and opportunities than any other single happening in his life. In time it will become, out of more than three hundred *Tao Te Ching* translations, the most popular ever. In 1997, a twenty-fifth-anniversary edition will be published celebrating the book's success, twelve years after Gia-fu's death. And the book's evolution reflects another journey, beginning with Gia-fu's idea of the translation providing something good to do in morning meetings, then to thoughts of perhaps publishing it, and finally to in fact publishing it with accompanying photographs and calligraphy—this last an inspired addition. This evolution will culminate during the five-month stay in Vermont.

Although he's leaving friends and important places behind, this dislocation, unlike the upheaval preventing his return to China, occurs in the company of friends, community, his re-created family. It seems more relocation than dislocation, despite the reason for leaving Bear Creek Road. He has his Stillpoint, so moving with it seems okay. And of the fifteen or so travelers, eight will stay together for the next three years.

During the time Gia-fu has gotten Stillpoint under way and is relocating, the Feng family in China has been experiencing still another crisis, another revolution. Because of its nature and the nature of China's relationship with the rest of the world, Gia-fu knows very little about what's going on there and what's happening to his family. He won't know much at all until his return to China four years later when foreigners will once again be allowed into the country.

Chairman Mao, concerned internally about political rivals, threatened from the outside by Khrushchev's denunciations of Stalin, and true to his belief in continuous revolution, unleashes another horrendous campaign. This one, the beginnings of which can be traced to 1965, will turn into a force beyond even Mao's control, not ending until his death in 1976. During this time, untold millions of Chinese will be persecuted, killed, maimed, cornered into committing suicide. They will be encouraged, pushed even, through threats to their own lives, to betray those closest to them, making it difficult for anyone—husband, wife, child, parent, friend—to completely trust each other, making it safest not to share information or even thoughts.

This is the Cultural Revolution. Mao and his handpicked core of advisers, later called the Gang of Four, one of whom is his third wife, Jiang Qing, build on a complex series of events and circumstances to further Mao's control, to further what has become the cult of Mao. They capitalize on the steadily rising tension between outspoken scholars and writers and the most hard-line of the CCP as well as other conditions—the bloated, inefficient bureaucracy, members of which are accused of taking the "capitalist road." Mao exploits the country's youth: young people frustrated because of limited educational options due to a dearth of colleges and other educational opportunities, and the young who live in seeming confinement in the compounds of the Party elite. They especially have something to prove; they've had it easy and must demonstrate their purity and loyalty to Mao, to the China he stands for. In the mix are also those who have been sent to the countryside to work in communes. Mao will unleash the frustration and terrifying power of these young men and women and others forming his Red Guard. They terrorize without boundaries. They make a target of everyone—parents, teachers, elders— anyone who seems less than pure, anyone who represents tradition, the bourgeoisie, non-Mao thought. They humiliate, beat, kill, destroy—all with Mao's blessing.[1]

The Feng family, because of their education, their former riches, and their accomplishments, number among the targets. They're considered "class enemies." Feng Chong-ching, his home raided by the Red Guard, is confined to one room. The once grand residence of a proud, prosperous, and powerful family is now shared with other families. He suffers from a heart condition, and with his sons and daughters scattered overseas and across China, he mostly depends on his old, former servant An-uh to take care of him, making sure he eats and has the bare essentials. An-uh is with Feng Chong-ching at the end, in 1970. While still confined in his room, Feng Chong-ching dies of a heart attack. He is seventy-four years old.

A few years earlier, on his seventieth birthday, Feng Chong-ching had his picture taken with the diplomas of all nine of his children—all nine had bachelor's degrees and most had graduate degrees. A proud father, Feng Chong-ching referred to the diplomas as his treasures.[2] Some of his children he will never see again, and Gia-fu is one of these.

Now, because of the nightmarish situation, although Gia-fu's siblings contact him about their father's death via Hong Kong, there's nothing he can do. Certainly, there's no way for him to go there, to be with his family, or even to know all they are going through. And so, saddened by his father's death, unaware of just how dire his siblings' circumstances are, Gia-fu heads to new vistas, to the next part of his life.

The caravan travels to northern Vermont, where friend Elizabeth Kent Gay, who knew Gia-fu at the Institute for Transpersonal Psychology in Menlo Park, California, has a house they can stay in. And even better, Elizabeth's daughter, Susan Tarshis, has another house, better suited for this group, one with a perfect spot for a darkroom. They end up staying in this house, or camping around it, at Kents Corner in Calais through the summer far into October, into the autumn colors.

Shortly after they arrive, Chris Fessenden and Judith Bolinger, who most recently have been in Philadelphia, come to Vermont and join the group. They've been living in Philadelphia with a group of about thirteen people divided into two houses. Although they began the arrangement with high hopes, they now realize things aren't working out. A postcard from one of the Stillpointers brings them to Vermont where they find lots of new people, including Jane, who's with Gia-fu. They stay a few days and then return to Philadelphia, utlimately deciding to return to Vermont to be with Gia-fu.

At some point Gia-fu puts a question to Judith and Chris about their relationship. "Are you just in a holding pattern or do you want to make a commitment to each other?" he asks. They take the question seriously, reflecting, discussing, then concluding that they really do want to make that commitment, and they want to do it publicly. They talk with their parents and then make arrangements to hold the ceremony in the Pocono Mountains in northeastern Pennsylvania where his parents have a home. Setting the date for October 10, they ask Gia-fu to be part of the ceremony.

Soon after the first of October, Judith and Chris head to the Poconos where the group joins them a little later. There Gia-fu delights in walking in the beautiful forests, by the rushing streams, along the lake. As always, he walks for hours, always wearing or holding his bright orange raincoat, his protection against inclement weather. One day he walks on a trail near the Pocono Lake Preserve, a community built around the lake, one with a long-standing cooperative membership arrangement and very homogeneous membership. Somehow, he takes a trail and gets lost. Stopping, looking around, he realizes he's in somebody's backyard, and he's not sure how he got there. At the same time, the owners look out a window and see a stranger in their yard, what to them appears a wild-looking Chinese guy with mussed-up long hair, graying beard, holding an orange raincoat in one hand and looking around the place. They panic. They call the police.

Patrol car lights flashing, the police arrive almost immediately. They confront Gia-fu, question him—who is he, what's he doing here? Doesn't he know this is private property? Gia-fu tells them he's visiting, he tells them about Judith and Chris, who, when called, come right over. Judith and Chris establish who they are, telling them of Chris's parents who live here, vouching for Gia-fu. Eventually it all gets sorted out, and everyone goes home. But the incident leaves Gia-fu, Judith, and everyone else involved feeling discombobulated.

The day of the ceremony approaches. Gia-fu has suggested that everyone—that is, the Stillpointers and Judith's and Chris's parents and close relatives—come together the day before to talk about what this ceremony means. Judith's parents react differently to this idea and to Gia-fu—her father resonates to Gia-fu; her mother does not. But the afternoon and evening turn out well. And the next day brings the ceremony and additional people, including friends from Philadelphia, the whole group now numbering about sixty-five. The ceremony itself is simple. Judith and Chris have written their own vows, and Gia-fu offers a few words. Here in this beautiful place, among family and friends, in community, Judith and Chris are married.

Judith and Chris stay in the Poconos for another ten or so days while most of the others return to Vermont.

Taking advantage of being in New England, Jane and Gia-fu visit Jane's parents in New Hampshire. This may be the only time Gia-fu will meet the parents of any of his partners. Jane thinks he's a little uncomfortable around her parents but he seems to get along with them well enough. Not surprisingly, he continues his long daily walks, up and down the many back roads in the area. Mrs. English, unaccustomed to such devoted walking, asks her daughter, "Well, when is he coming back? Do you know where he is?"

Jane responds the only way she can. "He's out there walking. He'll come back. He'll find his way back."

Mrs. English accepts this, although she and her husband continue to be astounded by how far Gia-fu walks. Jane suspects Gia-fu's dedication is also his way of keeping his diabetes under control.

Gia-fu and Jane also visit Chögyam Trungpa, a Tibetan Buddhist who has begun Buddhist centers in the U.S. In time Trungpa, called Trungpa Rinpoche as a revered teacher, will develop an umbrella organization, Vajradhatu. Under this organization numerous centers around the world will grow, as will Shambhala for secular training and Naropa University as a contemplative university, both in Boulder, Colorado. Now Trungpa resides at a contemplative center he's established in Vermont, called Karmê Chöling. On learning that Gia-fu is in the vicinity, Trungpa invites him up for a visit.

Jane and Gia-fu do go to Karmê Chöling. It's the first meeting of these two teachers from other cultures, Chögyam Trungpa, exiled from Buddhist Tibet, and Gia-fu, now a self-styled Chinese Taoist. The occasion seems somewhat formal at first, with introductions and initial greetings. But then Trungpa offers beer to his guests and everyone relaxes into easy conversation. Watching them, Jane muses about these two seemingly ordinary people, each of whom has his own quirks and issues, both with important things to teach. Both are heads of their respective communities, both unconventional and spontaneous in the way they live their lives. And both Gia-fu and Trungpa are now, and will become even more so, cast into other images and roles by those searching for something, searching for a master, a superparent, a guide, a guru.

Trungpa's background and experience lie in the centuries-old tradition of lineage, the handing down through the generations of a spiritual role, the passing of the Dharma, the Buddhist teachings of the underlying order of nature and living in accord with it. Gia-fu isn't part of a lineage, and he doesn't want to be considered a spiritual master; his interests lie elsewhere. And he's most certainly not a Buddhist.

Despite the tendency for people to confuse Buddhism and Taoism, and despite their similarities—both are contemplative, both hold the importance of stillness and the inner life—they're two different philosophies, separate wisdom traditions, some would say religions. They emerged from two different cultures: Buddhism in India, around 500 BCE, Taoism in China, roughly the same time. When Buddhism came to China in the first century of the Common Era (also known as AD), the two wisdom traditions influenced each other significantly, and Ch'an (later in Japan to be called Zen) Buddhism, a Chinese version of Buddhism, was born.

Some people think of it as a matter of emphasis: Buddhism emphasizes the mind and working with one's mind; Taoism emphasizes nature. And yes, there are aspects of each in the other. Isn't that what that tai chi symbol conveys about the interrelatedness of things?

But we humans tend to make assumptions, and those who make assumptions about what Gia-fu is up to will routinely have those assumptions exposed and obliterated. Jane will sum it up decades later. "People would come to him with the idea that there was this wonderful Taoist sage they were going to come sit at the feet of and absorb all his wisdom. Instead, they got this encounter group stuff thrown at them!"

Trungpa and Gia-fu do find things in common; they respect each other and learn from each other on this visit, and on occasional visits in the future.

Back in the Vermont house, Jane and Gia-fu continue working on the *Tao Te Ching* manuscript. By now, the photographs-with-calligraphy idea has taken hold, so that's where they're headed. Both claim to have initiated the idea, and it's possible they both did. Jane will later reminisce, "It was one of those ideas that just became obvious. I remember even before I met him, I would think of my photographs as Chinese landscape paintings and imagined where the calligraphy would go."

The two work well together. Jane has set up a darkroom in the basement, where she can develop the photographs. She works on the photos and the layout, which doesn't interest Gia-fu. Gia-fu completes one chapter's worth of calligraphy each day, right on the photographs—a tricky proposition but he does it, and he does it beautifully. Because their interests differ but complement each other, no territorial battles intrude and they make steady progress. By August they're ready to send the manuscript to a publisher. Collier-Macmillan, the publisher for Gia-fu's first book, *Tai Chi—A Way of Centering & I Ching*, has the right of first refusal on Gia-fu's next book, so that's where they send the manuscript.

A couple of months after sending it and hearing no response, Gia-fu and Jane follow the manuscript. They've decided to go to Colorado anyway, and New York's on the way. Elizabeth has friends at Mineral Hot Springs in Colorado's San Luis Valley, and the Hot Springs is under contract, in escrow for the moment. The sellers offer to have Jane, Gia-fu, and the others stay there during November. Living at a natural hot springs in a beautiful part of the country and with the weather turning cooler sounds pretty good—Vermont's getting too cold for those living in tents—so they decide to do it. Jane and her family have often vacationed in Colorado and she loves the area. Now, October 1971, the trek back westward begins, some of the core group, such as Judith and Chris, traveling separately, some together. Gia-fu, Jane, Judith, Chris, Judith's sister and friends from Philadelphia, John Lyle,

Sue Blacker, Seichi and Emily Tsutsumi, and a few others Gia-fu knows—altogether a group of fifteen or twenty people—will all be together again at Mineral Hot Springs.

Gia-fu and Jane's stop in New York, although disappointing at first, takes a fortuitous turn. Arriving in the city, they go the Collier-Macmillan offices to talk directly to the publisher. There they meet the editor who's reviewed their manuscript. He likes it. But unfortunately, he's leaving the job at the end of the week. He's asked around, but no one else there has any real interest. There may be, however, someone else who will be interested, someone at a different publisher, and he has that person in mind. With encouraging words, he sends the two across Third Avenue to Alfred A. Knopf Publishers, telling them to speak to senior editor, Toinette Lippe.

Cautiously hopeful, Gia-fu and Jane follow the directions they've been given and find Toinette Lippe's office on the designated floor of the particular New York skyscraper. They speak to the receptionist, asking to see Ms. Lippe. Toinette, surprised to hear that two people she's never heard of are standing outside asking to speak to her, finds herself even more surprised that they have a manuscript she's never read—an inauspicious set of circumstances for aspiring authors. Editors like to read authors' work prior to sitting down to talk with them. Toinette will explain more than two decades later in a wonderful essay entitled "What Constitutes a Necessary Book," "Otherwise there is very little to discuss, since the author has read what he has written and you have not. In this case, not only had I not read anything by these people, I didn't even know who they were." In that same essay, Toinette will also recall, "But something stopped me saying, 'Tell them to leave the manuscript. I'm busy now. I'll be in touch when I've read it.'"

Not only does Toinette not utter the usual words, but she walks out to the receptionist and escorts Gia-fu and Jane into her office. She'll later describe her impression of the two as "a small Ho Chi Minh-like figure, complete with wispy beard, and his tall, strong American companion."

Toinette gets yet another surprise when she learns that the young man at Macmillan has sent them to her. She'd only met him a couple of times and didn't think he knew about her practicing tai chi. He, in fact, didn't know this. He only thought she might be receptive to their manuscript, this unique combination of text, photos, and calligraphy.

"He was right. I sat and turned the pages in wonder. Each verse was accompanied by Chinese calligraphy and an exquisite photograph. I persuaded them to leave the manuscript with me so that I could show it to the editor-in-chief."

The editor-in-chief agrees that the manuscript seems promising, while pointing out that Toinette's expertise isn't with photographic books. She concurs but says she "has a hunch about this book." He gives the go-ahead, and she starts working on it right away.

Meanwhile, Stillpoint-on-the-move arrives at Mineral Hot Springs at the north end of the San Luis Valley in south-central Colorado. High desert at 7,700 feet elevation with views of fabulous 14,000-foot peaks of the Sangre de Cristo Mountains to the east, forty miles from any town or store, the place seems funky and perfect. Gia-fu loves baths and hot water, so nothing could be better as far as he's concerned. The hot springs prove a source of joy for everyone, and they spend their days sitting in the morning, soaking in the springs, perhaps dancing in the evenings. Here at these wondrous springs, Gia-fu and Jane receive the contract from Knopf. It comes in the mail in an ordinary envelope. It is accepted with extraordinary delight.

Back at the publisher, Toinette starts studying the translation and decides it needs some work. To begin, she reads other translations, in the process learning that only the Bible has been translated into English more times than the *Tao Te Ching*. She selects a dozen or so translations, which she will later describe as "ranging from Arthur Waley's historically accurate version to Witter Bynner's lyrical poems which seemed to take liberties with the text while perfectly expressing the spirit."

Assiduously, thoroughly, Toinette works through each line, back and forth between Gia-fu's translation and others, making the changes she thinks will make the text flow more easily and better fit the photographs. To test her recommended changes, she reads the chapters aloud to a young Mexican friend. If her friend doesn't understand or thinks the lines don't read well, Toinette works some more on them. Toinette then sends the changes to Gia-fu for his approval, or occasional disapproval.

And finally it's time for publication. The jacket copy has to be written. Toinette puts off writing it until the deadline is only twenty minutes away. She's perplexed by the task, later putting her dilemma this way. "How could I possibly reduce this sixth century B.C. classic to a single paragraph?" But she does. She sits down at the typewriter and her mind goes blank, then she begins to type:

> Accept what is in front of you without wanting the situation to be other than it is. Study the natural order of things and work with it rather than against it, for to try to change what is only sets up resistance…We serve whatever or whoever stands before us, without any thought for ourselves. *Te*—which may be translated as "virtue" or "strength"—lies always in *Tao* or "natural law." In other words: Simply be.

It's perfect. The book is a hit. People from all walks of life read it, people for whom it will be the defining book of that period. Even *Time* magazine reviews it, although describing it as "the *Tao Te Ching* gussied up with photographs." Yes, Toinette, will say, "…but until it was gussied up with photographs, the *Tao Te Ching* had been around for 2,500 years and *Time* magazine hadn't bothered to review it."[3]

During the publication process for the *Tao Te Ching*, Gia-fu and Jane begin working on a second book, another translation of an ancient Chinese classic. This one, Chuang Tsu's *Inner Chapters,* will be a companion volume to the *Tao Te Ching*. Sometimes knowingly, sometimes not, the photos Jane now takes are destined for this next book. Some special photos she takes at a nearby spectacular anomaly of nature, the Great Sand Dunes. These photos are special not only because of the place but also because she shoots only one roll of film there and ten or twelve of the photos wind up in the Chuang Tsu book.

The Great Sand Dunes, destined some thirty-five years later in 2004 to become Great Sand Dunes National Park and Preserve, rise almost 750 feet above the high-mountain San Luis Valley floor and are the tallest sand dunes in North America. Nestled against the Sangre de Cristo Mountains, they cover about thirty-nine square miles. Breathtaking in their beauty and strangeness, they attract many visitors, but not so many in November when the Stillpointers hike around them and Jane shoots her one roll of film.

Their time at Mineral Hot Springs coming to a close means the group must decide what's next. Money is running out for some, so finding work must be one consideration. Being near mountains and good hiking also ranks high on the list. Teams of people go out to explore where to be next, a time Chris will remember as being open-ended, uncertain. And then they find Manitou Springs, where they rent rooms at a motel beginning December 1. Agreed on the move, when December 1 arrives the Stillpointers head to Manitou Springs. There they live, five to a room, in the motel for several months. The motel owner also has an apartment house where he and his family live on the first floor, and a few months later the Stillpointers find themselves moving to the second floor of the big old house.

What they find, once again, are wary neighbors, unaccustomed to groups like this one. The Stillpointers sit in the early mornings chanting for an hour, then have a sitting meditation, then chant again, sometimes spontaneously whooping and hollering, waiting for the sunrise. This activity, along with the currently unfamiliar daily tai chi in the park, probably causes some neighbors to wonder what's going on and, for some, it pushes imaginations into overdrive. The Stillpointers realize it's important to be involved in the community, which isn't all that easy since they're such an oddity. Gia-fu, however, stresses the importance of cultivating positive relationships with the neighbors. Selecting Judith as their ambassador, he tells her, "Judith, you have to go and talk to these people. Jane doesn't know how to do that. So you go and talk to them. You go offer them whatever they would like—babysitting maybe."

Judith does talk with the neighbors, and she and Chris end up doing a lot of babysitting for the landlord downstairs, but they realize it's going to be an ongoing problem and they just have to do the best they can. This holds true when they are renting and also when Jane and Gia-fu decide to buy a house there.

This surprising development begins when Gia-fu notices an old house on Ruxton Avenue near the Barr Trail, a rugged trail that winds thirteen miles upward, climbing seventy-five hundred feet to the top of

Pikes Peak. It runs partly along the cog railway that also travels up Pikes Peak, and Gia-fu loves going up and down it. Pikes Peak holds fame for several reasons, one of which is that on the peak in 1893, Katherine Lee Bates, teacher and author, wrote the lyrics to "America the Beautiful." This somewhat obscure fact, however, isn't what attracts Gia-fu to it. He's drawn by the ruggedness and beauty of the mountain and loves walking, usually at a fairly fast pace, up and down it, sometimes on the trail, sometimes not.

Lloyd Alexander later visits and will long remember hikes up the peak with Gia-fu. His first time there will remain engraved in his memory decades later. It starts with a simple suggestion by Gia-fu, "Well, let's go hiking."

Lloyd, who loves to walk and hike, says, "Okay!"—having no clue what Gia-fu means when he says "hiking." Lloyd just assumes the usual trek somewhere beautiful and interesting. He soon learns the error of his assumption as they go outside to begin their hike. Gia-fu takes off running up the mountain. All the way up. Lloyd, amazed, tries to follow. He'll later recall, "And I mean run, just straight out. Pikes Peak is a fairly steep incline, and he would just run. Even when there was no trail."

At the top, when Lloyd arrives, Gia-fu explains, "This is an old Chinese method." What Lloyd soon learns is that he means that you consciously can't miss the trees and boulders that are in your way. You just have to let go of your body.

Approaching a cliff, Gia-fu looks back at Lloyd and says, "Come on!" And down he goes.

Occasionally they pass some tourists, who stand gaping at the two as they zip down the hill. Lloyd thinks it's death defying, and he will remember the daredevil part of Gia-fu and his instinct to give things up to the natural body—like gravity. And they never have an accident. Not even so much as a turned ankle.[4]

One day, as Gia-fu heads up the mountain, he runs into Rudy and Catherine, an older couple he's met on the trail. He learns from them that the house on Ruxton Avenue is for sale. The owner, an older man, has died, and a bank is taking care of the estate. Seeing Gia-fu's interest, Rudy and Catherine tell Gia-fu how to contact the seller, which he does. And despite the shape the house is in—it seems to be sliding down the hill and needs a lot of work—he and Jane buy it, using their royalty advance from Knopf as part of the down payment.

Stillpoint now has a new home, one that truly belongs to them. The community will work on it, shaping it to fit who they are and how they choose to live. This big rambling old house will see seemingly infinite comings and goings as the community shifts, sifts, and thrives on this mountainside under the blue sky of Colorado.

CHAPTER ELEVEN

EBB & FLOW

The world is ruled by letting things take their course.
It cannot be ruled by interfering.

—from Chapter 48, *Tao Te Ching*

It's early in 1973. Gia-fu, Jane, and the bank that financed them now own the big old house on Ruxton Avenue, in Manitou Springs, Colorado, right in the middle of an area once considered a holy place by the Ute, Cheyenne, Arapaho, and Kiowa. The springs that drew those Native American nations and served as the town's namesake are closed now and have been for some years, but these nearby, century-old, three stories of rambling rooms and porches perched on the hillside offer a strong enough draw in themselves to be Stillpoint's home base for the next five years.[1]

As Gia-fu, Jane, and the other Stillpointers move to their new home, Gia-fu senses a lingering impression of the deceased previous owner. He wants to acknowledge that the house belonged to someone before him and to make peace with this man so he can truly move into his house. All of his attention turned to his task, Gia-fu pulls out some of the man's left-behind clothing and puts it on. The past owner's shirt and trousers hanging loosely on his slender frame, Gia-fu now prepares to acknowledge the man and show respect for him and his life in the house. Turning to the others, he tells them he must talk to this man "in order to receive this house and these clothes" and in a simple observance he does so, making that peace with him and acknowledging ownership of his first bit of land, the first home he has owned in his adopted country.

The house now theirs, the enthusiastic Stillpointers soon begin the cleaning, repairing, and remodeling that this ramshackle house so desperately calls for. Jane's parents have remodeled two houses so she has some experience, which comes in handy, as does the experience of a few others. The Stillpoint core—among them Arthur Kuper, Charles Gagarin, John Lyle, Judith Bolinger, Chris Fessenden, Seichi and Emily Tsutsumi, Jane and Gia-fu—presses on. At a steady pace, especially during the first year, they draw on all their budding and some more well-developed skills. John Lyle, for one, has a background in heating and air conditioning. Despite the Los Gatos experience that brought complaints from neighbors for their non–building-permit buildings, they work mostly without benefit of building permits, except for the electrical system. They need to upgrade the electrical circuits and wisely decide to do this by the book and very early on. Much of what they design and do is through some sort of consensus, which seems to produce good results.

Looking back from a distance of seventeen years, Judith Bolinger will remember:

> And so we were there for the next two years, building, adding to the place, and walking up the mountain every morning. So it was kind of a ritual. We'd get up at five thirty or six, and we'd sit for an hour, and then we'd all take hikes and come back. We'd usually take something to eat, come back around noon or one, and have the rest of the day to do our projects.[2]

Chris will long remember that Gia-fu's one constant was walking, and other interests ranging from volleyball to the Watergate hearings would come and go, all in the context of a healthy lifestyle.

During this time the core remains steadfast as others come and go, drawn by word of mouth through the ever-growing web of relationships that began in California. These years of social upheaval, continued protests against the Establishment and the Vietnam War, and ongoing social experimentation bring seekers through town, in and out of Stillpoint. The core Stillpointers, a close group, have little patience for anyone who shows up "blissed out," quickly helping them get their heads out of the clouds and their feet back on the ground.

Yes, the neighbors wonder what's going on, who these strange people living in that big house are. Stillpoint's differences put off some locals and attract others. One couple Gia-fu and Stillpoint attract is a dean at the local community college and his wife, whose names have since been lost in time's shuffle. They spend a good bit of time at Stillpoint, bringing their credibility in the community and other practical benefits with them. The dean has some machinist training, and he puts it to use during the summer when the height of the remodeling is underway.

His wife, very much respected in the community, willingly offers her respectability when Jane plans a visit to the police chief to reassure him about what they're up to and what they're not. It's a smart move in these hippie-commune, counterculture, drug-prevalent years; Jane wants to distinguish between who they actually are and rumors, stereotypes, and false assumptions.

Jane and her respectable companion arrive at the station and ask to see the police chief. He happens to be in and agrees to see them. As they take their seats across the desk from him, Jane introduces herself. He knows her companion, trusts her and, therefore, seems willing to listen to what Jane has to say. He settles back in his chair, seeming relaxed and curious.

Jane, in her straightforward, no-nonsense way, lays all the cards on the table, saying, "Okay. Here we are. We know you have questions, so ask us whatever you want to know about us."

"Drugs?" he asks, equally straightforward.

Jane responds, "We don't have any dope. In fact, we have a strict rule about it." He raises an eyebrow and Jane adds, "Once I caught someone with drugs, and that person was gone within a day."

They talk a little more with Jane describing the Stillpoint community and its intention to sustain a simple and honest way of living together, peacefully with the rest of the community. At the conclusion of this brief conversation, the relieved and reassured police chief thanks the two for coming in. He now knows he has contacts, a means for communicating directly with this unusual group, and he appreciates it. The visit accomplishes its important goal, the echoes of which twenty-five years later will be seen on the city's website in its history: "The counterculture movement found an accepting home here and alternative lifestyles are still appreciated." The visit also confirms that Jane can, in fact, talk to the neighbors, something not too long ago Gia-fu said she couldn't do.

But it's not completely clear to Jane just what Gia-fu thinks. She's in a kind of manager role for Stillpoint, and she has acquired the reputation for being "the bad one," enforcing the rules just as she described it to the police chief. Even twenty-five years later, musing about what Gia-fu may have thought, Jane will recall, "I don't think he quite knew what he wanted me to be. Sometimes he wanted me to be a cute little girl, and sometimes he wanted me to do all the dirty work. Like down in Manitou I was his hatchet lady. I was the one who threw people out." She does throw people out when necessary, and now in the still early 1970s her ability to organize, enforce the rules, and maintain order isn't yet tempered with an abundance of tact; she's still growing into being her own person.

Life in Manitou Springs bears some resemblance to life in Los Gatos, although Chris will later think of the days at Los Gatos as less structured. In Judith's eyes, Gia-fu remains true to his cause and passionate about it— that is, to create a new social living style, an honest, natural way of being together, underscored by Taoist philosophy. Gia-fu talks about this often, about the importance of nature and the importance of being "up front" about things, and about not taking oneself too seriously. He also prides himself on being what he calls a charlatan, his way of scoffing—reminiscent of his theatrical pronouncements in the Esalen dining hall—at those who do take themselves so very seriously, whether as spiritual leaders or intense spiritual seekers. A favorite topic targets where various leaders have gone wrong and particularly New Agers, all trying so hard.

Jane aids Gia-fu in not taking himself too seriously. On more than one occasion when he's wound up talking about something, she quietly walks up behind him, puts her arms around his slight frame while holding his arms down, picks him up, and unceremoniously carries him off to the side of the room, saying, "Oh! A portable guru." Laughter meets this act, Gia-fu's along with everyone else's.

The idea of "guru" is one Gia-fu wrestles with. He does not want to put himself in that role, nor does he promote himself that way. He does, however, think gurus have their place; the Taoist that he is sees both sides of the matter, yes *and* no. In a 1977 New Dimensions Radio interview, while Gia-fu refers to himself as a Taoist rogue, he will acknowledge that gurus are here to demonstrate they have reached a certain stage, like a master or a tai chi master. He will say, "Actually there is not an outside master. But you can see the essence of the practice of Taoism in some people. You can see the essence of Taoism in someone who is further along the path." Not the adoration, but the learning is what is important. "Every three men who are walking [by me], there's always one that's my teacher. I would say that every man is my teacher." But most importantly for Gia-fu, "Nature is my teacher."[3]

With nature as the central teacher, he also learns and profits from meditation, group meetings, walking, tai chi, calligraphy and, in the first year in Colorado, completion of the Chuang Tsu book, *Inner Chapters*. A small group works with him and Jane on the translation in the evenings. When it's time for calligraphy and photographs, Gia-fu and Jane work as they did in Vermont on the first book, each on his or her respective tasks. This one seems harder because Chuang Tsu, in Jane's eyes, "is very strange...less accessible" than Lao Tsu and the *Tao Te Ching*. Chuang Tsu, who allegedly lived from about 370 to 301 BCE, was to Lao Tsu what Plato was to Socrates. The *Inner Chapters* of his teaching consist of the part of his work that scholars acknowledge to be written by him because of the consistency and coherence of form and expression. Some of the later chapters, scholars believe, could have been written by other people.

Humorous, skeptical, and elusive, Chuang Tsu is much appreciated by Gia-fu. He resonates to Chuang Tsu's words, parables, and startling insights. Jane illustrates the translations with her funny, odd pictures of bones, chickens running around, cow weathervanes. They all fit the text perfectly.

In addition to the general routine and working on the book, Jane and Gia-fu continue to take a few trips. Sometimes other Stillpointers travel with them; sometimes they go alone. They travel to Newfoundland, San Francisco, Santa Fe, and the Grand Canyon. A few months prior to one trip to the Northeast, Gia-fu encourages his friend Tran Van Dinh, journalist, professor, and former diplomat with the Embassy of Vietnam in Washington, DC, to meet him at Amherst the next summer. He writes "I want you to come to assist me in Taoism workshop—your 'Tao of Watergate' [essay] is very beautiful."[4]

Gia-fu and Jane also spend quite a bit of time at home in the community. As happened in Los Gatos, the whole community sometimes goes camping. One place especially memorable lies over the Sangre de Cristo Range west of Cottonwood Pass, a few hours' drive from Manitou Springs. A beautiful, pristine area, it's full of aspen groves and beaver ponds, a perfect setting for walking, hiking, fishing, and canoeing. They set up tents and create Stillpoint in that setting for a week or two.

Because of her experiences with summer camps and canoeing trips in New England and Wisconsin, Jane instigates many of these community outings. One winter she even gets Gia-fu on cross-country skis. Strapping on the long skis, he stands up uncertainly and tries to follow her instructions. He feels uncoordinated with his feet tied to these boards and alternately putts along and falls down. But he doesn't care about that; he gets up every time and keeps at it, enjoying the surprise of it all, and of course, he does it with all his being.

The Stillpointers all have jobs of varying kinds and for varying lengths of time. Judith and Chris sometimes teach tai chi at the Y, and she teaches bread-making, too. Others work when opportunity and skills match. In 1973 Gia-fu and Jane begin doing some teaching. First, through their ever-expanding network, they're invited to teach during the spring quarter at Thomas Jefferson College in Allendale, Michigan. Gia-fu teaches tai chi; Jane teaches a comparative course in Chinese philosophy and modern physics. Gia-fu's tai chi class fills with a hundred students and he has to hold class in the gym.

Gia-fu and Jane stay for a brief time in a house near the campus, but they soon decide they don't care for the house. It seems too dreary. A biology professor, Henry Cameron (Cam) Wilson, invites them to stay at his small home and they do, although they sleep on a mattress in the back of their station wagon parked just outside the house. It's a small-world encounter when Josie, Cam's wife, and Jane discover they had known each other back at the University of Wisconsin in the sailing club. And the small world turns unpredictable when, years later, Cam becomes a swami called Anantananda Muktananda.

In the summer of 1973, long before Cam makes the transition to swami, he brings a group of students to Stillpoint in Manitou Springs. There, the Stillpointers find the influx of new energy refreshing, and with the newcomers they continue their outdoor adventures—hiking, camping, fishing.

Gia-fu, however, seems to want more solitude, more quiet time, and more time to work on translations. After a couple of outings he begins to stay behind, working or hanging out in the sauna. At Esalen he had the renowned hot springs for soaking and at Los Gatos the hot tub and sauna, all of which he's missed. Here in Manitou Springs, it's not until the group builds a sauna that he can resume his treasured and, to him, essential practice.

During the 1973–74 academic year, Jane and Gia-fu teach a term at Colorado College, a small liberal arts college in nearby Colorado Springs. Again, Jane teaches a comparative course of quantum physics and Chinese philosophy, and she and Gia-fu coteach a tai chi class. The classes are a huge success; some of the students will remember them decades later. Long after Gia-fu's death, they will contact Jane to tell her how important she and Gia-fu were in their lives.

Because of his time at Esalen, his tai chi book, and now the *Tao Te Ching*, which is being translated into numerous languages and sold in many parts of the world, Gia-fu's name has become a familiar one in circles associated with tai chi and Taoism. There's a ready market for him in Europe, and he happily accepts invitations to teach there. Beginning in February 1974, he travels alone for a few weeks teaching his workshops in the Netherlands, Greece, Portugal, and Spain. He'll soon meet up with Jane in Paris, where together they'll lead more of the tai chi workshops.

While Gia-fu's schedule takes him to Barcelona, Jane is in London being hosted by Oliver Caldecott of Wildwood House, the British publisher for the *Tao Te Ching*. While there, Jane meets Fritjof Capra, a fellow physicist with interest in the Tao. It's during this visit that Jane encourages her publisher to publish a manuscript he showed her, Capra's book *The Tao of Physics*. Soon it will be published and will turn out to be another exceedingly popular book of the time, an innovative book linking physics and Taoism.

Flying to Paris to meet Gia-fu, Jane will later recall that she felt "a little scared, but eager to see him." She keeps a journal of the trip, not knowing that three decades later it will become a source of information for a book about Gia-fu. Gia-fu himself writes little about this trip.

Meeting in Paris, they're both glad to see each other's familiar faces in these foreign lands. They wend their way to their hotel and their hosts, Gabriel and Anne, who then take them out for what Jane describes as a "crazy supper" and post-supper singing in the park. Between Jane's rusty schoolroom French and Anne's rudimentary English, the two manage to communicate in "franglais."

This initial stay in Paris is a brief one, and the next morning Gia-fu and Jane make a mad rush by Métro to the Gare d'Orléans to catch a train for Blois in the Loire Valley. Even the smallest transaction takes effort, but Jane summons up French words to ensure they're on the appropriate train and to pay the fare.

The ancient town of Blois brings delectable food, good walking, and perfect scenes to photograph, including large trees and black-building silhouettes. It also becomes the scene of an intense argument springing up suddenly between Gia-fu and Jane. Later, it's hard to remember how it started, probably from some seemingly benign conversation, perhaps Gia-fu's assessment of the Barcelona workshop. The genesis fades but the angry moments remain etched in memory.

"Stop this ego trip!" Jane says to him. "You're playing 'guru' again!"

"You're the one who's sucking off who I am!" he angrily flings back at her.

"Who's really sucking off whom here?" comes the retort.

Another few verbal shots fired, the two realize they have to talk reasonably about whatever is underlying this anger. They talk at length, about the two of them together, about what Jane calls the "guru trip," about how Gia-fu sometimes feels used, too. Finally, the air feels clearer, some of the tension Jane's been feeling is released, and Gia-fu's more relaxed for the moment.

Gia-fu, however, struggles now and will continue to struggle with the tendency of others to put him in the guru role and his own ambivalence about it. On the one hand, he says he doesn't want to be considered a guru, a master. He himself doesn't believe in the kind of self-styled guru so popular these days. He rejects the adoration aspect of willing, seemingly mindless followers, yet he knows he has something to teach. But in the currency of the times, it's easy enough to be lured into the whole package. People long to adore someone, to put someone above themselves. And Gia-fu's personality, his way of drawing people in, the ancient wisdom he exudes, combined with his affinity for drama, for being on stage, make it even more difficult. Possibly even more so when he's in a new environment and the main attraction. The multifaceted Gia-fu will continue grappling with this issue off and on for the rest of his life, and it's most certainly a recurring theme on this trip.

The next day, February 26, to see the sights, they travel by taxi to Chambord, a Renaissance château that once served as a retreat for kings, particularly Louis XIV. It's huge, sprawling, and multistoried, full of ornate tapestries, furniture of the Louis XIV period, and numerous ceramic and porcelain pieces. Feeling saturated by all the riches they've seen inside, they leave the massive gray stone castle and walk in the woods and by the lake, Jane stopping to shoot photos. The sun's out, but the February wind blows cold and damp and leaving the chateau grounds for a big dinner seems a good idea.

This day, they're both feeling, acting odd. Gia-fu picks up on the discussion they've been having about each other, about the two of them together. He's trying to understand the trouble, acknowledge the bumpiness in their relationship, how they're getting along, or not. He tells Jane, "We're both kind of unmarriageable, so we have to try hard to tolerate each other." And for a while they do, because they also care about each other. Gia-fu even goes out to get travel information for their next few days, even though he doesn't particularly want to.

The travelers see the town of Tours before going back to Paris on a snowy March 1. Back in Paris they have a good part of the day to themselves. They walk past the Louvre, in the Jardin des Tuileries, down the Champs-Elysées, by the Arc de Triomphe, beautiful in the snow, "all like an etching," Jane writes. The beauty and sense of tranquility, however, become lost in a confused evening when they feel they're back among disorganized people. Traveling in a strange place and negotiating every transaction—small and large—in a foreign language, exhaust them. Here the bathtub's not clean and there's no breakfast except a scant bit of yogurt.

They're feeling tired, depleted even, and tension again bubbles up between them. And now they have another workshop. But before it begins, Gia-fu returns again to their earlier relationship discussion, how they affect each other. This time, he bluntly tells Jane, "You drag me down at workshops," his voice fast, staccato.

Jane thinks this is true sometimes but not always. She often has trouble during the first part of the workshops; she thinks the first part's awful. This may be because of her judgments about how Gia-fu is leading them.

But then she gets into them and moves with the energy there. She knows that if she's having trouble, that affects Gia-fu. And this holds true for the one coming up now.

The workshop begins, with Jane tired and hungry. For the first hour and a half she has trouble attending to what's going on. And then, finally, as she later writes, "flow starts—one of G's crazy dances—much better than tai chi, with which I'm somewhat bored." The workshop goes well and, for Jane, ends well, too. She feels even better after the excellent lunch of hors d'oeuvres, good red wine, mocha cake, and café au lait they share with an American history professor and a masseuse from the group. Jane thinks her French improves when she's "drunk a bit."

The afternoon begins with two hours of fine chanting, followed by a good talk about the yin and yang of masks and oneness, then more tai chi, push hands with partners. Workshop over for the day, the pair walk through the Paris evening to a mass at Montmartre's Basilique du Sacre Coeur, the Romano-Byzantine style basilica built atop the hill. Afterward, they visit a small Roman Catholic church, then have coffee in a Montmartre club before turning in for the night. Both are ready for sleep.

The next day brings more of the workshop and its completion. Then, workshop done, they're off to Scotland. Years later, when asked what the workshops were, Jane will say, "Tai chi, encounter…I don't remember. They were Gia-fu workshops!"

In this trip of less than a month, Gia-fu and Jane cover a lot of ground, geographically and emotionally. When they arrive at the airport to depart for England, they discover flights are delayed due to a British European Airways strike. It makes sense to spend the few extra hours in Paris, so they return, visiting Île de la Cité, the heart of Paris. There, to their delight, they see a bird market. Then to Notre Dame, lit and glowing in the sunset, an organ concert in progress. Later that evening on the boat train bound for London they meet three British men there for a British-French rugby game. Talking with these young men, they learn that eighteen of their friends from their home village, teammates, have died in a Turkish plane crash, just this past noon. It was a flight they took because of the same BEA strike that has put Gia-fu and Jane on the boat train with them.

How can they comfort? What can they say? But because they are Gia-fu and Jane, they offer what comfort they can in words and sit quietly with their grieving new acquaintances.

Arriving in Dover, Jane whizzes through immigration. For Gia-fu it's another story. He's taken aside and endures an hour's questioning: What is your business here? Why are you traveling from France to England? Where are you really from? Again and again. For an hour he patiently responds to questions. Finally, he's cleared to go.

Now in London via train, they then fly to Glasgow where they have dinner with a friend's parents. They stay the night in a cold rooming house where it's easy to imagine how cold, dark, and long the winters must be in this part of the world.

March 5 finds them in Edinburgh for a day and a night. Walking through this classic old city, they see the castle looming atop the hill, trees bare in the park, and the museum of Sir Walter Scott, Robert Burns, and Robert Lewis Stevenson in a sixteenth-century house. Another backdrop for another argument, the cold, cloudy day another setting for airing the unsettled feelings between the two.

As Jane later will write, she "hassles Gia-fu a lot" this morning. She thinks it may be because she's unsure about why she's here with him. Maybe deep down something's telling her it's time they part. But she doesn't know for sure.

They argue about the same things, the same themes. "You drain me."

"You're always putting yourself in the spotlight."

"You take too much."

Again, they talk. "It's difficult, us together. But at least we can be honest with each other."

"Yes. We have some major differences and they keep coming up. But because of that, we learn from each other."

More talk, more self-examination, more softening. They get it sorted for the time being as they walk down Royal Mile and up through Holyrood Park to Arthur's Seat. Jane takes pictures—the blacks, grays, and greens of the landscape and the funny-looking sheep. The light's good most of the time, now with some sun filtering through the clouds.

Next day after a hearty breakfast during which they see an old Scot put his cap over his teapot to keep it warm, they press on back to Glasgow and then to Dunoon. They're going to Dunoon to visit Jane's father's cousin, Paul Worth, a rugged eighty-two-year-old man who lives with his wife, Betty, on Loch Eck among snow-covered hills and fantastic scenery. The setting reminds Jane of northern California. There are even redwood trees, and they see two swans flying down the loch.

The visit, brief but delightful, includes a long drive in the highlands over narrow, winding lanes. Gia-fu takes it all in stride, including the long drive, which usually makes him antsy. Paul and Betty treat Jane and Gia-fu well, which Jane appreciates, especially since she's never met them before. For their part, Jane and Gia-fu put their problems aside to enjoy this wild, beautiful place and Paul and Betty's kindness.

Then it's back to Paisley, Glasgow, and on to London for an eventful last few days there. In London they go first to Wildwood House, sign books at the Village Bookshop, and then prepare for the final weekend workshop. It's a whirlwind.

A rainy Saturday and the last workshop. The small room won't allow for much tai chi, not with twenty people. All twenty sit in a circle on the floor. There's a psychiatrist; a fifty-seven-year-old Scot who hates his wife; a couple in their forties each with three marriages under their belts, who now are splitting up—he's tried suicide; a thin, wispy girl just out of a mental hospital; one hippie writer; one matron; one increasingly likeable tough girl; and others, one of whom Jane thinks of as "the usual bleeding heart, groovy-tripper mother."

Gia-fu starts the workshop, as usual. He gets the group talking, airing their feelings, then up and moving with some tai chi despite the cramped space, and more talking—encounter. The battling couple air some of their problems, some of their confusion. And although everyone does the same, it seems more intense for these two. Gia-fu coaxes it all out—the anger, disappointment, bitterness, and resulting misunderstandings—all of it out for inspection. From Jane's perspective it goes well, even the first part of the day that she usually thinks is awful.

The work continues the next day, addressing the confusion, working through emotions, both in group sessions and the limited tai chi, clearing that confusion away. And in fact the whole group seems clearer, lighter. Some express strong interest in coming to Colorado, to Stillpoint. This happens in most workshops; people appreciate the experience and they want more. Over the next few years, quite a number from the various workshops and tai chi camps make it across the Atlantic to Stillpoint.

And now on Monday, an auspicious event for Gia-fu. He and Jane are to have lunch with Joseph Needham, chemical embryologist and renowned Western sinologist whose life's work lies in the multivolume, pioneering *Science and Civilization in China* series.[5] A groundbreaking, ongoing work, it's Needham's response to the question that accompanied his startling discoveries about Chinese scientific and technological sophistication while directing the Sino-British Co-Operation Office in Chongqing during World War II. Printing, the magnetic compass, gunpowder, among many others inventions, were made in China long before the West even thought about them. So why, Needham asks, given traditional China's spectacular achievements, did the scientific and industrial revolutions occur in Europe and not in China? This question will continue to occupy him until his death in 1995, and his colleagues will carry on the research and writing even after.

Not knowing Jane would join them, Needham had planned to take Gia-fu to the dining commons at Cambridge University. But here in 1974, women are not allowed in the dining commons, so they agree to meet at a local restaurant. A big man with a shock of white hair parted on the right, he looks every bit the scholar he is. Walking into the lunch place, an old wine cellar with a good salad bar, he has to duck to clear the low white brick tunnel leading into the room. Seeing him, Gia-fu feels awed by the man's presence. It's his turn to feel that he's sitting at the feet of the master, this one a man of great intellectual accomplishment, one that furthers the West's understanding of the world's oldest civilization by leaps and bounds.

Gia-fu does manage to converse, although he drinks too much wine and acts a little odd, not quite himself. But the meeting goes well enough for Gia-fu to feel they've established a contact for possible future ventures. Sadly, this will turn out to be the only time Gia-fu and Joseph Needham meet.

The remaining few days in England give Gia-fu and Jane a chance for a little more sightseeing—Cambridge, East Anglia, Thetford Forest, Brandon Country Park, Castle Acre, and some priory ruins, which Jane thinks fantastic. She takes lots of photographs of the ruins on this cold, raw day, a day of soft light and a gloomy feeling helped along by stark trees and stone and brick buildings. Her very pores absorb how "the land feels old and very much lived in." And as always, while Jane takes pictures, Gia-fu walks.

Before returning to the U.S. Gia-fu and Jane meet again with Oliver from Wildwood House. He has copies of *Inner Chapters* fresh off the press, and he's quite pleased with it. So are the authors. They have supper with Oliver and Fritjof Capra and afterward go to Capra's lecture, "Taoism and Modern Physics." Jane thinks the talk quite good—a complex subject clearly put, and dear to her heart. Gia-fu also finds it good, stimulating. It seems a fitting way to finish their stay, for the next morning, March 14, 1974, they fly back to the U.S.[6]

So ends Jane's and Gia-fu's big trip. It has been their first time abroad together and, though they don't know it, also their last. The workshops will continue into the 1980s, though they won't be leading them together. Within a very short time they will part. But for now, the two wanderers head back to New York, then home to Stillpoint.

At Stillpoint, Judith notices that Gia-fu and Jane seem always to be fighting. It seems there's never a week in which they don't have a really hot confrontation over something. His patriarchal side and fiery nature come out in these arguments, really heating things up when it collides with Jane's own fieriness.

He yells, "Well, you do this! It's what the woman does! Why do you always deny this part of yourself?"

She yells back, matching his ferociousness, her anger fueled by her feeling that here the feminine gets distorted into traditional roles; women are not appreciated for their deeper aspects, their true nature. Yin balances yang, and it seems that here yang isn't balanced at all. To Jane, nature seems the only aspect in which yin can enter the equation here. That's good, but it's not enough.

This period holds conflict, seeds of which had been planted the previous fall, and it also holds change. Last September, Emily and Seichi had a baby, fitting with Gia-fu's ideal of beginning a hundred-family community. But over time the tension rises, not only between Jane and Gia-fu but also, in the eyes of some, between Jane, Emily, and Seichi. Tension seems increasingly to permeate the atmosphere. In retrospect, Chris will come to think that much of the community's energy went into trying to hold on to how things had been among them, attempting to keep things the same. The situation, however, is not the same. As recognition of this creeps in, it punctures their hopes, and their dreams for the long term slowly slip away. The point arrives when Emily and Seichi decide they cannot raise a baby in an atmosphere so full of tension and conflict, and they leave Stillpoint.

Judith observes that Gia-fu seems very much into himself. He spends his days walking and translating, spending time with the community in morning sitting meditations and when he returns from walking around four for his tea. After tea he works on his translations, one of which is a new translation of the *I Ching*, but this time with a more thorough, less hip approach. Then he sleeps.

And now others who have formed the core of Stillpoint for the past three years seem ready to go on to other things, to their next chapters, and they begin drifting away. Judith and Chris to California, others on their various, separate ways. Judith will later reflect that during her time at Stillpoint, she found in it a refuge, an opportunity to be still, to examine her life and what she wanted to do with it. Others shared this appreciation of the stillness and learning to listen to oneself, all part of the environment Gia-fu created. Judith's words, spoken two and a half decades later, point to what her time at Stillpoint and with Gia-fu meant in her life, and it's not unlike what many others will also say.

> It was kind of a pit stop. While I was there, my father died. It was a perfect environment for me to be able to integrate all that into my being and be in that. When I came out here [California] and was writing, I wouldn't have done that I don't think, if I hadn't kind of stopped in my life.[7]

For Chris, it's been a satisfying time, not the least of which was being with Gia-fu and being part of this community and its dynamics. And during this time he discovered carpentry, which will become his work for the future.

As these transitions are occurring and people are starting to leave, a few months after their return from Europe, Gia-fu and Jane receive an invitation to teach at Esalen from Gia-fu's old friend, Dick Price. Dick has been to Stillpoint to visit, both in Los Gatos and in Manitou Springs, but Dick and Gia-fu haven't seen each other often and this looks like a good opportunity.

This is the second time Gia-fu and Jane have been to Esalen together. The first was a brief trip a couple of years back. Now, in the summer of 1974, they plan to stay a month. It turns out to be a pivotal month, for when their workshops are done, the visit over, and the time comes to leave, Gia-fu leaves alone. Their creative work together on the *Tao Te Ching* and *Inner Chapters* completed, their arguments increasing in number and intensity, Gia-fu and Jane end their time together and go their separate ways. Jane stays on at Esalen, intent on following her own path, beginning with a deep exploration of what it means to be Cesarean-born. She will stay there, exploring, examining, taking workshops and trainings for the next couple of years, after which she will devote herself to writing, photography, and publishing. One of her books will be entitled *Different Doorway: Adventures of a Caesarean Born*, to be published in 1985, eleven years from now.

Her path will cross that of Anne and John Heider again at the Human Potential School in 1976 to 1978, in Mendocino, California, continuing the thread of her early connection with Anne at Girl Scout camps and the private school they both attended. She will also live with Judith and Chris in San Francisco for a year at the end of the decade. During her stay with them, her darkroom will burn down, destroying photographs, negatives, her work of many years.

Now in 1974, Gia-fu returns to Colorado, to his Stillpoint. And although most of the core group are now gone, new people continue to arrive. A new core forms. The community ebbs, flows, and continues on. Things continue to run their course.

CHAPTER TWELVE

A WORLD NEITHER
MADE NOR CHOSEN

When there is confusion, there is anxiety.
With anxiety, there is no hope.

—from Chapter 4, *Chuang Tsu: Inner Chapters*

H e can return to his homeland. Political machinations on the world's stage affect the Feng family again but, unlike those of the late 1940s and 1950s that stranded Gia-fu in the U.S., the current series of events works in their favor in some ways. Now in 1975, finally, after twenty-eight years away from China and his family there, Gia-fu can return.

The events leading to the reopening of China began officially with the 1972 week-long state visit by U.S. President Richard M. Nixon. Behind-the-scenes diplomacy and a substantial amount of unofficial advocacy, including years of effort by groups such as the Committee of Concerned Asian Scholars to loosen the U.S.'s rigid views of China, created an opportunity for Nixon's visit.[1] This happened despite U.S. involvement in Vietnam, despite the continuing Cultural Revolution, and despite the tension between China and the U.S. over Taiwan. Historic and auspicious, the president's visit capitalized on others' efforts and helped soften the hard lines between the two countries, reopening communication a little, eventually making it possible for some trade to resume. Most importantly for the Feng family, it eventually unlocked the doors allowing distant family members to write to each other and, ultimately, for Gia-fu's return after half of his lifetime away.

When Gia-fu learns that he can once again return to China, he writes to his family. And although their letters are vetted, censored, they continue for some time until Gia-fu can arrange his trip. It's enough in the meantime that they can at last hear from each other, see each other's handwriting, be in touch again.

Gia-fu knows the China he'll be returning to is different; what he can't know is how different. And indeed, he finds it profoundly altered, with changes he may never be able to fathom.

When he lands at the Shanghai airport on October 22, 1975, Gia-fu's anxiety increases. He struggles to suppress his expectations, alternating between overwhelming joy and the fear that coming back to this place, after all that's happened, brings. He wears a long beard, just like his father wore. He wears a big down jacket, the kind only foreigners wear. And most blatantly, he wears red trousers like a Taoist priest might wear. No one in China wears such clothing now. The clothes worn here come in dark neutral colors, dark blue, brown, and they're mostly made of cotton.

In the week that Gia-fu stays in Shanghai, he tries to learn all he can about what has happened to his family—to his father, his sisters, his brothers, nephews, and nieces in these years he's been away, especially in the years they couldn't communicate. He learns some of the story, but a high degree of distrust exists—not necessarily of the person but of telling anything to anyone, because a person with information, however seemingly innocent, is vulnerable. He can be persecuted. He can reveal something ostensibly unimportant, ordinary even. And this innocent information can cause harm to himself and others. Gia-fu understands that the siblings he's seeing again are not the same ones he left when he set sail on the USS *General Gordon*. These people, his family members, while happy to see him, are cautious, guarded, and more subdued than before.

Elder Sister's son suggests that perhaps Uncle Gia-fu will shave his beard. He tells his uncle that if he doesn't do this the Red Guard will likely do it for him. Gia-fu shaves, probably for the first time in many years. His nephew also suggests that Gia-fu wear less conspicuous clothing, and some of the time he does wear a blue Mao suit, but even so he still carries the air of a foreigner.

The family fortune is long gone, and their home belongs to the state. Many families now live in the formerly lovely, now run-down house on Avenue Foch. The idea of personal property belongs to the past, to a past his family believes is best forgotten. The 242 valuable paintings, even the very rare ones? Gone. The exquisite vases? Precious jade carvings, beautiful antique furniture? Disappeared. The library of 7,705 books, including many very rare ones from the Tang Dynasty and from other dynasties past? All vanished. All has been confiscated and taken away. But how? Gia-fu wants to know. The response is always a shrug. Well-founded fear of retribution, of further persecution, brings only silence about the atrocities and losses his family suffered.

Asked directly, "Brothers and sister, have you suffered?"

"Well, yes. The Red Guard stepped on our backs and then went away. But let's forget about that now. We are here together." Stepped on our backs? Gia-fu immediately grasps the literal and metaphorical meaning of these words. "Yes, Father died in 1970, and he was confined by the Red Guard. There is nothing more to say."

What further to ask, what to say?

Gia-fu goes with his young nephew to see Shanghai and its surroundings. His nephew takes him to various places, including the Friendship Store, and serves as a necessary guide to his uncle's once familiar home. As a foreigner, Gia-fu can buy things for himself and his family in the Friendship Store, things people who live here aren't allowed to buy and certainly can't afford. They're not even allowed in the store. These stores are for foreigners and Gia-fu is one. He feels he's treated somewhat like an official guest because he's a U.S. citizen, because China wants to put its best foot forward to show the world how advanced, how civilized it is, at least on the surface. It's a kind of "revolutionary diplomacy," Gia-fu thinks, through which China believes it's protecting itself from attack and criticism while continuing to pursue its revolutionary goals.

This revolutionary diplomacy gives Gia-fu special privileges—access to the Friendship Store, to hotel rooms, and to restaurants—but it prevents him from intimate contact with ordinary Chinese outside his family. It's an easily enforced segregation because when people learn he's American, they become careful, cautious; they pull back, afraid they can be accused of something through too close an association with this capitalist, imperialist foreigner. He sees this response fairly often when he shows up for early-morning tai chi in the park, even though he wears his Mao suit.

Gia-fu notices that Shanghai people in general, including his siblings, seem not quite "with it." He surmises they're not exactly unhappy or miserable but under considerable strain. Maybe, he thinks, it's the overcrowded situation almost everywhere. The parks are jammed with people. He sees hundreds of people meeting in storefronts after business hours, some of them spilling out onto the streets. To have their required daily meetings, people sit on counters, in alleyways, and down every lane. They simply have no other places to meet.

Everyone belongs to a unit, a group that one is assigned to, with group leaders who make sure members attend these daily meetings or study sessions. Certainly, this is a different kind of group than Gia-fu has been involved in and has led at Esalen, Stillpoint, in travels in Europe. These groups are mandatory, and everyone, everything, has to be accounted for, often in written reports. There's lots of self-criticism; people get a chance to criticize themselves before others take their shots. There's no real privacy, and there's an overall air of personal restraint. At the same time, people seem to feel they're in a constant state of emergency. Tranquility no longer exists in the China Gia-fu's now seeing. Mao's goal of shaking things up so everything is in what he calls a state of *luan*—chaos or confusion—seems to be working. And because of it, people are extraordinarily vigilant.

Behavior toward foreigners holds special importance in the study sessions, especially for tourist guides and others in close contact with tourists. These people are required to report in minute detail every contact with a foreigner. Gia-fu observes that when he walks into the hotel restaurant, he often finds everybody busily writing like school children in a classroom. Once he's noticed, one of the staff stops writing long enough to wait on him.

He also finds people less polite, more outspoken, and very accustomed to criticizing anything foreign. When he brings the French bicycle he's bought for his nephew to his hotel, people stand around criticizing the French workmanship, giving the impression this foreign bicycle is worthless. Exasperated, Gia-fu thinks that now there's no such thing as doing a favor or being polite in Shanghai.

The week in Shanghai up, Gia-fu leaves without all the answers he craves, the same answers he fears. He travels to Beijing where he's planning to meet another brother. They're meeting in Beijing because at this time foreigners can travel only to approved places in China, the more attractive and prospering places, and Beijing is one of these.

Now, after almost thirty years apart the two brothers meet in cold, wintry Beijing. The years alone do not separate them. Each brother's experiences create a gulf in understanding that cannot be completely bridged despite their deep bond and unwavering caring for each other. Perhaps this closeness makes it even more difficult to comprehend the impossibility of sharing what has really happened.

However, they share what they can as they walk Beijing's main streets for hours. In the bitter cold of the bleak wintry day, they learn much from each other, with Gia-fu sensing that complete freedom to speak does not exist for them.

Even so, Gia-fu pleads, "Brother, tell me what has happened. What have you suffered? What torture have they put you through? Please tell me all you can."

His brother gives only a cursory reply but Gia-fu can begin to guess, to glimpse what his family has endured. But it's difficult for him to grasp how their family background and education have put his siblings under such a microscope of suspicion. The very accomplishments in which Feng Chong-ching gloried for his children place them in the worst possible light in this China, a situation unimaginable for any proud parent, particularly one who values education as highly as Feng Chong-ching did. Now there's the next generation to wonder about. What will their chances for education, for a full, satisfying life, be?

Just as Gia-fu's trip to his homeland makes possible his first meetings with his China-born nephews and nieces in Shanghai, in Beijing he meets one of his nieces, Yun ke. As with many Chinese youths, Yun ke's education has been interrupted by the Cultural Revolution and the consequent demise of China's educational system. Now in 1975 at age twenty, the bright, diligent Yun ke works a machine, punching out electrical components in the Bureau of Beijing's Electrical Components Number Nine Factory in a Beijing suburb. She's allowed to join her father and Uncle Gia-fu in Beijing and will also go on the tour to other approved sites with them.

Gia-fu and Yun ke hit it off immediately. He sees that she isn't wearing the ubiquitous dark clothes and comments on this. "Why is everybody wearing the dark-colored clothes, but only you wear the red square shirt? This should be the right cloth for a girl!"

Yun ke responds with a smile, happy to finally meet this charming, charismatic uncle she's heard so much about. She impresses him with her nascent independence, her willingness to stake out what territory she can for herself without going over the line, quite a feat in this environment. His comment to his brother understates his assessment, "This one is normal!" But Yun ke considers it high praise indeed, remembering her uncle's words three decades later.

Having brought gifts for his family, Gia-fu asks Yun ke what she would like to have. Her response pleases and surprises him. "Nothing. I'm just happy to see you."

A few more days together seem to solidify the almost instant bond between Gia-fu and his young niece. He worries that she won't have an opportunity to get a good education. Perhaps it's the combination of their rapport, his concern for her future, and his tendency to do things off the cuff that push him to ask if he can adopt Yun ke. Whatever his motivation, he puts forward the startling request to his brother and he also talks with Yun ke.

To Yun ke he says, "You have to take more study. If there is not a chance in China, you can go to the U.S., and I can help you." He advises her, attempting to nurture the seeds of independence he's detected, "You should not always do things just because others tell you to. You should be thinking for yourself." Reflections of what Gia-fu's worked so hard to do himself, the freedom he's sought in his life.

Gia-fu's words make an indelible impression on his niece. The regime under which she lives drums just the opposite into everyone's head and metes out harsh punishment for disobedience. This exotic uncle of hers, however, seems very definite about the importance of not blindly doing things just because people expect you to, of not following the rules without giving them any thought.

While these words impress Yun ke, they also reveal another reason for Gia-fu's difficulty in understanding and accepting what's going on in China and what's happened to his family. He's traveled a long way to find freedom for himself, invested in years of self-examination and reflection in San Francisco, at Esalen, at Stillpoint, his own community. He bases his whole existence on this internal freedom. He's unable to accept the reality of such incredible external control, the fact of the overwhelming powers at work in China now, and the dire consequences awaiting anyone who strays from the rule, the word of Mao. He hears about it, he sees it at every turn, but somehow he still can't accept it. His experience in such different circumstances has led him to an ever-expanding sense of self and of freedom. His niece's experience has not.

Her father feels the wrenching conflict of wanting the best for his daughter and not wanting to be so far apart from her. But acknowledging to himself that Yun ke could have more opportunities, especially for education, and considering that Gia-fu has no child of his own, he agrees to Gia-fu's request. "Yes," he tells his brother. "She can get further education if you can take her to the U.S." Agreed on the goal, the brothers understand that numerous steps lie between the intention and its becoming a reality. This will take a little time.

The travelers soon set out on the trip planned primarily by Yun ke. The challenge has been to plan an interesting route in light of limitations on where foreigners can travel. Even the Chinese need special permits to leave their home, to go to another town, city, or province. They'll go by train to Dazhai, a model agricultural farm in Shanxi Province in the north, then west and south to Xian in Shaanxi Province. From there they will head on to Changsha, where Mao attended the Hunan Number 1 Teachers' Training School and was later teacher and principal, and nearby Shaoshan, Mao's birthplace—both in Hunan Province in south-central China. If time permits they'll also go to Guilin in the Guangxi Zhuang Autonomous Region in the south. Given his keen interest in history, Gia-fu particularly wants to go to Xian because of its role as capital during thirteen dynasties, including the fascinating Tang Dynasty (618–907 CE). It's also the eastern end of the Silk Road. He's to be disappointed, however, because he'll find many places in Xian closed, and even more closed to foreigners. Revolutionary diplomacy?

They visit the Dazhai farm where farmers are sent to learn about the best, most forward-looking techniques, following Mao's directive "Learn from Dazhai." Known for its plentiful crops and well-maintained fields, Dazhai also features engineering feats with dams and aqueducts. The farmers here seem to work day and night, literally moving mountains to make more area for farming. Loudspeakers have been installed to blast out music and motivational slogans to encourage the workers. Gia-fu seems impressed, although he can't know that in only a few years Dazhai will be seen as the failure that all the large-scale Chinese farm efforts become. The pressure to be perfect, the overworking of the fields and people, and construction with shoddy materials will all take their toll.

But for now, he learns about plans and dreams from the young guide, and he watches the commune workers hard at it. Their backbreaking jobs seem endless, causing Gia-fu to think of philosopher Martin Heidegger's words, "Man is always in a world he neither made nor chose." Despite the world they find themselves in and with little hope of changing it, these workers labor on, and to go forward they believe they are working for something beyond themselves. Gia-fu thinks about how this differs from his own situation in his adopted country, where he's free to maintain his own life space and his freedom of choice. Although born into this world not of his own making, in his adopted country he's free to remake it as best he can. He may not have chosen to be born, but he can choose his own lifestyle.

But he thinks his adopted country could learn something from the communes, perhaps something about togetherness, the communal bringing up of children, and the general enrichment of human relationships. He acknowledges the mistakes the U.S. has made and continues to make but places great value on his ability to choose, to speak out, and to promote or participate in new ideas that emerge. "The soul of the United States of America is still alive and well after two hundred years," Gia-fu writes.

The guide, a local peasant, tells him that in five years the farming will be 100 percent mechanized. She literally glows as she talks about the commune, impressing him with her sensitivity, strength, and toughness. He even considers her elegant. This is a far cry from his attitude toward other peasants in his earlier years, and he's very aware of it. He recalls being fifteen and visiting his ancestral village. There he treated the farmers and their families condescendingly, as if they were stupid—or worse. And they dared not speak up at that time. The social gulf was too wide; there were too many strictures and experiences telling them not to. His attitude toward the local girls in Kunming also comes to mind. Yes, he realizes, he's changed, and he's glad of it.

Yet his own internal landscape still holds puzzles, some prompted by being in this land that should be so familiar, but isn't. In this China the way people address each other has changed, and the manner of address naturally affects how one relates to others. It therefore causes him to think about who he is in relation to others, in relation to himself in the varied circumstances in which he's found himself in the five and a half decades of his life. He knows he can no longer call people *Xian Sheng*, meaning "before born," or *Fu Ren*, meaning "assisting person," or Mr./Miss/Mrs., which soon will mean "wife of" or "Madame," or *Xiao Jie*, small sister. The demand for equality in this classless society overrides these traditional forms, forms that reflect the old inequality of a hierarchical, class-based society.

Addressing people as "comrade" turns out to be not quite proper either. Eventually he learns the correct method, which is to use *Lao* for males and *Siao* for females. *Lao* means "old," and Gia-fu recalls that in his younger days males used this term when they referred to their intimate contemporaries and male members of the lower classes—servants and others. But then the term was impolite if used in formal or official meetings. First names are not often used here as they are in the casual West. Lao in front of one's name now suggests informality and equality.

Siao means "little." In his earlier days, people used Siao to refer to youths, like juvenile servants or errand boys. No comparable term exists for females; thus Siao is used to evoke a sense of equality between the sexes and among age groups.

Remembering that linguist Benjamin Lee Whorf discovered it is language that determines what we think, that the structure of language structures our thoughts, Gia-fu muses on what he's learning about names and forms of address now. And he recalls an exercise at Esalen in which participants walked around the room calling their own names, whether nickname, first, or last names. When Gia-fu called himself Feng Gia-fu in the Chinese way, he felt a much stronger sense of identity than when he called himself Gia-fu Feng.

The travelers find further opportunities for constrained sharing as they travel, and they take photographs in approved areas, of approved subjects, capturing memories of their limited time together. Gia-fu has trouble understanding that he cannot take pictures of anything he wants. He's told this again and again, sometimes by his niece, sometimes by others who aren't as polite. The government does not wish to have pictures taken of anything traditional or, in their eyes, primitive or antiquated; these scenes are not for Western eyes. Anything classic, traditional, or quaint is off limits. They want only to project the image of glorious China as modern, prosperous, and efficient.

A photo opportunity obviously on the approved list features a statue of Mao. The resulting small black-and-white photo shows the travelers in Shaoshan standing by a typically enormous, highly idealized statue of Mao. Posing by the dominating figure, Gia-fu wears his Western-style down parka and the stubble of a newly begun beard. He stands by Yun ke, whose long braids rest on the shoulders of her modest plaid jacket. They face the camera with unflinchingly neutral expressions.

Gia-fu envies the ability to converse with interpreters in different languages and dialects. He tries to say the right things, and once while in Mao's home village he comments to their guide, "It is important that one work thoroughly through the thought of Chairman Mao."

The guide approves, but he voices his approval not to Gia-fu but to Gia-fu's companions. Gia-fu desperately tries to break through this formality, to have a direct, spontaneous conversation. He sings some old tunes he remembers from his youth. A mistake. The songs are considered romantically decadent, and the situation becomes even more awkward. Gia-fu tells himself he should have learned some revolutionary songs before coming here.

Again asking about the Cultural Revolution, Gia-fu signals that he knows it's been a difficult time and he wants to know more. But what he hears are not the kinds of things he's heard in the U.S. about the Cultural Revolution. In the U.S., it's been romanticized by some, denounced by others. But no one there knows the full situation. Gia-fu's concern about his family and his homeland deepens. And there's nothing he can do about it.

In Changsha City, the third stop on the tour, the cold, rainy weather depresses the travelers. Yun ke, having only ten days off from the factory, must return before their tour is complete. Although Gia-fu doesn't want her to go, he's learned enough to know she must, that he can't interfere in these matters.

After a sad, resolute farewell, Yun ke flies back to Beijing, and Gia-fu continues alone to the beautiful Li River in Guilin. But it's a lonely trip, and after a day or two he writes to his brother to tell him he has no interest in traveling alone, so he's going on to Hong Kong to visit their sister before going home to the U.S.

Hong Kong. "Fragrant Harbor" in English. Still a Crown Colony of the United Kingdom courtesy of the British-instigated Opium Wars of the early 1860s, it will remain so for another twenty-two years. In 1997, it will revert to China's oversight as a Special Administrative Region. Then it will have special autonomy under the "One China, Two Systems" policy until 2047. The territory comprises more than 260 islands, but it's to Hong Kong Island, the place people think of when the name Hong Kong is mentioned, that Gia-fu's bound.

It's the first time in many years that these two siblings have so much time to spend together, to talk, to catch up. His sister has visited him a few times in the U.S. because she and her husband, whose work involves travel, periodically go there. But this time is special. Brother and sister can spend hours talking, just the two of them, and the hours they spend sharing their thoughts and innermost feelings renew and strengthen the bond between them. Neither has been subjected to the kind of persecution other family members have endured. Neither knows the full story, but they tell each other what they do know about family and share much more about themselves.

Knowing her brother's habits of taking long walks and not eating supper, Younger Sister fends off social arrangements with old friends and relatives for much of the five-day visit. Her maid prepares Gia-fu's food as he likes it, without salt or soy sauce, which Gia-fu very much appreciates. And he does take long walks. Fortunately, footpaths near his sister's luxurious high-rise apartment in Hong Kong's hills lead to a lovely park on The Peak, a favorite and beautiful high point of Hong Kong.

But aside from these more peaceful walks, the chaos of the city, the noise, the industrial fumes bother him. And although Younger Sister takes care to provide private, quiet time for the two of them, Gia-fu still finds the steady phone calls, the requests for help, the social demands on her because of her high social status a dramatic contrast to the kind of life he's chosen to live. Still, Gia-fu appreciates the time with his sister and his brother-in-law, when he's not working.

When it's time to leave, his sister takes him to the airport. There's a long line at the ticket counter, and Gia-fu takes his place at the end. But Younger Sister goes up to the counter and waves his passport and ticket in front of the clerk, shouting something that Gia-fu can't quite discern in the surrounding chaos and noise. The clerk knows what she wants, and acknowledging her VIP status, he beckons Gia-fu to come forward. He quickly leads Gia-fu through the routine, and since he carries only a knapsack and no luggage to check, he's through in minutes. Uncertain about how he feels with this special treatment, Gia-fu nonetheless appreciates his sister's efforts on his behalf.

Brother and sister know they love each other, and they also know their lives seldom bring them together. Gia-fu recognizes how they both detach from their emotions to cope with this situation, trying to hold the reality of their lives and the emotion they feel in some kind of balance. They've had plenty of practice in their difficult years of leave-taking, not knowing when or if they'll see each other again. Gia-fu's recent partings with siblings in China still haven't completely prepared him for yet another one. But they say good-bye, and on this twenty-second day of November 1975, he boards the huge airliner to return home.

The flight home brings an encounter with a new immigrant on his way to the U.S. Gia-fu asks how it's possible for a Chinese to emigrate these days. The young man refers to the official line of revolutionary diplomacy that's intended to win the hearts and minds, as well as the money, of the overseas Chinese. His father owns a restaurant in New York City and must have connections.

Gia-fu is asked by his fellow travelers to ask the young man, who hasn't yet learned English, how he feels about his newfound country. Gia-fu reluctantly asks him and he responds, as Gia-fu roughly interprets, "Do I need to say anything! It goes without saying." He's left his wife and five children behind in their home in Fukien Province, and he proudly shows Gia-fu their picture. Another family separated.

Back at home, Gia-fu writes Yun ke a letter of invitation to the U.S. Using the letter, Yun ke gains acceptance to Washington University. She completes her visa application, and to everyone's surprise is very quickly granted a visa. She tries to contact her uncle Gia-fu in the U.S. with no luck. As days, weeks, and months pass without a reply, her distress grows. The visa's expiration date drawing near, Yun ke applies for a renewal. It's granted, and again everyone's surprised. But still no word from Gia-fu. Yun ke can only wonder, bewildered by her uncle's silence. So many questions arise for her: When he saw his family in China, what did he really see? Is he so ambivalent about the family after the China visit that he can't face the situation directly? Did he blame the Cultural Revolution's victims for loss of the family's fortunes? Is it just a horribly unfortunate coincidence that her uncle cannot communicate at this critical time?

Abandoned by her uncle and potentially stranded in China unless she takes quick action, Yun ke turns to her fourth aunt—her mother's sister who lives in Hong Kong. She asks her aunt if she can come stay with her and attend the university. Her aunt gladly takes her in, and although it's in Hong Kong and not the U.S., Yun ke does get her education.

Never knowing what happened, thirty years later Yun ke will surmise that Gia-fu must have changed his mind about having his niece come to the U.S., about adopting her. She will never know for sure. That Gia-fu always sends postcards from the various places he travels in Europe and other parts of the world adds to her puzzlement.

A decade later, in 1984, when his younger brother comes to the U.S. on a business trip, he telephones Gia-fu. He's unable to come to Colorado, and Gia-fu's unable to travel to Indiana, but Gia-fu phones his brother often while he's in the U.S. They have good conversations, full of care and concern for each other.

But Gia-fu's struggle with his feelings about his family have surfaced and continue to surface along the way: the recurring dreams, nightmares about not getting to his mother's side before she died, his flight from being "a bird in a cage" to Kunming, his changing relationship with his father upon his return to Shanghai after the war, and again in 1963 when Eldest Sister and her son first arrive in the U.S. and Gia-fu avoids meeting them, leaving for Japan only two days after their arrival. Eldest Sister assesses Gia-fu's behavior thirty-two years later. "When he came to the U.S., he changed. He was afraid to see me because I would not approve of how he dressed and his long hair."

Yet Chao-hua—that is, C.H.—said, "Gia-fu [was] her pet."

To which, Eldest Sister responded, "Yes, because we [had] the same interest. We love literature, but all the others are engineers."[2]

When he returns from China, he tells Eldest Sister and C.H. that things are not good in China. He's worried. Yet he writes, "I find myself gradually detached from my siblings and my old traditions." Further, he writes about being relieved when he's denied a pass to visit his parents' graves. But was this detachment or too much grief to bear? Or does one follow the other?

He asked to adopt Yun ke. He took gifts to his siblings, nieces, and nephews. He continues to write, albeit brief notes, to his brothers and sisters there. He continues to call and write occasionally to C.H. He may try to distance himself in various ways, but he remains Third Brother. And in his own way, he still expresses caring for his family.

Upon his return from China, fellow Stillpointers and other friends observe Gia-fu's depression, his sadness. It doesn't begin to dissipate for a long, long time, and it never fully disappears. Yet when he writes of this visit, he often writes glowingly about the changes there, about Mao, about all the things that restrict the freedom he so loves. One thing among many that he writes is this, rationalizing Mao's theory of keeping people feeling a sense of constant emergency:

> Psychologically, it is a part of the idea of continuous revolution to keep people from complacency by creating emergencies. The concept of emergency is now very much a part of [the] human potential movement. Studies show that we produce much more efficiently during the wartime than during the ordinary years when we are only operating with a few percentage points of our real potential…

> The violence sounded repulsive at first, but after I saw some creeping corruption surfacing, such as a slight overcharge by the tourist guide and petty stealing by the hotel maid when I passed through Kwang-chow on my way out, I am convinced that the people have to be kept constantly vigilant…

Not having known Gia-fu myself, the contradiction leapt out at me decades later as I read his papers and talked with his friends and family. I wondered if he was trying to protect his family in China. I wondered if he really believed what he wrote, if he believed that comparison between Mao and the human potential movement, if he thought people needed to be treated violently to avoid corruption. This was the puzzle that prompted me to turn to Fourth Brother Chao-hua, C.H., his response becoming a thread, a theme throughout my search. Again, I remember. "Uncle," I asked, "how could Gia-fu write such positive things about what was going on in China, knowing the troubles your family experienced, and at the same time be so depressed when he returned?" And C.H., cogitating on this question for a moment, replied with a sigh. "Ah, Carol. People are multifaceted. And Gia-fu, even more so."

CHAPTER THIRTEEN

TRICKSTER AT WORK

…Emperor Fu Shi was calm and tranquil when asleep, and simple and direct when awake. Sometimes he would take on the spirit of a horse, and sometimes that of an ox. His wisdom could be trusted. His virtue was genuine. He was beyond distinguishing between what a man is and what he is not.

—from Chapter 7, *Chuang Tsu: Inner Chapters*

The rhythm of life at Stillpoint on Ruxton Avenue in the second half of the 1970s sees the continued ebb and flow of community, the comings and goings of Gia-fu as he continues his tai chi workshops all over Europe, always returning home to Manitou Springs. This half of the decade also holds a gradual movement toward another step in Stillpoint's evolution, evidence of which is to soon appear.

Micheline Wessler is now Gia-fu's companion and soon-to-be coteacher. He and Mich, as she's most often called, met at one of his tai chi workshops in Louisville, Kentucky, in the mid-1970s, after Jane left Stillpoint for good. It was Gia-fu's only workshop in Louisville, and Mich attended with a friend.

Gia-fu took an immediate interest in Mich, impulsively inviting the interesting twenty-four-year-old to go with him on his upcoming European tour. But she didn't have a passport, so she couldn't go. Instead she moved to Stillpoint. Easily, naturally, their relationship grows, reflecting their closeness in heart, spirit, and their work together. For her, as a young adult, the relationship helps bring her further into realizing who she is. For Gia-fu, Mich can be a tender companion, a partner, and the current female head of Stillpoint. More than thirty-five years later, future Stillpointer Tomi Smith will recall how Gia-fu would say, "Mich and I are of one mind."[1]

At Stillpoint Gia-fu teaches Mich to teach tai chi so they can both work with the camps, which they do within a year or two. Gia-fu likes teaching in Europe more than in the U.S. and, mirroring this preference, his popularity there continues to grow. Germany, Holland, Denmark, Spain, and France number among the countries with centers and communities interested in the kind of work Gia-fu does. Through word of mouth, interest snowballs as different students continue to set up ever more camps. Mich and Gia-fu spend about two weeks in each camp, flying from place to place. A continual outgrowth of the camps, numbers of European students come to Stillpoint, some for weeks, some for years. In the mid-1970s Americans outnumbered Europeans. Over the years this ratio steadily shifts to more Europeans, reflecting Gia-fu's growing overseas reputation.

In characteristic Stillpoint cadence, new people as well as regular Stillpointers arrive and leave. Of those who come for frequent extended stays, several will hold memories and images of the time that decades later will help tell Gia-fu's story. One such person showing up at the Ruxton Avenue Stillpoint in 1976 is Tomi Smith, also called Onny. From Texas and newly divorced, Tomi records in her journal that she's seeking "the next chapter" of her life. She arrives on Monday, March 29, wanting to see what Stillpoint's all about. Gia-fu happens to be home, and he's the one to greet her. As bookkeeper, Mich responds to Tomi's questions about the fee structure for staying there: seven dollars a day for the first week, and after that, if she works, it's three dollars a day.

On this first visit Tomi stays only one night. Awaking for morning meditation, she joins others in the east-facing meditation room while it's still dark. As the dawn fills the glass-enclosed room, Tomi and the others finish their meditation, leaving the room as the sun ascends, its rays now streaming through the windows. Anyone who had been at Los Gatos would notice similarities between early morning meditations there and those experienced here.

After breakfast and a walk up the mountain, Tomi returns to find Gia-fu, who wants to show her the library. The scholar in him prizes books, journals, newsmagazines, and he's always encouraging Stillpointers to read, to consider, to know what's going on in the world. He gives Tomi a book he thinks explains Tao well. It's Philip Rawson and Laszlo Legeza's *Tao: The Chinese Philosophy of Time and Change.*[2]

In the day and a half Tomi spends at Stillpoint, she watches and also participates in its daily life: one Stillpointer gives a massage to another; a guy who comes in for a tai chi lesson later plays the guitar and sings for a while; she takes a sauna with another, and they shower; people go out to walk, to work, they return, and the next morning, there's the group meeting again. Tomi's heard a little background on the group sessions: that they focus on the here and now, and how members function in the Stillpoint community.[3] She's had some experience with group work at Esalen, back in 1972. Participants realize the sessions present a safe, controlled opportunity to release anger and resentment that build up in a community living closely together. It's no different here at Stillpoint. Tomi notices that as some problems start to come out, attention shifts to a couple of people. One tells another what he thinks, what's bothering him: "Get off my back about what I eat. You think you know what's good for me?"

More comments come, direct, not softened in any way. Gia-fu acts as the mediator or bridge, keeping the talk going. But at an acutely timed point, in his usual blunt style, he lobs a comment of his own at one of the guys—Bob, "You suck, but you won't be sucked in."

It's quiet in the room. The feeling is thick but to Tomi, not uncomfortable. It feels to her as though an *expression* of feeling fills the room. Gia-fu directs a further observation toward Bob: "You won't accept what people say, but you change it, try to control it *and* whoever says it."

Gia-fu's approach is pure Gestalt, first encountered at Esalen with Fritz Perls and others. It of course has his own touch, in keeping with Gestalt beliefs in the critical dimension of the group leader's authenticity. And further reflecting Gia-fu's authenticity, doctor, writer, and Gestalt practitioner Claudio Naranjo will later explain that a Gestalt/Taoist approach means "a course of appropriate action dictated by deep intuition." He will describe Gestalt with the following formula, which, depending on who one asks, fits Gia-fu well:

$$\text{Gestalt therapy} = [\text{Awareness}/\text{Naturalness} + \text{Support}/\text{Confrontation}] \text{ Relationship}$$

Gia-fu is confronting Bob, and in Naranjo's terms "eliciting genuine expression and confronting the dysfunctional," using negative reinforcement or "ego reduction."[4] This approach seems to hit home for Bob, who sits uncannily still, as if absorbing the shock of its truth. It hits home for Tomi, too, who immediately thinks of a particular person in her life who, in her opinion, does this very thing. As for Bob, he continues sitting silently, as if unable to find a response. The exchange is left at that for now, to be continued later.

With only a taste, an appetizer, of what Ruxton Avenue and Gia-fu offer, Tomi leaves after little more than twenty-four hours, driving back to Texas to take care of some things. By April 10 she's back at Stillpoint, where she'll live for extended periods over the next decade. At morning meditation a couple days after her return, she and Gia-fu are the only ones there. He shows her another tai chi form, Cloud Hands, and asks about the massage work she does and her interest in touch. She demonstrates with face massage, something she'd learned recently at an Esalen work-study program. He shows her Oriental massage, what she describes in her journal as a "type of pressure on my knees—could feel the energy." Stillpointers, learning from each other.[5]

Gia-fu remains, as always, clearly the male figure at Stillpoint, echoed in the way he later signs a letter to Richard Hoffman: "The Patriarch of Stillpoint Global Village."[6] And from the mid-1970s to the decade's end, Mich is the female figure in running Stillpoint and helping people through their issues—another young, bright, interesting woman, similar to Jane in these aspects but possessed of a clearly different personality. Both, however, during their respective times at Stillpoint, are placed in roles calling for experience beyond their years.

Stillpointers will long remember how adept Gia-fu can be with groups and individuals, how he can be very social and playful. He can meet and speak with parents of students at Stillpoint in ways they can understand. His love of theater and his skill at taking any number of different parts, most likely attributable to his devotion to Chinese opera, fuels the role playing that goes with Gestalt. And he has an ability to step out of his traditional Chinese upbringing yet bring the ancient teachings into modern daily life in ways that help people make sense of who they are and how they want to live their lives. This skill is that blend of Taoism and Gestalt, the possibilities within which so captivated Gia-fu early on at Esalen when he first encountered Gestalt therapy.

Now in the summer of 1977, as many as fifty people live in the house and about 75 percent of them are Europeans, mostly from Scandinavia and Germany. Everyone in the Stillpoint community has a part in making it run smoothly, whether it's doing yard work, shopping, cleaning, gardening, errands, or other regular tasks. Assignments vary, but the critical thing is that people take their responsibilities in and to the community seriously, even if they aren't particularly skilled. Tomi, however, devotes her considerable skill to making the kitchen function—organizing, baking, cooking—but she also does yard work, errands, and other things at times, including the bookkeeping for a while. Mich is the overall manager, and others—Don LeVack in particular, a recent graduate with a psychology degree from Ohio State University who moved to Stillpoint in March 1977—will soon take on an increasingly active role.

When Don moves in he immediately feels at home. Perhaps it's because of the dreams he'd been having about the big old house—vivid, recurring dreams about specific rooms and arrangements of rooms, immense rooms that he feels dwarfed by, dreams that came a few weeks before he sets foot in the house. When he actually enters it he feels the cloak of familiarity all around him. Later reflection will bring him to feel the dreams signified his "having a place to grow up in."

Soon Don is taking care of financial matters. Gia-fu seems to trust him, maybe because Don can be detached and doesn't idolize Gia-fu. He, as with so many others, appreciates the environment Gia-fu provides—the quietness and solitude, as well as the emphasis on walking and reading. Two decades later, Don will also recall the way Gia-fu worked with people, how he could "get right in there—get through all that crap." He'll ascribe Gia-fu's skill in part to "his civility toward others, which could be attributed to his Asian upbringing. He made people feel so comfortable, they each felt special." And through all of Don's numerous departures to various other places and returns to Stillpoint, Gia-fu will always give Don "the feeling of being extremely welcomed." Being at Stillpoint with Gia-fu will always feel like home. He can go there anytime, with no questions asked.

Of course, Gia-fu's other dimensions stay front and center, especially his use of "a confrontive kind of therapy," a signature Gestalt approach. He'll recall that Gia-fu's "major focus was on interaction and getting through people's bullshit" to destroy their preconceptions about how things are. Getting rid of preconceptions allows more realistic and authentic functioning, makes it possible to take life as it comes rather than building up images of what one thinks it is, fears it is, wants it to be. Encounter and role playing both help with cutting through such baggage. To do this, Gia-fu takes a certain attitude or stance and the group responds. The sessions can get pretty heated, with people becoming very angry—screaming and crying. But Gia-fu seems to have a knack for knowing who can handle the heat and who can't. And after the session Gia-fu and the others can just "drop it and be friendly." [7]

Sometimes after an intense session, Gia-fu will prepare breakfast for the group—eggs, tofu, spinach—or the group cooks breakfast together. The contrast between the intense encounter experience and the pleasant breakfast—confrontation versus civility—is so great it leaves a lasting impression on some group members. These extremes may, indeed, be one factor that keeps people at a distance from Gia-fu. Perhaps he does off-the-wall things sometimes to counter the guru image. Along those same lines, Don thinks the extremes help Gia-fu keep the group from devolving into some kind of a cult around him as a leader.

Two decades later Don will recall a typical scene: One person hadn't done his part for the group meal. He tried to explain to Gia-fu, "I thought it would be better for people to just get what they want for the meal, let their hunger direct them to the food their bodies are needing now. And besides, I was just letting the day unfold naturally. I'm into that."

Gia-fu shouted—loudly, forcefully, spitting out the words in a staccato-like tempo, "That's part of your problem, that's part of why the beans weren't cooked today, or the showers weren't cleaned. It's only natural to people who never lived in a family, who never had warm feelings toward anyone in their family, who never had responsibility to work with people and live with and love their uncles and grandparents, so that everyone helped together and everyone worked together." And he peppered his comments with swear words. Something he did only in situations like this.

Despite the irony of his own privileged upbringing, Gia-fu's aiming at a favorite target: the idea that one's particular sense of reality and lifestyle is the only one possible. In some cases the prevailing notion of reality includes excuses for drugs, which Gia-fu just won't tolerate. How people live, participate in, and contribute to the community reveal much about who they are and how they can respond to the vicissitudes of life. The well-defined duties provide stability. It's a kind of "kibbutz therapy," as Lloyd Alexander will later describe it, rather than a theoretical model—responsibility to and learning from the community.[8] Drugs can have no role in this.

Many who come to Stillpoint during the mid- to late 1970s and early 1980s come from difficult family situations. These people are looking for help in some way or, at the very least, an environment in which they can work things out for themselves. Don understands this, and when asked more than two decades later about people who sought out Gia-fu and the Stillpoint environment, he recounts:

> We had quite a variety—a number were on the "humanistic trail," especially those from Europe. There were well-educated people, some working on their PhDs, and others from various professional disciplines. And among the variety were those who were in pretty rough shape. The aura [at Stillpoint] was definitely anti-establishment. A lot of these people had been through more shrinks than you could count. A lot, probably a third or a quarter in this group, were in pretty bad shape. Gia-fu didn't necessarily treat them as wounded. He'd often give them excessively high standards. Once they said yes, he'd get on them, keep reminding them of this, like a parent. He could be amazing; he could be nasty and throw people out. Sometimes [their staying] was conditional, say on their quitting drugs.[9]

Some who come are wounded from other experiences—disillusionment with a guru, Vietnam, a major illness, cancer perhaps. And there are those who seek a different experience, a community, a way to be in nature.

Don and Gia-fu get along well, and he never harasses Don as he does others. Don likes Gia-fu and feels he can learn from him. He knows he benefits from being around Gia-fu. And Gia-fu appreciates the way Don can be detached and "see other people's buttons." Not that Don ever confronts Gia-fu. The only one who seems ready to, as Don describes it, "jump on" Gia-fu is George, an older Stillpointer noted for his temper. And that never lasts long. Gia-fu just doesn't respond to it.

But what Gia-fu seems to be responding to now is a need to find someplace more remote than 616 Ruxton Avenue. He likes to be in nature. He likes solitude, an increasingly rare commodity in Manitou Springs. Even on his long walks he sees too many people, and sometimes they even try to talk to him. It's intrusive, disruptive. No, he wants some place farther away from town, more removed from all the constant, bustling activity. Having limited cash flow, he obtains commitment of the necessary financial support from Lorraine Kirk and Michael Burton, former Stillpointers who return in the summers. Then he engages a realtor and, in the early fall of 1977, he begins the search.

One day the realtor calls asking Gia-fu to go check out a place four miles south of the tiny village of Wetmore, seventy or so miles southwest of Manitou Springs. Gia-fu, Lorraine, Richard Bertschinger—here from England—and a couple of others head out, driving toward Wetmore. From the base of snow-covered Pikes Peak, they pass through high, red-clay foothills, out across the sage-dotted plateaus, dropping down into the Arkansas Valley, heading into the antediluvian Wet Mountains. Some fifteen miles from the site, Gia-fu suddenly shouts, "Yes, Yes! This is it! I can feel it in my belly. Yes! This is it!"

And arriving at the site, seeing it with his own eyes only confirms what his belly has already told him. This is it.

One hundred sixty-six acres of meadows, forest, and mountains with small, gurgling Middle Hardscrabble Creek running through it. Transitioning from ponderosa pine, gamble oak, sagebrush at seven thousand feet altitude to spruce and aspen forests at eight thousand feet. Signs of deer, an occasional elk, mountain lions, bears, wild turkeys, fox. In the geologically ancient Wet Mountain range, this property abuts San Isabel National Forest on the west and south, unpaved County Road 387 on the east. To the north, Pikes Peak rises in the distance. Cattle graze in adjoining fields. This is ranching country, not a tourist destination, and it's in Custer County, the second least populated county in Colorado. Twenty miles east are the spectacular Sangre de Cristo Mountains, on the west side of which lies Mineral Hot Springs where Jane, Gia-fu, and the rest of the Stillpointers stayed when they first came to Colorado five years ago—forty-some miles as the crow flies to the southwest. Now, here on the eastern side of Hardscrabble Pass just east of the spectacular Wet Mountain Valley, Gia-fu finds what he's looking for.

The Stillpointers call it the farm. And indeed, the property has most recently been used for dry-land farming by Paul Burnham, the seller. A method used by farmers in semiarid regions, certainly fitting this part of the country, dry-land farming focuses on growing wheat, leaving the fields fallow during the summer and—for another decade, until practices begin to change—tilling the soil during the fallow period. Dry-land farming isn't what Gia-fu has in mind, but he appreciates that the land has been used for this purpose. In addition to all the land, the property includes a big barn, a trailer, and a shed. But just as the buildings on the land will soon change, so will the land's use.

With Gia-fu's genius for "making something from nothing," as Don will later describe it, the community finds itself tearing down a military administration building at recently closed Ent Air Force Base. They'll use the materials to build cabins at the farm. Mich has negotiated a fifteen-hundred-dollar contract to purchase the materials, with the proviso that the community dismantle the two-story building that yields a thousand two-by-twelve, eighteen-foot-long boards, plus windows and doors, with an estimated value of twenty thousand dollars. That's a lot of material, and it all gets moved temporarily to the parking lot on Ruxton Avenue. It fills the parking lot, in some places with wood stacked six feet high. These materials will build six or seven cabins at the farm. Transporting them from Manitou Springs is a slow, laborious process, but eventually, over the next year and a half and with a great deal of effort, it happens.

Among the first cabins to be constructed will be Gia-fu's. Building commences gradually, but once begun it progresses steadily. In the winter of 1978, Gia-fu writes to friend Richard Hoffman, who has been to the Ruxton Avenue Stillpoint on several occasions and is someone with whom Gia-fu has become close:

> The farm is progressing slowly in a Taoist pace. No big building. Barn is under renovation. My cabin is being built—just a little one. Each one's cabin is built by oneself. Most people sleep in the barn and a friend of mine in California gave us a small trailer which will be for babies. I don't know how the adults can stand the cold. Some of us still in tents however, everyone is high. There is something in the air...[10]

That something in the air invigorates Gia-fu. It energizes everyone. Gia-fu's delight about the land, the quiet, the air adds to the general feeling of intoxication.

In his letter he also reports, "Mich is busy trying to sell Manitou property. We cut it up to many pieces." Some of those pieces he's sold to the County Parks Department for access to Bar Trail. Others are ultimately sold, and Don LeVack eventually buys the house, which he will later turn into a bed and breakfast.

For the present, however, Don, Jim Wolfendon from California, and Fleming Fontel from Denmark work on Gia-fu's cabin that begins as a simple eight-foot-square structure topped with a peaked roof. Other stories including a loft will be added later. Fleming will help with the later alterations. Reminiscent of Taoist hermit cabins of old China, this simple abode sits atop a hill overlooking a meadow to the east and meadows, hills, and distant Pikes Peak to the north. On the south and west, tall pines shelter the cabin, adding to the hermit-like atmosphere. With plenty of windows for warmth and light from the sun, it will in time also house a bathtub in which Gia-fu can soak to his heart's content.

For a while Stillpoint continues at the Manitou Springs house, as the transition to the farm gradually unfolds. Don spends the second winter, the coldest on record, there in a tent. It's during this time that he builds an appealing little cabin by the creek that will become known as the Dragon Cabin. As they're built each cabin will have a name. This one reflects the fierce dragon Don's friend paints on the back window. To build in the freezing weather, Don has to make little fires to thaw the ground enough below the frost line to dig holes for the foundation posts. The slow, grueling process brings worthy results as the little cabin takes shape.

During these years, just before and right after acquiring the farm, Gia-fu's work in Europe really takes off. He's scheduled for two tours in Europe this year, 1978, one in July–August and again in September. In May Gia-fu again writes to Richard Hoffman telling him that in July he and Mich are leaving for the Riviera, the Black Forest, Amsterdam, and other destinations. He announces, "By the way, Michline [sic] & I (also) are married." This development might be surprising if anyone cared about or paid attention to Colorado law, which acknowledged Gia-fu and Jane's common-law marriage. But these formalities never enter Gia-fu's mind, and they certainly don't interfere with how he's choosing to conduct his life.

And confirming his enthusiasm for the European camps, he writes, "Much demand for my service in Europe. I also [find] these sessions stimulating. It is a different kind of energy compared to the U.S. The chemistry is different. They also pay well!"[11]

Another event Gia-fu relates to Richard concerns Stillpoint's evolution. Although he's still using the name Stillpoint University for some purposes, he's now calling the farm Stillpoint Hermitage. "We finally got incorporated as non-profit religions organization."

Further, he decides to create a "New Taoist University in Colorado" at the farm, calling it a "Hermitage & Hostel," which especially appeals to the Europeans. He tells Richard about the new enterprise, asking him and his wife to be part of it. He, along with others, has even created a press release:

Stillpoint University invites all those interested to come and get involved in the building of a new Taoist village in Colorado. A University is expanding into a new dimension with 180 acres of virgin land, including forest, meadows, streams and natural springs in the Wetmore valley bordering on the San Isabel National Forest, the pearl of Colorado. The aim is to form a Taoist Utopian "hundred-family village".

Stillpoint University was founded by Gia-fu Feng, a unique man [imbued] with the Chinese classical culture, one of a vanishing species…

Stillpoint University is concerned with the development of the whole person through self-discovery. It is an organism rather than an organisation. If you need further information write to 616 Ruxton Avenue, Manitou Springs, Colorado 80829.

MEMBERS OF THE FACULTY
Dr. Richard Hoffman (Medical Science)
Peggy (Medical Management)

Dr. Lorraine Kirk (Cultural Anthropology)
Dr. Michael Burton (Social anthropology)
Onny Smith (Social Architecture)
Micheline Todt (Building Construction)[12]

While this venture attracts some interest, it never becomes formalized, but Gia-fu's many facets, his numerous interests, continue to influence Stillpoint's development. Lorraine Kirk and Michael Burton, both co-owners of the farm, now Stillpoint University, never teach a regular course of study, nor do the others listed. But people still come and go as the ripples caused by Gia-fu and Stillpoint reach ever outward.

As for the European camps, they provide much-needed income for Stillpoint. By 1978, Gia-fu is spending several months teaching the camps, and that will only increase for a while. And because he doesn't do tai chi on a regular basis when he's not conducting camps, he brushes up for a few weeks before leaving for them. In October of this year a letter to Richard, whose work in medicine has now taken him to Santa Fe, New Mexico, brings him up to date on Stillpoint affairs and Gia-fu's own travels.

> This morning we read your article on medicine. Our schedule here is 4 a.m.–8 a.m. class, break for Tai Chi & eat, 10–2 p.m. work; 3 p.m–7 p.m. walk. We have moved "completely" here on the farm. We have goats & chickens, about 10–20 people. Our 5 weeks in Europe was fruitful. Mich & I were enlightened— We want to call it "Tai Chi Revival." I just got a call from Kohn (International Dance Institute) to have 2 weeks teaching next summer. I am planning a month long camp next May in Greece. I have attracted many dancers in Europe. It is exciting!
>
> During the morning classes, we also translate *I Ching*, a version I have been doing for the past 4 years. Still lots of changes. I wish you could join us, you can make specific & important contributions. I refuse to publish it until I've got it all down pat "perfect."...
> So much happening here, I don't what [sic] to start. I sleep much

sounder here than in Manitou even though I felt good there. One can always feel better!

. . .

Still many Germans are coming. They come & go. Dutchman too. New Zealanders & Australians as well. Richard from England is coming for Christmas. (10/15/78)[13]

At the England camp, referred to as a retreat, a young Englishman by the name of Alan Redman shows up. He arrives early in the evening to find no one in sight. Finally he comes across the caretaker who tells him everyone's asleep already because they're starting the session at two thirty in the morning. Alan goes to bed wondering how he's going to sleep at this early hour, but the time passes and two thirty a.m. arrives. Dressing, then finding the appointed place, Alan walks into the room where a log fire is burning in the huge fireplace. By the fire sits a little man with a beard. As he finds a seat, Alan hears this man, Gia-fu, talk about circulating the chi and about meditation. Alan is spellbound, listening as Gia-fu's voice transports him far away to a mountainside in China. He feels as though he's hearing one of the ancient Taoist hermits, sitting just outside his cave breathing in the dew and the mist.

At eight when the session ends, Gia-fu stands. Alan notices that he's wearing old, baggy corduroy trousers and a sweater. He will come to know that Gia-fu often wears clothes that are too big for him. Alan thinks he's not overly concerned about clothes, or how he looks, but pays attention to more important things like those he was just talking about.

Gia-fu suggests that people walk, but because it's foggy and raining very few do, except for Alan, who's needing some fresh air despite the rain. After a few minutes, he takes the plunge and starts down a path. Through the misty fog he sees a small figure walking ahead. He's sure it's Gia-fu but he's not so sure if he should try to catch up with him, if he should try to talk with him. Maybe Gia-fu's doing walking meditation. Or maybe he just wants to be alone. But Alan takes a chance and catches up, greeting Gia-fu and asking if it's okay to walk with him. It is.

The two talk as they cover miles in the rain. Alan tells Gia-fu about himself, about how hard things have been for him, how alienated he's felt from everyone, everything. He feels different, like he doesn't fit in. He's really captured by what Gia-fu has been talking about in the early morning session and wants to know if he can become a Taoist. What does he have to do?

Gia-fu turns to him, looks directly at him, and says, "Oh no. You are a Taoist. You don't become a Taoist. You're born one."

During the retreat, Gia-fu and Alan walk every day. Alan learns much—that it's those people who often don't fit in who are Taoists, that the important thing is to become who you are, not to try to be like somebody else. Everyone is unique—not special. Gia-fu tells Alan to learn from nature. The trees in the forest don't want to be like each other. A particular pine tree is that pine tree, not the bigger one across the way; another tree may be an aspen, perhaps a tall aspen, or a short aspen, but the trees don't try to imitate each other, nor do they compete with each other. Each follows its own course.

Alan wants to learn more from this unusual person. When Gia-fu returns to the area several months later, Alan is there. He asks Gia-fu to take him as a student. Gia-fu responds, "Oh, you already are. And there's a three-year apprenticeship."

Alan sees Gia-fu every year when Gia-fu comes to England, through 1981. He's aware that Gia-fu has a unique way of teaching, and that tai chi is only one expression of his work. Tai chi serves only to engage, to get students moving, to get the chi flowing. It's one approach among many, including walking, meditation, walking meditation, sleeping meditation, bathing meditation. But Alan doesn't yet know this. He's been working on his tai chi, and he's getting pretty good.

When Gia-fu returns a few months later, Alan wants to show him what he's learned. Other people want Alan to show Gia-fu how he's improved. They tell Gia-fu that Alan's tai chi is really good. But three or more days go by and Gia-fu doesn't ask Alan to demonstrate. Then one day he comes upon Alan alone, grabs him, and pulls him behind a building where there are lots of geese. Startled, Alan looks from the geese to Gia-fu, wondering. Gesturing to the geese, Gia-fu tells Alan, "Show us your tai chi!"

And Alan does tai chi for the geese. It scares them half to death.

This isn't the only unusual situation in which Gia-fu summons Alan to demonstrate. After a day-long session Alan, Gia-fu, and a couple of others go to a pub that serves real English ale, which Gia-fu really likes. It's late in the day, and they're sitting outside in the pub garden along with many pub regulars. Gia-fu takes a sip of ale someone's bought him, and because he likes only a sip he then passes it around to share. Turning to Alan, Gia-fu says, "Alan, do tai chi for us."

Seeing no alternative, Alan stands and begins the form here in this garden of an English pub, surrounded by so many regulars, who stare in wonder. They don't have a clue what the man's doing.

Recognizing the wisdom in what Gia-fu asks of others, even with the discomfort it sometimes causes, Alan knows Gia-fu is teaching him something important, and he understands it. There's something far deeper than tai chi going on here, and because Gia-fu creates situations that point Alan in a deeper direction, Alan can go much further into discovering his true nature than doing perfect tai chi can ever take him. Over the few years he will have with Gia-fu, he will see Gia-fu find just the right approach for the situation, not only for him but for others as well.

At one of the retreats a young man Alan will later describe as "one of those English people who'd been to public school [same as private school in the U.S.] and who'd read all the books" keeps asking Gia-fu questions. He poses the questions in a way quite obviously designed to illustrate his own knowledge, to put himself on an intellectual level above the others. Finally Gia-fu turns to the man, giving him his full attention, and says, "You know, John. You're such an asshole." The questions end, and Gia-fu gets on with the session.

Incidents like these occur back home at Stillpoint continuously. There's the young guy who's never done any work and who whines about anything too difficult. Gia-fu asks him to dig a shallow ditch for irrigation near the garden. He finally finishes it, after considerable complaining. Gia-fu surveys his work, looks around the garden and says, "Hmm. It's in the wrong place. Cover it up and dig one over here." The guy does it and this time, without the whining. He finally gets the lesson.

Gia-fu's range seems wide. He can create dramas to get the energy moving, and he can just as easily approach situations quietly. When in the first retreat Alan always chooses to sit in the back, Gia-fu picks him out and asks him to bring him a cup of tea. As Alan hands the tea to him, Gia-fu says, "Stay up here. Sit by me." Alan's shyness eventually loses its grip as Gia-fu continues finding ways to draw him out, unobtrusively, effectively.

An old theme emerges when Alan calls Gia-fu "Master."

Gia-fu responds, "No, I'm not your master. Your master has to be traditional. I'm not traditional."

In other settings Alan hears Gia-fu assert, "I'm not a tai chi master. I've never claimed to be a master."

Gia-fu still reacts strongly when people try to put him in that role. He thinks they want a master, a guru, so they don't have to make their own decisions, but he still simply does not want to be put on a pedestal, be made something he's not. On the other hand, he knows being considered a master or guru can come in handy. He'll be heard saying, "People will lie to their therapist, but they won't lie to their guru." There's no arguing with a Taoist.

Two and a half decades later, Alan will reflect, "If you were straight with him, he would be straight with you. If you played games with him, then you were asking for trouble."

And about the master role Alan will say, "He was more the trickster. That was him. A unique individual. He was like a character from a Chuang Tsu story. He's there all the time in Chuang Tsu. He's the one who wipes you out."

Trickster. Author Lewis Hyde will later write, "The best way to describe trickster is to say simply that the boundary is where he will be found—sometimes crossing it, sometimes erasing or moving it, but always there, the god of the threshold in all its forms."[14] Coyote in Native American lore, Hermes in ancient Greece, Ananse in Africa, Jamaica, and other scenes of that diaspora, Monkey for the Chinese. Elusive, complex, ever changing. Doing anything to get you to do what's needed. Showing up as a Taoist rogue.

And as far as that marker referring to the master that the Stillpointers will put on Gia-fu's grave, Alan will say he's got no problem with that. It is the natural sequence, and Gia-fu, whatever anyone called him, "was like the bird that flies his own path. You can watch him fly, but he leaves no path to follow. You have to find your own."

Even now in the late 1970s, Alan sees that it's easier to go along with being put on the pedestal, being called and considered a master, than not. At the same time, he recognizes the true wisdom in not getting caught in that trap. In another twist on the theme, Don Workman, a Stillpointer, will later conclude, "Gia-fu was a master of Life."[15]

Of course, there are people who think Gia-fu's crazy, or a weirdo, or both. They only see some little, bearded Chinese man in baggy clothes sitting, eating peanuts, doing or saying outrageous things. At the beginning of a camp or retreat, Gia-fu usually says something that makes people uncomfortable, and if they leave, it's okay. He knows these aren't the people who will honestly work with him. The remaining ones he can really move with, and many of them will return to the camps time and again.

As for Alan, because of Gia-fu he'll continue on his own path, and years later it will take him to China where he'll be ordained as a Taoist priest, taking the name Shi Jing. He'll become involved with the British Taoist Association and will dedicate the summer 1997 issue of *The Dragon's Mouth*, the Association publication, to his teacher, Gia-fu Feng. And after a 2001 visit to Stillpoint, Alan, or Shi Jing, will observe, "Stillpoint is perfect. Gia-fu knew what he was doing. The environment, the place you do the cultivation is part of the cultivation. You can't do it just anywhere. These mountains remind me of ancient China. The buildings are in special places: one in the valley with the valley spirit; one by the running water; one allows a view over the treetops. It's like the Dragon Gate Caves in China. You can just see it." Nature, nurture, cultivating the mind, body, and spirit.[16]

Stillpointer Don LeVack will echo Alan's observations, underlining the spiritual aspect of Stillpoint and what Gia-fu created there:

I will always remember the experience of awe/joy at times, i.e., sitting in group meditation in the morning as the sun came up in Wetmore...

This experience of awe was also experienced on our daily walking trips, which was part of the Stillpoint program; everything would become crystal clear, the colors brightened, cares fall away. The experience of awe/joy was not a pursuit but a natural consequence of our lifestyle which would happen periodically without warning, without desire of its pursuit. Our daily work activities, such as building cabins, working in the garden, shopping, paying bills would also be opportunities to experience that all is well in the world, everything is perfect.[17]

Knowing his friend Gia-fu has found a remote place for Stillpoint, longtime friend Lloyd Alexander stops by Stillpoint en route from San Francisco to Denver. With him is Margaret Susan Wilson, just finishing law school and also a graduate of the California Institute for Asian Studies, formerly the Academy of Asian Studies where Gia-fu spent some pivotal years back in the mid-1950s. As Susan and Gia-fu talk, their mutual acquaintances, teachers, and friends number many through this web of Asian Academy/Institute relationships. Gia-fu also finds Susan's legal mind and her depth of interest in what he's doing added attractions, and Susan's returned interest in this intriguingly insightful and complex person opens the way for friendship. She's also quite taken by the setting—the quiet, the stillness, the beauty. This place invites reflection and meditation.

Even so, this time Lloyd and Susan stay only a short while, a long afternoon, long enough to launch a fledgling friendship between Susan and Gia-fu and long enough for Lloyd and Gia-fu to enjoy each other's company. Both Susan and Lloyd will come back at different times. Neither will stay for more than a few days. And just as Lloyd has never become a part of the community, nor will Susan, although her eventual effect on the community itself will be profound.[18]

In 1981, Gia-fu's again off to Europe, a trip he's made every year since 1974. This one takes him to England, West Germany, Switzerland, Spain,

Italy, Denmark, and Holland over a seven-month period. The camps bring more visitors to Stillpoint, which Gia-fu writes about to Richard on New Year's Eve 1981. "I'll have 50 foreigners here from Jan. 15–Feb. 15." He also tells Richard, "Hundreds of people came to me in Berlin—7 moons in Europe—one camp after another." And he signs the letter, "Exciting & Excited—Gia-fu."

The spring of 1982 finds Gia-fu off again to Europe, and this time also to Australia and New Zealand. This turns out to be his last year of travel. The August 10, 1982, JFK Airport stamp in his passport, his fifth passport as a U.S. citizen, marks the end of almost a decade of camps abroad. They've been wildly successful. They've brought people from all over the world to Stillpoint. Writing to Richard, he refers to the number of Europeans and others at Stillpoint. "Now our members of Stillpoint Global Village are mainly Europeans, with some Americans. My dream of cross-fertilization of different cultures has come true today."

Carmen Baehr is one of the Europeans who in 1983 contribute to Gia-fu's continuing realization of his dream. From Germany, Carmen's a young student therapist who has been supporting herself by working in nursing homes and with dying children. Critical, intense work, perhaps even more so for the daughter of a Holocaust survivor. Sensing she's on the threshold of a psychologically intense period, Carmen is feeling over-whelmed. She's looking for a place that's emotionally and psychologically safe and to be with someone who can offer support. Twenty years later, Carmen will think about events that led her to Stillpoint, recalling, "I did have that moment of sanity where I dreamt…about this guy, maybe a ship's captain, picking me up and taking me across the ocean…and I fol-lowed through on it. I interpreted it as going to America, and I did… Instinctually, I knew that Germany was not the place where there was the support to fall apart." She's heard of Gia-fu from his camps in Germany, that he is a tai chi teacher. From the little she's heard, she's intrigued, in-terested enough to come to this distant place.

So now she's here at Stillpoint, thousands of miles from home. It's four a.m. and she's in the barn, in the big, open room that's been remod-eled for use as the meditation and meeting room. It's a simple, sparsely furnished room with weathered wood floors and walls and a high barn ceiling. People sit around, either on meditation cushions or just on the wood floor, huddled in their sweaters and jackets. She will later recall, "I was cold and tired. I was freaked out with all those strangers and wondering what was I doing there anyhow? And I heard these steps. It felt familiar, an inbody, physical experience of knowing those steps. I knew who that was."

Having climbed the stairs to the second floor, Gia-fu enters the room. Looking around, he spots Carmen. Kindly, sweetly, he welcomes her. But then there's a complete shift. Carmen won't be able to forget, even two decades later, what happened next. One of the Stillpointers, Bronco, was supposed to pick her up at the bus station in Manitou Springs, but instead, when she called, he told her to take the bus to Wetmore the next day. This left Carmen to wander the unfamiliar streets alone on her first night in America. Gia-fu turns to him.

> And then basically he proceeded pounding on this six-foot, three-hundred-pound man. It was Bronco, a blacksmith from Copenhagen. He was screaming at him, what he'd not done. And there was all this drama going on after the meditation. It was like, whoa! Gonna go pack my bags! I'd never heard anything like that. I mean, I come from a normal, repressed background. And this guy was a maniac and everybody else there just seemed like mental health patients, literally.

When the session's finally over, Carmen sees the shift in Gia-fu that has puzzled so many before her. He's kind again. Gentle even. But perhaps a little more distant than when he welcomed her, engaging in small talk. Responding to her comment about the inner blocks she feels, he tells her, "I have the Rocky Mountains in my chest."

He shows Carmen the cabin she's to stay in and leaves her there alone. Not surprisingly, she's baffled by what's happened so far, but she's here, and she knows it's going to take some paying attention to accustom herself to this unusual new environment.

She falls into the Stillpoint rhythm, morning meditation and group sessions, perhaps some translating, breakfast, chores, walking. Some people go out to work at neighboring ranches. And now that she has the physical space that is Stillpoint—all those meadows, mountains, and forests—she also senses the emotional space she's needed and craved. Within the space, without the distractions and structure of her demanding work and her overly full schedule, she watches herself begin to fall apart. She feels she's coming undone. She questions her reality. During the first one hundred days, she feels her energy overwhelm her as she unravels. And although she won't think in these terms at the time, she'll come to know it's kundalini energy, psycho-spiritual energy, the energy that uncoils serpent-like in a spiritual awakening.

In one of the morning sessions, Gia-fu makes a comment. Looking back, she'll remember his words hitting the target, how what he said was crucial, but she won't be able to remember what it was. She will, however, always remember the effect—that it causes her to crumble, completely, thoroughly, finally. And somehow she knows this is what she's been seeking; she now knows what she must face—she must face her fears. Slowly, day by day for months she stays with the fears, not pushing them away, not glossing over, not denying they're there but living with them, working through them.

Gia-fu sees it right away. And somehow he energetically holds the space, not touching, not talking, just being there, assuring her that it's okay to go through this here, providing a container so she can complete the transformation. This tiny little guy can deal with unbridled, raw energy and it doesn't scare him a bit, whether it's spiritual transformation or unleashed anger.

At some point, Gia-fu tells her to read a book in the Stillpoint library, *Kundalini: Psychosis or Transcendence* by Lee Sannella, MD.[19] She reads it, and it's as if a cloud passes by. She will recall her reaction, "This is me! He knew—exactly! It felt like a light bulb or something." She realizes that what she's been experiencing is only a matter of not running away from oneself, that this is "just normal experience."

> And then, Gia-fu saw me that next day, and he said, "Now you're here." Never even said anything real specifically, but he knew. That was the thing. I felt "held." Like they say, a holding environment that you have for a baby? I felt that there. There's a big net of energy in

that place. It's like this umbrella of protection where that whole un-
doing could happen without a lot of interference. It was just normal
process. I mean it wasn't that intense intellectual blah, blah, blah. It
was just like something that happened, that just was right. And he
definitely noticed when it had run its course, and it shifted. So then,
then he asked me to stay. Well, I was there. That was my home.

Carmen sees what has happened in this situation as very different
from relying on purely Western psychological concepts. In this situation
there've been no labels, no intellectualizing of what's been going on with
her. Gia-fu doesn't label the states of mind she's been experiencing as un-
healthy, as counterproductive. Instead, Carmen thinks of what he does as
entirely different. In her eyes, "He would ride it like a wave. And he would
teach people one way or another. That makes people really strong…It
really isn't therapy, it's just true human relationships. Like in the tribe
where people work things out amongst themselves, and they care enough
to do that, even if it gets messy."

While Carmen's experiencing all of this, others at Stillpoint are also,
in Carmen's words, "chewing on their stuff." This chewing causes people
to support each other in the sense of respecting what one is experiencing
and what it takes to get through it. But even that, the way they support
each other, isn't conventional. It's not the "lovey-dovey 'I support you'
and then listen to your story" sense. No, this is different. People are present and allow you to do what you need to do, and they all know the courage it takes to do it. There are recognition of and respect for the common,
yet difficult, hurdles human beings face.

Carmen appreciates the acknowledgment by Gia-fu and the others
that we all carry hopes, fears, memories, preconceptions, misconceptions
and that we all need "to let go of that stuff." This attitude's clear one day in
the group when she's crying. She sobs, almost uncontrollably. The others,
sitting in the usual circle, don't quite know what's going on, but they sit
with her and whatever it is that's touching her. After a while, Gia-fu looks
around the group and, quietly, simply says, "Her father was in a concen-
tration camp."

223

Gia-fu directs his talents to other aspects of life at Stillpoint. He's interested in relationships—after all, his idea of a hundred-family community means there should be families within the larger Stillpoint community. For those already in relationships, he nudges them to look at their respective roles: Is one person overpowering the other? Is this person terrified of being thought of as homosexual? Sometimes the questions come directly. Sometimes they appear as an exaggerated situation in group session. But they come. And people respond to the various approaches differently. Any defensiveness gets worn down, or else the person leaves. They know more will be coming.

For the unattached, Gia-fu can quickly get to the sense of who an individual thinks he or she is and who a mate might be. He often suggests, "Why don't you go out with so-and-so?"

The response, often unspoken, but obvious in body language and facial expression: "That's the last person in the world I'd think of going out with!"

It doesn't matter what actually happens as a result of the question because the attitude is there, and Gia-fu takes it in, which becomes quite clear, and he works with it, working on the person.

A favorite line of his is, "Why don't you marry so-and-so?"

Doesn't matter that A and B actually do or don't get together. What matters is getting to the issue—"Marriage? Me? I'm waiting for my prince!" And so the subject has an opportunity to look at her- or himself. The individual in question gets to see his or her unrealistic expectations, whether he or she wants to or not.

But sometimes people respond differently. At Gia-fu's suggestion Gabi, another Stillpointer, and Fleming do get together, and eventually they marry. They have a baby, whom they name Christina. Gia-fu loves to watch Christina and finds great joy in her.

One day as Gabi teaches tai chi, Gia-fu takes care of baby Christina. He's holding her when, much to his embarrassment, she begins to cry. She's crying wholeheartedly, probably because she's been constipated for about a week, but Gia-fu doesn't know this. He only knows she's unhappy, maybe uncomfortable. He holds her up and gently bounces her, cooing and saying soothing things.

She stops crying. Her eyes widen as if she's startled by something. There's a release. Her constipation ends, leaving Gia-fu and everything around covered by the resulting catharsis. Tai chi stops as laughter takes over. Even Gia-fu finds the messy situation hilarious.

He's in the kitchen one day, and Carmen's there, too. Cooking some food and doing the daily work, she feels lonely and unloved. Although she doesn't say anything about her feelings, she knows they're obvious. Close to lunch time Gia-fu leaves for his usual walk. But a few minutes later the door opens, and Gia-fu pokes his head back in to say, "I love Christina very much. And she doesn't expect anything in return from me."

This incident stays indelibly etched in Carmen's memory, as does another in which Gia-fu pushes her boundaries. Her community duties include cooking. She's a vegetarian. But Gia-fu has her pluck, clean, and bake chickens they raise at Stillpoint or get from a neighboring ranch. Pushing even further, she has to hold a chicken while Sue Bailey chops its head off. It turns out she's not so good at holding the chicken, and she ends up wishing, however horrible it might be, that she had been the one to just chop its head off.[20]

Even before Carmen's arrival at Stillpoint, a friend of Gia-fu's from the San Francisco days turns up. Robert Breckenridge has come to Colorado to visit his mother. Having heard Gia-fu interviewed on a 1978 New Dimensions Radio program in San Francisco but not seeing him for many years, he decides to find Stillpoint and visit Gia-fu. He goes to the Manitou house and is directed to Wetmore. Arriving around four in the afternoon, he learns that Gia-fu has retired to his cabin, now referred to as the hermitage, for the evening, so he'll have to stick around to see him in the morning.

Robert stays in a little A-frame cabin by the creek, the closest one to the other buildings. It's winter, and it's cold. He crawls in under several sleeping bags and snoozes until four in the morning when some Stillpointers stop by to take him to morning meditation.

Robert opens the window, one from the Ent Air Force base building that now serves as a door, crawls out, and with the help of his flashlight follows the others up to the teahouse. The teahouse, the largest cabin they've built there, consists of two fair-sized rooms and a loft. A woodstove warms the place. As Robert climbs the ladder, which currently serves as the stairway, he sees others around the stove, already meditating. Despite the darkness, Robert can see straw on the floor and blankets on the straw, piles of assorted old furniture, pillows here and there. Finding some pillows for himself, he gets into some sort of meditation, some amalgam of approaches that seems to work for him. He meditates for a while. Then he hears somebody fussing around with teapots and cups. He hears a noisy slurping sound. It's a familiar sound. He thinks, that must be Gia-fu! Who else would dare be noisy in a meditation session?

Gia-fu, delighted to see Robert, invites him to stay at Stillpoint. He entices him with a scholarship, but Robert stays only for breakfast, which they have in the trailer. The trailer, one of the buildings here when Gia-fu bought this place, serves as kitchen, bathroom, central place for community activity. Robert and Gia-fu sit on the floor cracking peanuts, still a favorite of Gia-fu's, and eating oatmeal with the peanuts.

Not long after this brief visit, Robert returns to Stillpoint. This time he's part of a walk across the U.S. called Walk for the Earth. Leaving from Point Reyes, California, and walking to Washington, DC, the walk's organizers and participants hope to bring attention to ecology, disarmament, and Native American rights. The route takes them on Colorado Highway 2, relatively close to Stillpoint. Robert, fellow walker Priscilla Johnson, and several others decide to take a side trip to Stillpoint, Robert having written in advance.

Arriving at Stillpoint in the afternoon, Robert is met by Sue Bailey, Gia-fu's current partner. Gia-fu and Mich had gradually drifted apart, and Mich has now left Stillpoint. Sue does most of the bookkeeping and shopping and in Robert's words, "acts as Gia-fu's right-hand assistant."

In her twenties, Sue comes from Australia. She's had her share of problems, and after she came to Stillpoint, Gia-fu helped her face them. Robert will remember twenty years hence that Sue "was very friendly and good spirited, enjoying her life. She seemed to be, in many ways, much, much more attuned to Gia-fu than the others. She didn't take him too seriously, and she apparently wasn't afraid of him. She was having a good time, and she was being responsible."

Now, greeting Robert, Sue delivers a surprise. "Gia-fu and I are getting married tomorrow morning, and you're going to do the ceremony."

After all, Robert has a minister's license from the Universal Life Church, an organization that offers a license to anyone who sends in a dollar. Designed with the destruction of church hierarchies in mind, it licenses anyone who wants to be a minister, provided they pay the price.

Even so, Robert protests an official role. "I don't do ceremonies! I was always frightened in church, anyhow!"

Reassuringly, Sue tells him, "Oh, don't worry about it. We'll do something. It doesn't matter to us."

And while Robert spends the night thinking about what to do, others there make preparations for the event. Wabi-sabi is the art of elegant simplicity, of seeing the beauty in the ordinary, in imperfection, incompleteness, a culture refined by sixteenth-century tea master and Zen monk Sen no Rikyu.[21] In keeping with these principles, Gia-fu wants the flowers to be columbines. Twenty-five years later, Colleen Corbo, at Stillpoint during 1983 and 1984, will reminisce about how Gia-fu wanted only columbine, for it was columbine season and Stillpoint had an abundance of the varying shades of blue and purple wildflowers. She'll remember the absolute beauty of those masses of flowers at the wedding.[22]

All assemble in the barn, sitting in a circle in typical Stillpoint fashion. Gia-fu and Sue sit on a platform to one side. Robert passes a talking stick, an Indian tradition: when you get the stick you can talk, or you can pass it on the next person.

It begins with Robert. He gives a little prepared speech about love, but he won't remember what he says. He hands the stick to the next person, and so it goes, the stick making its way around the circle. People talk, or not. Gia-fu is the last to hold it, and he speaks:

> This isn't a marriage for romance, because romance doesn't last. It's there for a little while, and then it's gone. I'm not marrying anyone for romance. It's not a marriage for sex either, because we don't have to marry for that. I'm marrying Sue Bailey to have a matriarch for Stillpoint. This is important.

Sue and Gia-fu exchange jackets, as sometimes happens in Chinese weddings. As Gia-fu dons Sue's jacket, he begins prancing around, seemingly in parody of an effeminate man. Sue laughs and soon everyone else does, too. Two or three people with guitars and someone playing an old piano back in the corner provide music for the ensuing merriment. Wine flows. Somebody brings out a whole turkey on a platter. It's passed around the circle and, because there are no knives, forks, or plates, each person pulls off a piece of the turkey and passes it on the next person. Robert's memory will be of a "hilarious, marvelous wedding. I thought I had never seen such a wonderful wedding."

Later Sue Bailey comments to Robert, "The only reason I married Gia-fu is he's the most outrageous character I've ever met in my life."[23]

Gia-fu—outrageous character, gentle mentor, trickster, monkey king, master-guru or not, patriarch of Stillpoint.

CHAPTER FOURTEEN

A SIMPLE
SEQUENCE

Returning is the motion of the Tao.
Yielding is the way of the Tao.
The ten thousand things are born of being.
Being is born of not being.

—from Chapter 40, *Tao Te Ching*

A photo album of Stillpoint lies open on the table, its pages filled with smiling images, laughing children, weddings, picnics, goats and kids, chickens, bucolic landscapes, the waterfall. Taken mostly in 1983 and 1984, some photographs feature Gia-fu. Gia-fu in a flowing black and gold Chinese robe and yellow baseball cap, waving a fan toward a couple seated facing him. Gia-fu in the middle of a group of children and adults crowded together on the steep steps of the tea house, all wearing bright smiles, matching the sunshine that also illumines their faces. There's even a picture of Gia-fu with Kalahari, the Arabian horse someone rode across multiple states to present to him as a gift. And there are some of a bear nosing through trash left out by the tea house. All together, the photographs tell of individuals and families living simply, close to the land as a community, and of their relationships with Gia-fu, founder of Stillpoint, patriarch of Stillpoint Global Village.

And now that he's no longer traveling, now that he's home to stay, Gia-fu turns his full attention to Stillpoint, his translations, and other new ventures—hopes for a Stillpoint Press, for one, and heightened interest in health and medicine for another. For the first, a friend in Germany expresses interest in financing Stillpoint Press, although unfortunately, this will never work out. But Gia-fu doesn't know it won't, and planning for it buoys his enthusiasm for translating even more. He'd like a first edition of a new *I Ching* translation in a larger format, "so that each hexagram will occupy two sides—one in calligraphy, and the other in English." Echoes of the highly successful *Tao Te Ching* translation. He's completed an *Art of War* translation and is working on others.

Along with continuing his translations, Gia-fu has been working on his autobiography. Having written about the first part of his life, he sends a draft to China scholar Roxane Witke at the East Asian Institute at Columbia University in New York, with whom he's previously corresponded. Gia-fu appreciates Dr. Witke's scholarship and resulting publications, among which is a 1977 book about Chiang Ch'ing, Mao Tse-tung's wife. Dr. Witke provides, along with suggestions on style and content, encouragement for his project, "You've had a fascinating life...You're insightful and unpretentious, and the latter trait is rare in an autobiographer."[1]

He does continue writing, primarily revising and condensing material about the years from his birth in 1919 to 1949, after he's come to the U.S., into another draft entitled *One Hundred Pages of Feng*. This draft, less than one-third the length of his original manuscript, will have an unpredictable future. Some thirteen years after Gia-fu completes it, Stillpointer Jerry Coulter will leave *One Hundred Pages of Feng* on my doorstep, following our surprise meeting on a trail at Stillpoint. It will be a much-appreciated gift, despite my several years' work organizing the three hundred completely random pages, not knowing a condensed version existed.

Now in the early 1980s, Gia-fu's escalating interest in spreading knowledge about Chinese medicine and Taoist medicine, which really mean the same thing, parallels concerns for his own health. The last trip abroad left him with a severe case of what seems to be bronchitis, due to the congestion and coughing he's constantly experiencing. A letter to Richard expresses his desire to hold a conference on the subject, but not just a theoretical one. "Chinese medicine (Daoism) is becoming increasingly significant [sic] in my life. It has to be done here at Stillpoint, where alchemy can take place, not just talked about."

Alchemy. That aspect of Taoism devoted to "the transformation of body and mind toward health and longevity," as later explained by Taoist Eva Wong.[2] Now in August 1983, Gia-fu asks Richard to visit, and it's not only their warm companionship and friendship he seeks but also some medical guidance from someone he trusts. Richard does visit, as he will do another time or two in the next year. His work in Columbia, Missouri, precludes his staying at Stillpoint, but he does as much as he can from afar and during the times he's at Stillpoint. He examines Gia-fu and on one visit, at Gia-fu's request, does a general checkup for most of the other Stillpointers there at the time.

Gia-fu's long interest in foods and eating habits that promote health remains strong. The focus on yeast at Los Gatos Stillpoint continues even now, along with avoidance of salt, oil, and sugar coupled with ample exercise to control diabetes—a necessity if one doesn't take insulin. Also important as givens are not eating too late in the evening, plenty of walking, long warm baths, and sufficient sleep. After all, attention to health goes hand in hand with Taoism. In general, preventive medicine appeals to him: what he calls the curative medicine, a kind of medicine little emphasized in the West.[3] And although he never criticizes Western medicine around Richard, he avoids going to a doctor. Some Stillpointers have even heard him express a fear of doctors. Delving ever further into natural healing, he continues corresponding with Richard and also, briefly, with another out-of-the-ordinary doctor who has expressed interest in a "Taoist type of wellness and growth center." But it's Richard with whom he communicates most often, by phone, letter, or on Richard's occasional visit.

In accordance with Chinese medicine, Gia-fu pays attention to his body signs—the color in his face, the length of his coughing spells and time of day they occur, the color and quantity of the mucus he coughs up. And by July 1984, he lets Richard know he's "ready to try a more traditional form of antibiotic." He wants Richard to prescribe one, although he's most willing to take full responsibility in case of any side effects. At the same time, he tells Richard, "By the way, all my teeth fell out during the last 2 years, only one left in my upper jaw." He ends with, "I take 5 hours walk & 5 hours bath every day," signing the letter, "I love you. Gia-fu."

Returning to Stillpoint in October 1984, Richard gets Gia-fu to consent to a chest X-ray. Quite a feat, but perhaps telling, Gia-fu doesn't even resist Richard's suggestion. Richard writes a prescription for the X-ray, and he sees the resulting report: "AP chest film reveals that the chest is emphysematous. There is a right lower lobe pneumonia. The heart size is normal." The general impression summarizes, "Chest showing pneumonia."

Gia-fu also coughs up some sputum that's examined under the microscope for tuberculosis, just as he's cultured for bacteria, tuberculosis, and yeast. All prove negative. Cancer and tuberculosis appear to be unlikely diagnoses.

He gets his antibiotics, prescribed by Richard, who thinks they might help and with little to no side effects. No one knows if he ever takes them, and sometime later he tells Richard he thinks he doesn't need antibiotics. He does, however, heed Richard's other suggestions. After that October visit, he asks Sue Bailey to let Richard know that he's following all his other advice to the letter. He's changed his sleeping position, added a few things to his diet—drinking two small bottles of beer a day to stimulate his appetite—and is beating his right lung three times a day. His spirits high and energy level increased, he's grateful for and most appreciative of Richard's help.

The community knows Gia-fu's been having health problems, but they want to believe he's getting better. He does, in fact, show some promising signs, some improvement from time to time, an increase in energy for a while or a better appetite for a bit. He doesn't say much to the community, doesn't tell them about exactly what's going on with him, so it's easy enough to think this continuing illness is something he'll weather.

All the while, life at Stillpoint continues as usual. It's at full occupancy right now. As usual, folks are up around four for meditation, which now takes place in the trailer. It's easier for Gia-fu to get there than to the tea house, the trailer being closer and not so much of a climb. Whoever shows up first has responsibility for starting a fire in the woodstove. A new arrival this May 1985, Nathan Meier, often gets there first, so for the week he's there he starts the morning fire.

By the time the fire begins heating the room, two, three, or four people are sitting and meditating. The trailer is set up with walls removed all the way from one end almost to the other—from the kitchen to the office, with the bathroom in the middle of the two rooms—tub, toilet, and all out in the open. The nicely carpeted meditation hall sits just a step down from the bathroom. A big warm, comfortable place, the meditation hall has big windows up to the sides—bad for insulation but good for light during the day.

Sue runs Gia-fu's bath and he gets in, splashing around a bit. This leisurely bath lasts maybe twenty minutes or so. Soft darkness fills the room, broken only by the sparse glow of a single candle. The woodstove crackles. Gia-fu soaks. Others meditate.

While it's still dark Gia-fu emerges from the water, bundles up, and sits with the rest of the group. When it's light enough they all work on translations. He leads the translation session, beginning by reading a chapter in Chinese, then explaining what it's about. Someone has a dictionary handy in case it's needed. The session is seminar-like and free flowing, and anyone who wants can contribute. Once the vocabulary suggestions are voiced, Gia-fu pounds it all together, clearly comfortable with English and Chinese. The whole group discusses the passage until it's right—and Gia-fu coughs through it all.

Nathan, whose background includes a degree in Asian Studies and work in printing, has come to Stillpoint to do calligraphy and meet Gia-fu. When they meet, perhaps because he hasn't seen him before, it surprises him that Gia-fu looks older than he expected. He can also see that his health is deteriorating, and he senses, regretfully, that Gia-fu may not be here much longer. He's very thin, weighing less than eighty pounds. Twelve years later on a return trip to Stillpoint, Nathan will recall, "I knew he didn't have long to teach. Some of his physical infirmities were taking their toll on him. He seemed less patient [than I expected], though he was still sharp. But it was a disappointment that he wasn't going to be around for long studies."

Despite Gia-fu's weakened health, Nathan's one week at Stillpoint with Gia-fu proves more than memorable, illustrated by the reflection he'll share during that 1997 return visit. "It was an important week in my life. Everything I've done with my life since then has echoed that week."

Not serendipitous, that May 1985 visit to Stillpoint. Nathan was there, at that time in that place, for a specific purpose.

> I needed to see it, see Taoism as something functional. And then, his Taoism was sometimes angry Confucian propriety. Sometimes it was Gestalt psychotherapy. Sometimes it was letting things be the way they were gonna be. And really, [at this point] the group dynamics developed without his input, as they're supposed to. I mean at least in the Zen context, as I've discovered since then, people learned to harmonize together without having to bother the master with these issues. In fact, I think that was a lot of his anger. He was perceiving that he needed to be involved in the dynamics of the place because it wasn't running as well as it had been.[4]

But while Nathan notices these dynamics, some of the more permanent Stillpointers have been noticing how Gia-fu seems even gentler, how the quality of his love and compassion has grown. They see this reflected in daily interactions and in special gestures. A few months ago, Gia-fu sent a picture of Sue Bailey and himself to his family. Carmen will later interpret this as reassurance to his family that he's not alone, that he's settled. Concerned for his family, he doesn't want them to worry or feel regrets.

He even has another toilet installed, this one semi-private, despite his previous efforts to suggest people learn to let go of rules about bodily functions—about going to the bathroom—to give up those inhibitions. He gives away much of his clothing and signs some stocks over to Sue. And he moves from his cabin on the hill, his hermitage, to a small travel trailer one of the Stillpointers has brought there.

Even these gestures and his increased weakness fail to alert the community about the gravity of the situation. As Carmen will later recall:

> Even though Gia-fu got weaker, he still told people off to the last breath. So I think he knew…He was still doing incredible stuff a week before he died, twenty minutes before he died. If I learned anything from watching somebody die, it's that he definitely could be true to himself, pretty much to the end. If he was uncomfortable with something, you'd know![5]

It's June 12, early morning. The translation session's being held in the trailer, as it has been for the past several days. Despite his increasingly weakening state, as always, Gia-fu's still fully alert, fully here, fully living each moment. With his usual keen awareness and attention to others, he notices Carmen shivering. He says to her, "You're cold. Shall we close the window?"

The translation session begins. Together the group works to translate Hexagram 59, the next one in the sequence, the natural order of this ancient text so loved by Gia-fu. This hexagram, *Huan—Dispersion*. Auspicious for this day. Gia-fu has said on so many occasions that when he dies, Stillpoint as it is should die with him. Things can't be kept the same. Things grow, develop, and dissolve.

The translation session ends, everyone leaves. Sue returns, sitting with him, holding his hand. Quietly, gracefully, Gia-fu himself disperses; his life here at Stillpoint, on this earth, dissolves. Wind traveling over water, crossing the great river, evaporation, release.

> *dispersion*
> *grace*
> *the ruler approaches the ancestral temple*
> *favorable to cross the great river favor devotion*

> *wind traveling over water*
> *dispersion*
> *the ancient rulers sacrificed to the emperor*
> *and established ancestral temples*

in the early hours of the day
in the pre dawn light
we gathered
for what was to be
our last morning of translation together

> *disperse the self*
> *no remorse*

> *dispersing the group*
> *primal good fortune*
> *dispersed to reach something higher*
> *ordinary people are not able to understand*

> *dispersed*
> *sweating with great cries*
> *dispersion*
> *the ruler dwells no blame*
> *the blood dispersed*
> *gone far away*
> *no blame*

with this
on the morning of June 12, 1985
Gia Fu Feng died[6]

∾

Fourth Brother, C.H., awakens suddenly this morning, startled. A little while later the phone rings. Third Brother has gone.

Robert Breckenridge left a couple of days ago to visit his daughters in California. He's now camping in a state park southwest of Palo Alto. He feels Gia-fu—or is it his spirit?—here for a visit. When he calls Stillpoint, he's told that Gia-fu has died. Other similar experiences occur.

Gia-fu leaves a stunned and grieving Stillpoint community. He leaves shocked family members, brothers and sisters who had no idea he'd been so ill. He hadn't told them about his health, and those in the community either hadn't realized or were unwilling to accept that he had been this ill. They hadn't tried to contact the family, even if Gia-fu would have permitted it. Two decades later, his siblings still will not understand how this could have happened, how they could not have known—and not understanding that it was his choice not to go further with Western medicine, how something couldn't have been done medically for Gia-fu, their unconventional, one-of-a-kind, beloved Third Brother.

And capturing myriad feelings, Carmen will say:

Many people have been touched by Gia-fu, have a wound from Gia-fu—anger, grief, usually a reaction with some kind of pain. There is a brokenhearted quality with so many people. A vulnerability, a mystery. But there was some way of being touched, and not necessarily in a pretty way. Gia-fu could stand back and see what needed to happen for the situation. He could do the right thing at the right time without expecting anything in return. Many people try to come to terms with the legacy he left them.[7]

Sisters Mei-chi, Lu-tsi, and Ellen travel to Colorado from California for the funeral. Family members, Stillpoint community, friends, and neighbors gather for this farewell to Gia-fu, held June 16, 1985. Gia-fu has been dressed in his favorite clothes—a red silk robe and his baseball cap. The Stillpointers wear white, the Chinese color of mourning. The Feng sisters wear black, reflecting mourning in this, their adopted country. All honor the life of Gia-fu Feng. And mourn his death, the simple sequence of his coming.

Surrounded by meadows, forests, mountains, Gia-fu is buried at the foot of the hill on which his cabin, his hermitage sits. At the stillpoint of the turning world.

~

Lantau Island, Hong Kong. July 1985. On the other side of the world, a young man awakes early to the shouts and chants of monks in the monastery. Rising and dressing, he goes out into the dark morning to climb up Lantau Peak. As he walks up the misty hillside, he hears in his memory a high, ethereal, soulful voice singing the song he, Nathan Meier, sang at Gia-fu's graveside. As he reaches the peak and the dawn breaks, he sings the song again for Gia-fu, for what was evoked for him by being at Stillpoint for a single week, a single week that he will carry with him throughout his lifetime.

> Return, again. Return again,
> Return to the place of your soul.
> Return to who you are. Return to what you are.
> Return to where you are born and reborn again.
> Return again to the place of your soul.

EPILOGUE

SUSAN

The very highest is barely known by men.
Then comes that which they know and love...

—from Chapter 17, *Tao Te Ching*

How can I describe her, my sister, whose complexity continues to baffle me? Images come to mind. Her fury as a four-year-old, when she saw our brother's ten-year-old friend kill a bird.

"Damn you, Henry Harper! Damn you! You killed that bird!" she screamed at a startled Henry Harper. She was articulate even as a small child, especially when she perceived a wrongdoing. She was also physical—our mother had to park the car in which we all were riding and stop Susan's ferocious pummeling of poor Henry Harper.

At ten, she asked for and got a BB gun, which she learned to shoot well, usually wearing her Annie Oakley fringe jacket and aiming only at paper targets. While at Pensacola Junior College in Florida, Susan became captivated by Eastern thought, and especially by philosopher Sri Aurobindo. I recall her trying to explain his intricate writings to me. She could be very patient.

Variously called Susan, Suzi, Margaret, or Sue Margaret, she inhabited a slight frame of five feet, four inches. Long, dark hair, sky-blue eyes, and a finely sculpted face reflecting her Native American ancestry belied an iron will and unstoppable curiosity. Her incisive intellect, kind heart, and formidable temper would take aim at any injustice, as the unfortunate Henry Harper and later many others learned. A person of many facets and interests, her encounter with Gia-fu Feng accentuated these qualities. Their meeting spawned a chain of events none of us could ever have imagined.

Gia-fu and Stillpoint entered Susan's life in 1978. Susan and Gia-fu's meeting grew out of a web of relationships related to the San Francisco–based Institute for Asian Studies, where Gia-fu had first worked as translator for Alan Watts in the 1950s and Susan had completed a master's degree in 1976. The connecting thread was Lloyd Alexander, himself a fiery person and intimate friend of Susan's. Lloyd had been friends with Gia-fu for some time and also had many links to the Institute.

The meeting occurred in a serendipitous fashion during a road trip from San Francisco to Denver, when Susan and Lloyd stopped by Stillpoint to say hello to Gia-fu. The rapport was instant, both between Susan and Gia-fu, and Susan and the land. Gia-fu immediately showed

Susan around the place, hardly suspecting that some day this attractive law student would hold responsibility for it.

Susan had attended the Institute after completing a bachelor's degree in Asian Studies in 1974 at the University of Colorado at Boulder. Never following a predictable path, and ever managing to surprise family and friends, upon completing her degree at the Institute, Susan then entered Hastings Law School in San Francisco, where she earned a degree specializing in civil rights law. Further astonishing us all, in 1980 she joined the United States Army as a commissioned officer with the rank of captain, where she served a distinguished stint in the adjutant general's office. In this role, Susan directly and solidly pursued justice for those whom she felt to be innocent and those who had been harmed, especially women soldiers who were rape victims. Here she gained valuable trial experience, which would later serve her clients well. Stationed at Fort Carson, Colorado, for her three-year duty tour, Susan lived within an hour's drive of Stillpoint.

By the mid-eighties, out of the military, Susan had established a private law practice in Gallup, New Mexico, and her visits to Stillpoint became less and less frequent. But some irrevocable bond had developed between Susan and Gia-fu, some missing link in a mysterious chain reconnected, for when Gia-fu died in June 1985, he left Susan his share of the Wetmore property, royalties from his publications, and his publication copyrights. Susan was as surprised as anyone. But despite her bewilderment at this turn of events, she immediately knuckled down to the arduous work of sorting out the unruly affairs Gia-fu left in her hands.

I remember when I first heard of it. Susan unexpectedly dropped by my house outside Denver on a hot summer's day in 1985. Our warm, usual hug was made awkward by the large brown grocery sack full of papers she held in one arm. Her body felt thin and her muscles taut. Leading the way back into the kitchen, I stopped at the sink to get water for fresh coffee, hoping for one of our caffeine-propelled life debriefings. As I made the coffee she sat down at the small round table and sighed. Her long hair was pulled back in a ponytail, and I remember the light coming through the sliding glass door revealing a face that seemed a little pale and a brow a little furrowed.

Setting the coffee and mugs on the table, I pulled out a chair, but before I could sit down she said tersely, "Gia-fu died."

Her words and flat tone stunned me. It was as if she had been holding her breath and then finally exhaled, but I found myself unable to breathe at all. "What happened?"

"He's been really sick for a while with lung disease." She stopped as if to think about this, looked wide-eyed at me, then added, "But I didn't know he was *that* sick! He just died."

Again, she paused for a moment and then, her voice full of awe and panic, she said, "And Carol, he named me as executor and left a big part of his estate to me!" She took a deep breath and blew it out, adding, "He left me his share in Stillpoint and just about everything else. Two of his students own the other two-thirds of Stillpoint."

As we sifted through what had happened and what she knew so far, she made clear that she had no idea why he had left this to her. The dusty brown grocery bags full of receipts and papers, one of which was already sitting on my kitchen counter and a dozen others in the car, along with some years of unfinished tax returns, however, suggested that his affairs begged for a disciplined mind to attend to them.

Susan's legal knowledge may have played into Gia-fu's decision as well. Probably no small part was Gia-fu's insistence that the Stillpoint community disperse after his death. In contrast to the eventual grave marker suggesting he was a spiritual master, during his life, of course, he had tenaciously resisted being viewed and treated as such. At least ten Stillpointers I talked with about him a decade later told me this and referred to his refusal to set matters up to continue as usual after he was gone. He rejected the idea of a lineage for Stillpoint, yet his grave marker and its inscription I was to see a year later reflected what they wished he had been—and what Jane English so clearly said he was not.

Susan was not part of the community and had grown increasingly distant from it, nor was she someone interested in heading or leading such a community in any way. These circumstances may have signaled to Gia-fu that she would not try to keep things as they were, but rather would permit a natural and unfettered evolution of how the place would be used.

Although she never stayed at Stillpoint more than a few days, and she never became part of the community, she had served as Stillpoint's attorney and maintained a connection with Gia-fu over the years. She continued in this role despite periods of discord between her and Gia-fu in the first half of the 1980s. It's unclear what caused the discord. Perhaps Gia-fu wanted her to be more involved in Stillpoint than she was, or perhaps strained relationships between Susan and some of the Stillpointers caused tension between Susan and Gia-fu.

She was clearly devoted to her demanding work as a civil rights attorney, and I believe this took precedence over her attentions to Stillpoint. While in the Army she characteristically took on the difficult, unpopular cases. Later, during her 1983 work with Native American tribes in South Dakota, she worked relentlessly with her law partner, Vance Gillette, addressing countless injustices and difficulties there. Her commitment to aiding those who needed it did not wane in her work later in New Mexico.

But Gia-fu's will made clear that his share of the property (the other two shares belonged to Stillpoint community members Lorraine Kirk and Michael Burton) and remaining financial assets, accompanied by the bulk of his unresolved issues, went to Susan. That Gia-fu owned only one share in Stillpoint would later emerge as a major problem. For the moment, myriad immediate challenges sufficed. The assets helped but did not begin to cover subsequent costs.

As Susan worked to settle the legal and financial issues after Gia-fu's death, a few of the community who stayed tried to carry on. An excerpt from the Winter 1985 *Stillpoint Resonator*, a group journal, describes the situation well, and from the Stillpointers' perspective:

> A lot of people have been calling and writing to ask about the fate of Stillpoint now that Gia Fu has passed on. The situation is not entirely clear at this time but it appears that, unlike so many communities that were created around a powerful leader, Stillpoint will survive.
>
> Many of Gia Fu's ways could be labeled "creative chaos" and his estate was no exception. We have been fortunate that the lawyer

he chose to be executor and 1/3 heir is extremely competent. It appears that the estate will soon be out of probate, that various claimants have been satisfied without entering into litigation and that an IRS claim for tens of thousands in back taxes has been reduced to zero.

Currently land payments, taxes, insurance and utilities are being paid by the estate. Food, gasoline, odds & ends and miscellaneous living expenses are being paid by residents and visitors and by what little money we can generate from odd jobs, workshops, etc. Currently we are nine permanent residents: (alphabetically) Carmen Baehr, Sue Bailey, Robert Glenn Breckenridge, Flemming, Gabriela & Christina Fontel, Martina Gaith, Walter Meile…The power struggles that often destroy communities when the leader dies with no designated heir have been mild and non-destructive here. We have managed ourselves with no designated leaders and no formalized democratic or consensus processes. We really have been as we say, "organic" rather than "organizational". Soon, with our lawyers, we will be setting up a corporation to handle our business affairs. This may result in some kind of structure within the community itself. Keep tuned in for further developments…

There came a point, however, when conflict developed. Susan and many in the community came head to head in disagreement, as each had his or her perspective about an appropriate course of action. Another excerpt from the *Stillpoint Resonator*, this one Issue 3, reflects a changed atmosphere from that described earlier.

Gia Fu Feng, there is no doubt, left his estate as he did intentionally as he lived—interestingly creative in transcendent chaos: a final gift to all of us, each and every one…

Frustration for those seeking frustration. Legal problems for those seeking legal problems. Fear for those finding fear in un-pre-dict-abil-ity as well as enlightenment for those discovering freedom in it. Conflict for those wishing to hone their skills of intimidation. Mistrust for those projecting the untrustworthy. Humor for the numerous humerous [spelling intentional] ... A final stroke on his canvas of the unexpected, destined to slide its way into the cells of the left-brained robots of the highly organized ignorance of this great modern civilization. And also 180 [sic] acres of a cabin be-strewn Rocky Mountain Hermit Paradise—an island in the Tao, out of time, where wisdom is nurtured, intelligence subdued.

—Hoo Haw

A few months before the conflict peaked, however, the year 1985, though close to its end, still had more in store for Susan. In mid-December a car accident left both her and a friend with whom she was riding badly jarred and needing medical attention. Initially, Susan got the needed treatments, but then State Farm, the insurer for both Susan and her friend, began rejecting her claims while continuing to pay expenses for the friend. With all of her resources going into the law prac-tice, she was unable to pay for medical expenses. Her condition deterio-rated so badly she could no longer sit to prepare for trials nor stand in court to argue her clients' cases. Heartbroken, she watched all she had worked so hard to attain, her law practice and her home, slip away.

Never one to give up without a good fight, however, Susan regained her equilibrium and sued State Farm, filing the suit in federal court. As she prepared for the case she also tried to attend to Stillpoint. By this time the community had dispersed, eventually settling in various parts of the country and the world—Colorado, Texas, Guatemala, Germany. At Lloyd Alexander's request, Tomi Smith had been temporarily staying there, keeping an eye on the place.

Now Susan, having lost her home, moved to Stillpoint, living in the drafty, rustic teahouse, the log cabin that sat about one-third mile from Stillpoint's entrance. She invited people she knew, a family also seeking a new direction in their lives, to turn the upper floor of the barn into a home. They did this and lived there comfortably for more than a year, helping out around the place. A friend from Gallup, Joe Athens, also came to Stillpoint to stay for an extended time, aiding Susan by assuming the role of manager and providing her much-needed support.

After many months the State Farm case finally came to trial in Denver, in the federal courtroom of Judge Robert Matsch, who would later preside over the Oklahoma City bombing proceedings. Throughout the weeklong, exhausting jury trial, Susan remained focused and steady. I saw little of her during the trial, as it consumed her attention, and I felt awed by and superfluous to the process. Susan and her attorney, Patrick LeHoulier, prepared well, and the trial came out in her favor. After more than two years, the money for medical expenses and recompense for her lost professional life seemed a real possibility.

I visited her in her downtown Denver hotel room the night the trial concluded. Soaking in a hot bath, she exuded weariness, fatigue, and some sense of victory in a very hard-fought battle. I sat on the edge of the tub as she gave me an overview of major events in the trial, along with the results. She spoke of her local State Farm agent, who she said had tried to help her but subsequently had been fired from the agency. Fired, she said, because he had tried to help her.

She sobbed as she told me of one point in the testimony, "I had to tell them about the State Farm adjustor who came to my house to investigate this claim. It was at a time when I couldn't even get out of bed. He just tromped into my house, looked around for a minute, and called me a filthy Indian trying to get something for nothing."

My heart broke as she told me about this. I had not known about it, and her telling me then caused me to wonder how much more I didn't know. This incident had been hard enough for her to endure when it happened. She then had to relive the pain and humiliation of this experience in front of judge, attorneys, and jury. Endure his derogatory tone and language, she had, but she would not let them pass unaccounted for.

Victory, however, eluded her once again. Very soon after the trial, State Farm appealed the decision, and so, for the time being, the case remained unresolved.

Not knowing when the appellate court would review the State Farm case, Susan determined to carry on as best she could. She continued seeing to improvements at Stillpoint, cutting back the aggressive gamble oak to keep it from taking over meadows, restoring the twenty-plus huts, hauling off debris, replacing the makeshift electrical setup with a safer, more reliable system, ridding the forest of diseased trees, and other such things. Joe Athens, sometimes aided by the family living in the barn house, saw that these things were done. Local people helped as they could. Bill Donley and Jerome Weigel, neighboring ranchers, provided guidance as needed. Susan financed much of this work from royalties from Gia-fu's publications and a little legal work she could undertake from her Stillpoint base.

It was during this time that Susan met Clara and Margaret, two people who began their acquaintance with skepticism and soon became as family to her. Clara Reida and Margaret Locarnini bred appaloosa horses at their Singing Acres Ranch about ten miles up Highway 96 from Stillpoint. They viewed Stillpoint and Gia-fu with great suspicion, having heard talk about the unconventional lifestyles there.

Recommended by another neighbor, Susan contacted Clara about a sick Arabian mare. Clara and Margaret recounted their first meeting to me some months after I first met them in 1988. They had agreed to talk with Susan, but had reservations about anyone coming from Stillpoint. They saw the slender, long-haired woman, dressed in jeans and floppy shirt, and thought the worst. Not long after they began talking, however, they realized this person was someone who sparked their interest and with whom they would be willing to spend some time. The friendship developed quickly. They provided a much-needed haven for Susan, eventually turning a spare room into an office and bedroom for her so she could alternate between Stillpoint and Singing Acres Ranch. They also sent Margaret's canned vegetables, meat, and other goodies home with her and tried to encourage her to eat well, something she never could do on a continuous basis.

In the fall of 1989, as Susan attended to the many layers of tasks before her, she also began preparing for yet another trial. A local attorney had purchased the other two-thirds of Stillpoint from the former Stillpointers and had sold it to a couple who wanted to develop it for commercial purposes. The attorney was trying to force Susan to sell her share, and she was adamant that she would not. The case was to be tried in the Custer County Court. Thus entered all her efforts to improve Stillpoint, which she had tirelessly documented through photographs, receipts, and witnesses. Working with an attorney whom she had known for some time proved a disappointment to her when she felt he entered into the trial not well prepared. Another attorney with whom Susan had worked came into the case; Brenda Jackson, a young, thorough, and exacting lawyer from Cañon City. Susan prepared the final chapters of the case, and Brenda represented Susan in court.

Based on the nature of the dispute, the judge decreed a public auction, to be held in March 1991 in Westcliffe on the Custer County courthouse steps. The Custer County sheriff was to preside. In preparation, Susan, who had used all her resources and then some on Stillpoint, turned to me and also to friends. Together, Susan and I took out a mortgage, and then she also arranged for additional loans from friends—just in case. Susan undertook the bulk of the preparation work, with the support of Joe Athens, Brenda Jackson, Clara and Margaret, and others.

The auction was held early on a March morning in 1991. Susan didn't know I was coming, and when she saw me walk across the lawn in front of the courthouse, her face lit up. Her expression told me all I needed to know about whether I should be there or not.

The auction seemed like a scene from a western movie. The sheriff was tall and thin, wearing cowboy boots and hat. Several ranchers from around Stillpoint came to offer Susan moral support. Some were leaning on their pickup trucks parked nearby, waiting patiently. Two friends— Carmen Baehr, who had been at Stillpoint with Gia-fu for two years before he died, and Mary Wright—were there from Boulder. Mary was one of the friends who had generously offered financial support if needed. They both reflected Boulder more than Westcliffe in their flowing skirts and long, loose hair. The attorney on the opposing side, whom Susan had described as unctuous, was there along with his clients. No one had to point them out to me.

The sheriff laid out the rules, and the auction commenced. Bidding between Susan and the attorney progressed steadily. At a certain point the attorney signaled for a recess to confer with his clients. He returned shortly and began bidding again. Then after a few more minutes the attorney signaled they would go no higher in their bid. Susan had outbid them. Susan had bought Stillpoint!

Knowing of Susan's bankruptcy, the attorney didn't believe she had the resources to pay for the property, so he demanded to see for himself that she could. She produced the bank document showing the mortgage she and I had arranged. Then he insisted that she pay the full price—including that for the share she already owned, rather than only for the two-thirds that she had just bought. After some deliberation and consultation with the judge, Susan was required to pay the full amount. Our mortgage covered only the two-thirds, but with her usual thoroughness Susan had prepared for this turn of events. She signaled to Mary, who was standing a short distance away talking with her brother and Carmen. Mary strolled over to where we stood. Susan spoke to her briefly, and Mary reached into the pocket of her long, full skirt and pulled out a roll of bills. She handed over tens of thousands of dollars in cash to Susan. The attorney's eyes nearly popped out to see that much money produced on the spot, and from such an unlikely source! Later Susan and I giggled uncontrollably about that moment.

Susan, the attorney, and the judge spent much of the rest of the day haggling over details. The attorney seemed to make it as difficult as possible for Susan, and the judge was no help. After almost four hours of this, we drove to the Cañon City bank to finalize the mortgage arrangements.

After this event, for the remainder of March and early April 1991, Susan again turned her attention to Stillpoint. She also filed two lawsuits, one against the attorney for fraud and one against the judge. She felt they had used their offices unethically in this deal, and Susan was asking for recourse—more serious, grown-up shades of "Damn you, Henry Harper!" She then went to Gillette, Wyoming, to stay with her friend and companion, Mickey DeWeese. He and Susan had met through Clara, and he proved to be a steadfast friend and support for her. She and I saw each other several times during this period, and we talked often on the phone.

One Saturday in April, Susan left several messages on my answering machine. In the final message she said, "The doctor insisted I come to the hospital so they can find out what's causing these stomach pains. They just don't seem to go away in spite of all the yogurt I've been eating!"

Mickey picked me up at the Gillette airport, and we went directly to the hospital. Susan brightened visibly when she saw me. Those who knew her would not have been surprised by the scene. Sitting in bed, dark hair falling over the shoulders of the hospital gown, Susan was going through stacks of files piled around her bed and on the nearby table. She was at work. When I gently admonished her, she replied, "I have too much to do to just lie here!"

Susan told me they would be conducting tests the next day. After many tests, the doctor concluded that a benign tumor in the stomach was creating a blockage and recommended surgery. It was scheduled for Thursday.

During the surgery, Mickey, Susan's friend Judith, and I kept each other company in the very large, stark waiting room. Alternately staring out at the bleak landscape and talking with Mickey, Judith, or both, I felt the time drag by. None of us was willing to leave the waiting room for any length of time. Convinced by the doctor's pronouncement that the tumor was benign, we talked about what to do to help Susan recover from the surgery—where she should stay, who should be with her.

Hours later, when the doctor called us into his office after the surgery, we were completely unprepared and thoroughly stunned by his words. He told us they had discovered an advanced malignancy in her stomach. They were unable to remove it because it was all through her stomach lining. The doctor's words were so antithetical to what I expected, I couldn't believe them. His voice seemed to be coming from another planet. How could this be? The tumor was benign; they'd been so sure... Shivering so hard I could barely talk, I managed to ask, "What does this mean?"

Gently but firmly, he said, "The prognosis—under very good conditions, she might be able to live a year."

My insides turned to ice. I could not stop shaking. The doctor ordered me to be put under heated blankets until the shock wore off. It finally did, but I felt numb, moving mechanically through the strange world now before me.

I arranged to stay with her another week, and the whole time with her at the hospital. As she wished, we talked, watched movies she requested, and listened to music. Her favorite piece, Pachelbel's Canon in D, continues to evoke for me the tenderness and tragedy of that time. A long-standing consulting commitment caused me to leave, with the promise to return to Gillette immediately after. In the meantime our mother and brother, Bruce, were coming to Gillette to be with her.

I left with plans to return in a week. Calling daily to check, I learned her condition was not good, but I was unaware of how bad it had grown. Then, the day before I was to return, I received a midnight call in my Moscow, Idaho, hotel room. Mickey said I'd better come quickly. The earliest flight I could get departed from Spokane, sixty-eight miles away. Another person on the consulting team, Vickie Johnson, managed to get a car and dropped me there about two a.m. I went directly to the phone booth to call the hospital. Bruce took the call and told me things were not good. I told him when I would arrive, and we agreed that I would call periodically in the time before I boarded the plane, which was still some four hours away.

I could not tear myself away from that phone booth, for the phone seemed the only tangible, albeit slim, link between Susan and me. I was desperate for any connection and felt helpless with the physical distance. Telephoning was the only thing I could do, and I clung to that simple effort. Between calls, physically and emotionally exhausted, I dozed in the phone booth, my forehead resting against the phone itself, automatically awaking when it was time to call.

My flight, the first one out of Spokane, was to leave at six thirty a.m. I phoned again at six. My brother, his voice tightly controlled, holding back emotion as a weak dam holds back the rising waters, said, "Susan just died."

Too late. I was too late. Managing to board a flight, I wept my way back to Denver. I had planned to be with Susan that evening, holding her hand, sharing events of the past week, telling her how much I had missed her. Instead I was in Denver with my mother, Bruce, and friends Ellen and Celia, mourning for her.

Somehow, my mother, brother, and I got through the horrible first days. There were arrangements to make, family and friends to notify. We soon learned that in her will, dated March 27, 1991, Susan named me as executor, along with Joe Athens, and sole beneficiary, echoing Gia-fu's own actions. Stillpoint and all responsibility for it were then in my hands.

On May 13, 1991, three days after her death, family and friends from across the country gathered at Stillpoint to honor Susan's memory and spread her ashes, as she requested, "on a sunny hill" in the beautiful Colorado meadow she loved.

The legacy of Gia-fu Feng, "a final stroke on his canvas of the unexpected," continues. Not as Hoo Haw suggests, sliding "its way into the cells of the left-brained robots," but because of Susan's respect and her willingness to risk everything for "an island in the Tao, out of time…"

Inspired by my sister's commitment and vision and Gia-fu's legacy, Stillpoint: A Center for the Humanities & Community came to life in 1995. Friend Gary Holthaus, David, and I filed the incorporation papers to create a center for promoting a sense of community through the humanities, through the literature, history, art, philosophy, and music that both Susan and Gia-fu loved. The Center, the board of which includes former Stillpointers and Stillpoint friends, sponsors poetry and prose readings, musical programs, conversations, and other forums for experiencing and understanding the meaning of community in our lives.

A few years after Gia-fu's death, back in Australia, Sue Bailey and another former Stillpointer self-published the version of the *Yi Jing (I Ching)* Gia-fu and others had been working on at the time of his death. Perhaps most significantly, Gia-fu and Jane's translation of the *Tao Te Ching* continues to be the most popular English translation, with a smaller edition sans photographs published in 1989 and a twenty-fifth anniversary edition of the original-sized edition with photographs published in 1997. *Chuang Tsu: Inner Chapters*, having undergone several reprintings, remains of interest, as do the continuing calendars, cards, and journals Jane designs based primarily on the *Tao Te Ching*, with excerpts from *Inner Chapters* as well.

As for the land itself, Susan's fight to save it from development made it possible to keep it safe for others to experience its stillness, its special spirit. In 2005, through a conservation easement with the San Isabel Land Protection Trust, Stillpoint became free of threat of any development whatsoever into perpetuity. According to the agreement, the "property will be perpetually preserved in its predominantly natural, scenic, agricultural, and open space condition."[1]

Over the years, numerous people have taken the opportunity to be at, learn from, and give to Stillpoint. Public school, college, university and other groups, as well as individuals, have stayed there, always giving some service in return—repairing cabins, pulling noxious weeds, cutting the gamble oak away from the cabins. And inevitably, people come away with stories—peaceful, amusing, or wondrous.

And so I end with another story of Stillpoint, one that tells of an evening when David and I were privy to an unforgettable sight, one that underscores the spirit of Susan, Gia-fu, and Stillpoint and of how that spirit lives on. A late evening storm had moved in from the northwest, cloaking the mountains in its thickness. Sharp strings of lightning pierced the darkness, accompanying the staccatos of stinging rain. To the southeast, reaching to about a forty-five-degree angle, the sky remained perfectly clear, and in it the rising full moon shone brilliantly. The contrast between the northwestern and southeastern skies could not have been greater.

David stepped out on the back landing, wanting to watch the drama unfettered by window frames. Only an instant had passed when he yelled, "Carol, come see this! It's a streak of silver above the mountains."

I ran to join him and we stood, pelted by the hard rain, staring open-mouthed at the spectacle in the northwestern sky. As we watched, incredulous, a silvery, shadowy rainbow form took shape. "It's a rainbow, no, a moonbow!" David gasped. "How can that be?"

We stood, eyes glued to the phenomenon, as a second, paler bow formed above the more brilliant one. A double moonbow. And as our eyes became more accustomed to the sight, we could discern faint bluish, greenish, and pinkish glows from the more brilliant bow, as if it were a rainbow reflected in a silver bowl.

Eventually managing to drag ourselves away so that we could see the rest of the sky, we moved to the barn's other side for a direct view of the radiant moon. "The moon's so bright, it's acting as the sun to form this rainbow," David observed.

The wind cold, the pelting rain unrelenting, we moved inside to continue our vigil through the windows. The brighter bow formed a perfect arc, with the far end resting in a meadow across the way to the northeast and the other to the southwest, in the meadow by Gia-fu's grave. For almost forty-five minutes, the moonbow glowed and then very slowly began to fade, gradually giving way to the moon's steadily growing dominance in the changing night sky.

The moonbow's image often returns in my mind's eye, reminding me of the phrase "finger pointing to the moon" found in Eastern thought, suggesting that we not mistake the finger for the moon, as we so often do in our grasping for certainty, for answers to unanswerable questions. As if in recognition of the difficulties and dangers in too easily drawing conclusions, of pinning down certainties, I often wonder, was that moonbow the moon pointing its finger back? Perhaps to remind us, as Lao Tsu did some twenty-five hundred years ago,

> The Tao that can be told is not the eternal Tao.
> The name that can be named is not the eternal name...
> Darkness within darkness.
> The gate to all mystery[2]

NOTE ABOUT
NAMES and SPELLING

Chinese family names precede the given name, so the name Westerners would use to refer to Gia-fu Feng would be Feng Gia-fu in the Chinese custom. I have taken the liberty of referring to the Feng siblings primarily by their first names only.

I have used a mixture of the Wade-Giles and pinyin systems to spell Chinese words, matching the spelling to fit the times most associated with individuals in the Feng family, as well as various places referred to in the text. The family names are spelled consistently throughout the text.

Other Chinese words taken from Gia-fu Feng's notes and manuscript may not conform to a consistent pattern, so for both Gia-fu and myself, I beg the reader's forbearance.

CHAPTER NOTES

The *Tao Te Ching* quotations at the beginning of chapters are from the Gia-fu Feng and Jane English translation, *Tao Te Ching* (New York: Vintage Books, 1972). The Chuang Tsu quotations are from *Chuang Tsu Inner Chapters* (Mt. Shasta, CA: Earth Heart, 1997).

For the most part, personal information about Gia-fu Feng's years in China, including his return in 1975, was drawn from his autobiographical papers. Information from other sources is noted in the text or in the individual chapter notes.

TITLE PAGE

Quotation: Nicole Mones, *A Cup of Light* (New York: Dell, 2003).

CHAPTER 1

[n1.1] p. 10 This photo of Gia-fu was published in Anderson 1983.

[n1.2] p. 10 **Gia-fu describing Fritz Perls:** Gaines 1979, 170.

[n1.3] p. 15 **Patterns in our lives:** Bateson 1989.

CHAPTER 2

For a history of China and Shanghai, I drew heavily from the following: J. K. Fairbank 1992, 13–14; Spence 1990; Dong 2000; Seagreave 1985, 145.

[n2.1] p. 20 **Da Ching Bank:** The Ching Dynasty was Manchu and was established upon the defeat of the Ming Dynasty by the Manchurians in 1644.

[n2.2] p. 23 **Shanghai's Prime:** Dong 2000, 1.

[n2.3] p. 25 **Han-lin Academy:** Latourette 1946, 524.

CHAPTER 3

[n3.1] p. 36 **Japanese action in North China:** J. K. Fairbank 1992, 312.

[n3.2] p. 36 **Incident at Lou Kuo Bridge:** Spence 1990, 445.

[n3.3] p. 36 **World War II beginnings:** I. Chang 1997, 3.

[n3.4] pp. 36 **Japanese action:** Spence 1990, 445–447.

[n3.5] p. 37 **Numbers killed:** Dong 2000, 258.

[n3.6] p. 37 **Shanghai's International Settlement:** I. Chang 1997, 8.

[n3.7] p. 38 **Universities in exile:** W. Fairbank 1994, 98.

[n3.8] p. 39 **Japanese "new order":** Spence 1990, 451.

CHAPTER 4

[n4.1] p. 46 **Kunming environment and peoples:** China scholar William Doub interview, November 2004.

[n4.2] p. 47 **The Burma Road:** J. K. Fairbank 1982, 176; Spence 1990, 458; Tuchman 1970, 211.

[n4.3] p. 47 **Yunnanese ambivalence:** W. Fairbank 1994, 106.

[n4.4] p. 54 **Guanxi:** De Mente 2000, 22.

[n4.5] p. 58 **The Boxer Rising:** J. K. Fairbank 1992, 231–232.

[n4.6] p. 60 **Kunming Training Center:** Tuchman 1971, 263.

[n4.7] pp. 60–61 **General J. L. Huang:** J. K. Fairbank 1982, 202, 207–208.

[n4.8] pp. 62-63 **Kunming, SAU, and the KMT:** Spence 1990, 457.

[n4.9] p. 63 **Burma Road and Chinese workers:** Spence 1990, 458.

CHAPTER 5

[n5.1] pp. 70–71 **Shanghai after the war:** Dong 2000, 280–286.

CHAPTER 6

[n6.1] p. 75 **USS *General Gordon*:** See *Dictionary of American Naval Ships* website at www.ibiblio.org/hyperwar/USN/ships/dafs/AP/ap117.html

[n6.2] p. 76 **China and Western education:** Tuchman 1970, 29.

[n6.3] pp. 76–77 **The history of the Chinese in America:** I. Chang 2003, 132.

[n6.4] pp. 76–77 **Chinese students in America:** Ni 2002, 149, 159.

[n6.5] p. 77 **Complex relationship between China and the West:** Lian 1998, 19.

[n6.6] pp. 77–78 **The U.S. in the late 1940s:** Halberstam 1994.

[n6.7] p. 79 **China and U.S. relations/Korea:** J. K. Fairbank 1982, 320–321.

[n6.8] p. 80 **The Chinese and their food:** For a discussion, see Yutang 1935, 337.

[n6.9] p. 80 **Chinese restaurants in the U.S.:** I. Chang 2003, 163.

[n6.10] p. 81 **Chinese and class in the U.S.:** Professor William Wei interview, October 1999.

[n6.11] p. 81 **Wharton School:** See Wharton School website at www.wharton.upenn.edu/whartonfacts/

[6.12] pp. 82–83 **Pendle Hill:** Trueblood 1950, x; www.PendleHill.org.

[n6.13] p. 83 **Quaker emphasis on peace:** Rufus Jones quoted by Trueblood 1950, x.

[n6.14] p. 84 **Circumstances in China and the U.S. in the late 1940s and early 1950s:** Spence 1990, 514–533.

[n6.15] p. 84 **Proxy war:** Term used on *Wikipedia*, http://en.wikipedia.org/wiki/Korean_War.

[n6.16] p. 85 **Chinese students stranded in the U.S.:** Ni 2002, 151.

[n6.17] p. 86 **Difficulties with visas and work:** Ni 2002, 156.

[6.18] p. 87 **Prejudice among Chinese groups in the U.S.:** Chin, et al, 1972, 38. "The overthrow of the Manchus, the Sino-Japanese War, World War II, the success of the Communist Revolution, and the Cultural Revolution are five major events resulting in a China the Chinese of a hundred years ago, the ancestors of the fourth, fifth, and sixth generation Chinese-Americans, never saw and wouldn't understand. These new Chinese are emigrating to America. The assertion of distinctions between Chinese and Chinese-Americans is neither a rejection of Chinese culture nor an expression of contempt for things Chinese, as the whites and the Chinatown establishment would make them out to be. It's calling things by their right names. Change has taken place in China, in American Chinatowns and the world generally, changes that have been ignored and suppressed to preserve the popular racist 'truths' that make up the oriental stereotype."

[n.6.19] p. 87 **Margaret Olney friendship:** Margaret Olney interview, December 10, 1998.

[n6.20] p. 89 **Oliver Brown and Topeka law suit:** Halberstam 1994, 413–429.

[n6.21] p. 92 **Alan Watts:** Anderson 1983.

CHAPTER 7

[n7.1] p. 94 **American Academcy of Asian Studies:** For more information on the history and early faculty, see the American Academy of Asian Studies website at www.well.com/~davidu/aaas.html

[n7.2] p. 95 **Alan Watts:** Watts 1973, 306.

[n7.3] p. 95 **Refugee Relief Act of 1953:** Ni 2002, 152.

[n7.4] p. 96 **Chinese Communist Party campaigns:** Spence 1990, 541–551.

[n7.5] p. 96 **The Academy:** Watts 1973, 284.

[n7.6] pp. 96–97 **The Academy's founder, Louis Gainsborough:** See the American Academy of Asian Studies website, www.well.com/~davidu/aaas.html

[n7.7] p. 98 **Beat Zen:** Watts 1958.

[n7.8] pp. 100–102 **Robert Breckenridge, Gia-fu and the Academy:** Robert Breckenridge interview, July 15, 1997.

[n7.9] p. 102 **Watts's departure from the Academy:** Watts 1973, 315.

[n7.10] p. 102 **East-West House:** Ananda Claude Dalenberg interview, October 9, 1997, and letter from Robert Breckenridge, January 9, 1999.

[n7.11] pp. 102–103 **Hyphen House:** Chadwick 1999, 173.

[n7.12] p. 104 **Generation coming of age:** Watson 1995, 5.

[n7.13] p. 104 **Dinners by Gia-fu and Lew Welch:** Mertis Shekeloff interview, October 11, 1997.

[n7.14] pp. 104–105 **Human hygiene:** Joanne Kyger letter, June 1999.

[n7.15] p. 105 **San Francisco in the late 1950s:** Solnit 1995, 70, 76–77.

[n7.16] p. 106 **Joanne Kyger and Gia-fu:** Joanne Kyger letter, June 1999, also follow-up visit, summer 1999.

[n7.17] pp. 103–107 **Mertis Shekeloff:** Mertis Shekeloff interview, October 11, 1997.

[n7.18] pp. 107–109 **Great Leap Forward:** Spence 1990, 577–582. Also J. Chang and Halliday 2005, 448, 454.

[n7.19] pp. 109–110 **Pierre DeLattre, the Bread and Wine Mission, and Gia-fu:** Pierre DeLattre letter, January 2001.

[n7.20] p. 110 **Gia-fu Feng naturalization:** Original naturalization papers, September 4, 1962.

CHAPTER 8

[n8.1] pp. 112–113 **Michael Murphy and Dick Price:** Erickson 2005, 147. Also Tomkins 1976, 31.

[n8.2] p. 113 **Dick Price, Bonnie, and Gia-fu:** Anderson 2004, 39–42.

[n8.3] p. 114 **Dick Price description of his ecstatic experience:** Dick Price, interview by Wade Hudson, www.esalen.org/air/essays/dick_price.htm, April 1985.

[n8.4] p. 115 **Center for the exploration of new ideas:** Anderson 2004, 48.

[n8.5] p. 115 **Alan Watts's description of the Academy:** Watts 1973, 351.

[n8.6] p. 116 **Esalen, the name:** Anderson 2004, 18–19.

[n8.7] pp. 116–117 **Encounter at the Hot Springs:** (see note 8.1) Tomkins 1976, 40–41.

[n8.8] pp. 117–118 **Connections for the center:** Anderson 2004, 63.

[n8.9] pp. 118–119 **Gia-fu and the IRS visit:** Michael Murphy telephone interview, September 12, 1997.

[n8.10] p. 119 **Abraham Maslow:** Anderson 2004, 57. Also Tomkins 1976, 42.

[n8.11] p. 120 **First program series:** Anderson 2004, 68.

[n8.12] p. 121 **Michael trying peyote:** Michael Murphy telephone interview, September 12, 1997.

[n8.13] pp. 121–122 **Gia-fu and bodywork:** Anderson 2004, 87. (It's not clear just how much tai chi training Gia-fu received early in life. One sibling recalled a little during the summer months at the Feng villa.)

[n8.14] p. 122 **Program strands:** Anderson 2004, 79.

[n8.15] p. 123 **Gestalt therapy:** Perls 1976, 221. Also Anderson 2004, 86–87, and Bottome 1997, 2.

[n8.16] p. 124 **China and Chairman Mao—relationships in the world:** *Time*, September 13, 1963.

[n8.17] pp. 124–25 **Alternate view of China:** Committee of Concerned Asian Scholars 1972. Also Schurmann and Schell 1967.

[n8.18] p. 125 **Joanne, Mertis, Gia-fu, and woven mats:** Joanne Kyger letter, June 1999.

[n8.19] pp. 126–127 **Fritz Perls:** Gaines 1979, xii and 37.

[n8.20] p. 127 **Fritz and Gia-fu fight:** Michael Murphy telephone interview, September 12, 1997.

[n8.21] p. 128 **Gia-fu's pronouncements:** Michael Murphy telephone interview, September 12, 1997; quote from Feng and English translation, *Tao Te Ching*, chapters 42 and 7.

[n8.22] pp. 127–130 **Relationship between Friz and Gia-fu:** Gaines 1979, 145–146, 418.

CHAPTER 9

Much of the material in this chapter came from overlapping sources in the form of interviews and conversations.

[n9.1] p. 132 **One translation of Stillpoint:** Greene 2003, 116.

[n9.2] p. 132 **Taoism:** Berling, n.d.

[n9.3] p. 132 **Taoist approach to life:** Needham 1974, 83.

[n9.4] p. 133 **Quote:** Feng and English 1972, chapter 11.

[n9.5] p. 134 **Gia-fu and wholeheartedness:** Jane English interview, March 2000.

[n9.6] p. 136 **Anne Heider and Tai Chi book:** Anne Heider telephone interview, February 5, 2000. Also Feng and Kirk 1970.

[n9.7] p. 136 **I Ching Translations:** Legge 1963, 89. Also Feng and Kirk 1970, 41.

[n9.8] p. 137 **Tai chi and conducting:** Anne Heider telephone interview, February 5, 2000.

[n9.9] pp. 137 **Lloyd Alexander, Gia-fu, and Stillpoint:** Lloyd Alexander interview, October 9, 1994.

[n9.10] p. 139 **How Gia-fu leads group sessions:** Jane English interview, September 1994.

[n9.11] pp. 141–143 **Jane English, Gia-fu and Stillpoint:** Jane English interview, October 14, 1997.

[n9.12] p. 143 **Gia-fu's attraction to Jane:** Judith Bolinger telephone interview, January 1998.

[n9.13] pp. 146–147 **Judith and Chris at Stillpoint:** Judith Bolinger telephone interview, January 1998. Also Chris Fessenden telephone interview, December 19, 2007.

[n9.14] p. 148 **Composition of Stillpoint community:** Jane English interview, October 14, 1997.

[n9.15] pp. 148–150 **Natalie Ednie and Stillpoint:** Natalie Ednie telephone interview, March 10, 2007.

[n9.16] p. 151 **Tao Te Ching and Lao Tsu:** Feng and English 1972, front note. A more commonly accepted version is that Lao Tsu, sickened by the intrigue and corruption of the court, rode his ox out of China through the Chungnan Mountain Pass.

CHAPTER 10

Much of the material about the Stillpoint community in this chapter came from overlapping sources in the form of interviews and conversations with Jane English (1994, 1997, 2007), Judith Bolinger (1998), and Chris Fessenden (2008).

[n10.1] p. 155 **The Red Guard and the Cultural Revolution:** Spence 2006, 31–34. Also, for more information on Mao's campaigns, see Spence 1990, 602–617.

[n10.2] p. 156 **Feng Chong-ching:** Mr. Zhu-lei interview, translated by Feng Li, February 16, 1997.

[n10.3] pp. 161–163 **Toinette Lippe and the Tao Te Ching:** Lippe 1997.

[n10.4] pp. 164–165 **Gia-fu and Lloyd hiking:** Lloyd Alexander interview, September 1994.

CHAPTER 11

Again, much material in this chapter derives from interviews and conversations with Jane English, Judith Bolinger, and Chris Fessenden. Jane English's European trip notes were also a valuable source of information.

[n11.1] p. 168 **Manitou Springs:** See Manitou Springs' website, http://manitousprings.org/about/history.htm

[n11.2] p. 169 **Stillpoint routine:** Judith Bolinger telephone interview, January 1998.

[n11.3] p. 171 **Gia-fu on Taoist rogue, guru:** Gia-fu Feng *New Dimensions* radio interview, San Francisco, 1978.

[n11.4] p. 172 **Tran Van Dinh:** Letter from Gia-fu to Tran Van Dinh, October 30, 1972.

[n11.5] p. 180 **Joseph Needham:** See The Needham Research Institute web page, www.nri.org.uk/joseph.html

[n11.6] pp. 174–181 **Jane and Gia-fu European trip:** Jane English trip notes February–March, 1973.

[n11.7] p. 182 **Judith's time at Stillpoint:** Judith Bolinger telephone interview, January 1998.

CHAPTER 12

Information from this chapter comes primarily from Gia-fu Feng's papers, an interview with Feng Yun Ke, October 2005, Tai-an, Shandong Province, China, and from conversations with family who prefer not to be named.

[n12.1] p. 186 **Committee of Concerned Asian Scholars:** Interview with William Doub, former editor of the *Journal of Concerned Asian Scholars*, November 29, 2007.

[n12.2] pp. 198–199 **Gia-fu's siblings comment on Gia-fu:** Mei-chi Lee and C.H. Feng interview, January 1995.

CHAPTER 13

[n13.1] p. 202 **Mich and Gia-fu:** Tomi Smith telephone interview, January 21, 2008. A follow-up conversation with Don LeVack on January 22, 2008, also helped inform these passages.

[n13.2] p. 203 **Book on Taoism:** Rawson and Legeza 1973.

[n13.3] p. 203 **Gia-fu and morning sessions:** *Taoism and Gestalt Therapy*, article by Charles Gagarin, chapter 15, pp. 212–217. Unable to confirm source.

[n13.4] p. 204 **Gestalt therapy:** Naranjo 1993, xxx–xxxi.

[n13.5] p. 205 **Tomi and Stillpoint:** Tomi Smith journals, 1976–1978 and follow-up conversations and correspondence.

[n13.6] p. 205 **Patriarch of Stillpoint:** Gia-fu's letter to Richard Hoffman, August 23, 1983.

[n13.7] pp. 206–207 **Don LeVack and Stillpoint:** Don LeVack interview, July 27, 1999, and letter of January 2, 2008.

[n13.8] p. 207 **A kind of kibbutz therapy:** Lloyd Alexander interview, October 9, 1994.

[n13.9] p. 208 **People who sought Gia-fu:** Don LeVack interview, July 27, 1999, and letter of January 2, 2008.

[n13.10] p. 210 **The farm's progress:** Gia-fu's letter to Richard Hoffman, 1978.

[n13.11] p. 212 **Teaching in Europe vs. U.S.:** Gia-fu's letter to Richard Hoffman, May 22, 1978.

[n13.12] pp. 212–213 **Stillpoint University:** Stillpoint press release, November 1977.

[n13.13] pp. 213–214 **Stillpoint schedule and translation:** Gia-fu letter to Richard Hoffman, October 15, 1978.

[n13.14] p. 217 **Trickster:** Hyde 1998, 7.

[n13.15] p. 218 **Master of life:** Don Workman interview, November 27, 1999.

[n13.16] pp. 214–218 **Alan Redman:** Alan Redman/Shi Jing interview, August 13, 2001.

[n13.17] p. 219 **Awe and joy at Stillpoint:** Don LeVack e-mail correspondence, January 22, 2008.

[n13.18] pp. 219 **Margaret Susan Wilson:** Lloyd Alexander interview, July 25, 1997.

[n13.19] p. 222 **Kundalini:** Sannella 1976.

[n13.20] pp. 220–225 **Carmen Baehr, Gia-fu, and Stillpoint:** Carmen Baehr interview, October 3, 1997.

[n13.21] p. 227 **Wabi-sabi:** See www.resurgence.org/resurgence/issues/koren203.htm

[n13.22] p. 227 **Columbine only for the wedding:** Colleen Corbo interview, May 1, 2007.

[13.23] pp. 225–228 **Robert Breckenridge and Stillpoint:** Robert Breckenridge interview, July 1998.

CHAPTER 14

[n14.1] p. 230 **Dr. Witke comments on Gia-fu's autobiography:** Letter to Gia-fu from Roxane Witke, February 6, 1984.

[n14.2] p. 231 **Alchemy:** Wong 1992, viii.

[n14.3] pp. 231–232 **Gia-fu's interest in natural medicine:** Letter from Victor S. Sierpina, MD, Humana MedFirst Physician care, December 21, 1984.

[n14.4] pp. 233–234 **Nathan's experience at Stillpoint:** Nathan Meier interview, August 23, 1997.

[n14.5] p. 235 **Gia-fu in his last days:** Carmen Baehr interview, October 3, 1997.

[n14.6] p. 236 **Gia-fu's death announcement:** Death announcement used at Gia-fu's service; also found in Gia-fu Feng, et al., 1985.

[n14.7] p. 237 **Feelings about Gia-fu:** Carmen Baehr interview, October 3, 1997.

EPILOGUE

[n epi.1] p. 252 **Stillpoint land preservation:** Deed of Conservation Easement in Gross between Carol Ann Wilson and San Isabel Land Protection Trust, September 21, 2005, 3.

[n epi.2] p. 254 ***Tao Te Ching*** **quote:** Feng and English 1972, chapter 1.

BIBLIOGRAPHY

Anderson, Walter Truett. *The Upstart Spring: Esalen and the American Awakening.* Reading, MA: Addison Wesley, 1983.

Anderson, Walter Truett. *The Upstart Spring: Esalen and the Human Potential Movement: The First Twenty Years.* Lincoln, NE: iUniverse Inc., 2004.

Bateson, Mary Catherine. *Composing a Life.* New York: The Atlantic Monthly Press, 1989.

Berling, Judith A. "Dao/Taoism." Asia Society, n.d. http://www.askasia.org/teachers/essays/essay.php?no=40/

Bottome, Paula. *Completing the Circle: Taking Gestalt to Asia.* San Francisco: Clear Glass Press,1997.

Chadwick, David. *Crooked Cucumber: The Life and Zen Teaching of Shunryu Suzuki.* New York: Broadway Books, 1999.

Chang, Iris. *The Chinese in America: A Narrative History.* New York: Viking Penguin, 2003.

Chang, Iris. *The Rape of Nanking: The Forgotten Holocaust of World War II.* New York: BasicBooks, 1997.

Chang, Jung and Jon Halliday. *Mao: The Unknown Story.* London: Jonathan Cape Publishers, 2005.

Chang, Jung. *Wild Swans.* New York: Doubleday, 1991.

Chin, Frank, et al. "Aiieeeee! An Introduction to Asian-American Writing," *Bulletin of Concerned Asian Scholars,* Fall 1972.

Committee of Concerned Asian Scholars. *China! Inside the People's Republic.* New York: Bantam Books, 1972.

De Mente, Boyé Lafayette. *The Chinese Have a Word for It: The Complete Guide to Chinese Thought and Culture.* Chicago: Passport Books, 2000.

Dinh, Tran Van. "The Tao of Watergate." *New York Times,* Sept. 9, 1973.

Dong, Stella. *Shanghai 1842-1949: The Rise and Fall of a Decadent City.* New York: HarperCollins, 2000.

Erickson, Barclay James. "The Only Way Out Is In." In *On the Edge of the Future: Esalen and the Evolution of American Culture,* Jeffrey J. Kripal and Glenn W. Shuck, eds. Bloomington: Indiana University Press, 2005.

Fairbank, John King. *China: A New History.* Cambridge: The Belknap Press of Harvard University Press, 1992.

Fairbank, John King. *Chinabound: A Fifty-Year Memoir.* New York: Harper & Row, 1982.

Fairbank, Wilma. *Liang and Lin: Partners in Exploring China's Architectural Past.* Philadelphia: University of Pennsylvania Press, 1994.

Feng, Gia-fu and Jane English, tr. *Chuang Tsu Inner Chapters.* Mt. Shasta, CA: Earth Heart, 1997.

Feng, Gia-fu and Jane English, tr. *Tao Te Ching.* New York: Random House/Vintage Books, 1972.

Feng, Gia-fu and Jerome Kirk. *Tai Chi—A Way of Centering & I Ching.* London: Collier-Macmillan, Ltd., 1970.

Feng, Gia-fu, et al. *Yi Ching, Book of Change.* Mullumbimby, Australia: Feng Books, 1985. Copyright held by Estate.

Gaines, Jack. *Fritz Perls: Here & Now.* Millbrae, CA: Celestial Arts, 1979.

Greene, Eric D. *Recovering in the Tao: The Way to Healing and Harmony.* Wayne, MI: Tao Bear Books, 2003.

Halberstam, David. *The Fifties.* New York: Ballantine Books, 1994.

Hyde, Lewis. *Trickster Makes this World.* New York: Farrar, Straus and Giroux, 1998.

Johanson, Greg and Ron Kurtz. *Grace Unfolding: Psychotherapy in the Spirit of the Tao-te ching.* New York: Bell Tower, 1991.

Latourette, K. S. *The Chinese, Their History and Culture,* 3rd revised ed. New York: The MacMillan Co., 1946.

Legge, James. *The Sacred Books of China: The I Ching, The Book of Changes,* Dover ed. Toronto: General Publishing Company, Ltd., 1963.

Lian, Yang. "The Writer and the Party, Western Misunderstanding of Contemporary Chinese Literature." *Times Literary Supplement,* Nov. 6, 1998, No. 4988.

Lippe, Toinette. "What Constitutes a Necessary Book?" In *Tao Te Ching,* Feng and English, 25th anniversary ed. New York: Random House, 1997.

Naranjo, Claudio. *Gestalt Therapy: The Attitude & Practice of an Atheoretical Experientialism.* Nevada City, CA: Gateways/IDHHB, Inc., 1993.

Needham, Joseph. *Science and Civilization in China,* Vol. 2. Cambridge: Cambridge University Press, 1974.

Ni, Ting. *The Cultural Experiences of Chinese Students Who Studied in the United States During the 1930s-1940s.* Lewiston: The Edwin Mellen Press, 2002.

Perls, Laura D.Sc. "Comments on the New Directions." In *The Growing Edge of Gestalt Therapy,* Edward W.L. Smith, Ph.D., ed. Highland, NY: Gestalt Journal Press, 1976.

Porter, Bill. *Road to Heaven: Encounters with Chinese Hermits.* San Francisco: Mercury House, 1993.

Rawson, Philip and Laszlo Legeza. *Tao: The Chinese Philosophy of Time and Change.* New York: Avon, 1973.

Sanella, Lee. *Kundalini: Psychosis or Transcendence.* San Francisco: Lee Sannella, MD, 1976.

Schurmann, Franz and Orville Schell, eds. *The China Reader: Communist China, Revolutionary Reconstruction and International Confrontation 1949 to the Present.* New York: Vintage Books, 1967.

Seagreave, Sterling. *The Soong Dynasty.* New York: Harper & Row, 1985.

Solnit, Rebecca. "Heretical Constellations: Notes on California, 1946–61." *Beat Culture and the New America, 1950–65.* New York: The Whitney Museum of American Art, 1995.

Spence, Jonathan. "China's Great Terror." Review of *Mao's Last Revolution* by Roderick MacFarquhar and Michael Schoenhals. *New York Review of Books,* Sept. 21, 2006, pp. 31–34.

Spence, Jonathan. *The Gate of Heavenly Peace: The Chinese and Their Revolution 1895–1980.* New York: Penguin, 1981.

Spence, Jonathan. *The Search for Modern China.* New York: W. W. Norton, 1990.

Takaki, Ronald. *Strangers from a Different Shore.* New York: Penguin Book, 1989.

Tomkins, Calvin. "New Paradigms." *New Yorker,* Jan. 5, 1976.

Trueblood, Elton. "Introduction." In *Pendle Hill Reader,* edited by Herrymon Maurer. New York: Published in association with Pendle Hill by Harper & Bros., 1950.

Tuchman, Barbara. *Stillwell and the American Experience in China 1911-45.* New York: Macmillan, 1970.

Watson, Steven. *The Birth of the Beat Generation: Visionaries, Rebels, and Hipsters, 1944-1960.* New York: Pantheon Books, 1995.

Watts, Alan. *In My Own Way.* New York: Vintage Books, 1973.

Watts, Alan. "Beat Zen, Square Zen, and Zen." *Chicago Review,* Spring 1958.

Wong, Eva. *Cultivating Stillness: A Taoist Manual for Transforming Body and Mind.* Boston: Shambhala Publications, Inc, 1992.

Yutang, Lin. *My Country and My People.* New York: John Day Co., 1935.

Time, Sept. 13, 1963

INDEX

An educator for more than thirty-five years, Carol Wilson has served as high school principal, assistant superintendent, and director of a state-wide school university partnership. Her background in the humanities and culture provide a context for her writing. Currently, Carol's interests focus on promoting community through the humanities.